Teachers, Teaching and Control in Physical Education

Teachers, Teaching and Control in Physical Education

Edited by

John Evans

The Falmer Press
(A member of the Taylor & Francis Group)
New York ● Philadelphia ● London

UK   The Falmer Press, Falmer House, Barcombe, Lewes, East Sussex, BN8 5DL

USA   The Falmer Press, Taylor & Francis Inc., 242 Cherry Street, Philadelphia, PA 19106-1906

First published 1988

British Library Cataloguing in Publication Data

Teachers, teaching and control in physical education.
   1. Great Britain. Schools. Curriculum subjects:
Physical education.   I. Evans, John, 1952–
613.7′07′1041
ISBN 1-85000-410-2
ISBN 1-85000-411-0 (pbk.)

Jacket design by Caroline Archer

Typeset in 10/12 Bembo by
Mathematical Composition Setters Ltd, Salisbury, UK

Printed in Great Britain by Taylor & Francis (Printers) Ltd, Basingstoke

Contents

Contents

vi

Figures and Tables

1
Introduction: Teachers, Teaching and Control

John Evans and Brian Davies

It is now well over fifty years since the publication in Britain of the Board of Education's (1933) *Syllabus of Physical Training for Schools*. It is still a remarkable document, not only for the amount of detail it provides on the teaching of PE (no doubt necessary for a teaching force then predominantly untrained in the art of teaching PE) but also for the status and position it accorded Physical Education (then called Training) in the elementary school curriculum. In that document 'the development of a good physique' and the provision of an 'efficient system of Physical Training' were seen as nothing less than a matter of 'national importance', as 'vital to the welfare and even the survival of the race' (p. 8). The echoes both of war and of general economic recession even deeper than the more regional varieties we have experienced in Britain in recent years — and then, of course, unsullied and unsoftened by the supporting structures of a developed Welfare State — had much to do with this positioning of PE in the thinking of the Board. They reverberate with the emphasis placed in the syllabus upon the production, promotion and maintenance of fitness for health. Throughout the syllabus the social and medical functions of Physical Training loom large. In the Board's view an efficient system of PT could help compensate but not correct, alleviate or act as 'a remedy for all [Britain's social and economic] ills' (p. 8). Such was their magnitude that the Board acknowledged that PT had its curative limits. It alone could not reach those parts which political and economic measures were failing or not even attempting to satisfy. Even so, and somewhat optimistically, the Board went on to claim that the syllabus could, 'if rightly and faithfully used, widely adopted and reasonably interpreted yield an abundant harvest of recreation, improved physique and national health' (p. 8).

Some fifty years on the interested spectator on the educational and social scene in Britain could be forgiven for thinking that not much had changed in the country's economic position, at least in some regions, or in the social conditions of life for some of its people, or in the position afforded to Physical Education in the public thinking of prominent educationalists and politicians, or even in the emphasis given to 'health promotion' in the modern PE curriculum. Amid multi-million unemployment Physical Education has in the last decade once again entered the imaginations of politicians and educationalists as a legitimate subject of critical concern. However, as the contributions to this collection make clear, this concern has not always been supportive of nor evoked a productive debate about the development and promotion of PE in schools. Indeed, it has often been vilificatory, based on all but the crudest analyses and the most limited understanding of the actions and endeavours of physical educationalists in schools as we have them. In Britain and elsewhere teachers have been charged with bringing competitive games and with them the name of PE into serious disrepute, with endorsing or encouraging a fall in sporting standards and engendering low achievement, all in the cause of egalitarian mass participation, resting on an unthinking commitment to unsound left-wing ideas or fashionable but empty educational theories.

At least one advance wrought by recent debates on school processes has been to show that they have never been so innocent as Twain's metaphor involving the little boy and the log would have us believe (Davies and Evans, 1983). Physical Education is a social construct, 'a selection from culture, which contains explicit and implicit values about appropriate missions, goals and objectives' (Dewar, 1985, p. 160; Evans and Davies, 1986b). It is neither arbitrary nor immutable. PE, like all school subjects, constitutes what Dewar nicely refers to as an 'ideological statement', a way and not the only way of classifying, organizing, legitimating and transmitting knowledge in society. This classification benefits some and not others. PE like all other subject areas in the school curriculum is inevitably a site of struggle, a contest of and for competing definitions about what is to count as worthwhile knowledge, what the body, the individual, school and society are and ought to be. These values, assumptions and definitions held by individuals both within the profession and outside it influence, guide, facilitate and constrain the work of teachers and shape their and pupils' identities and practices. As such they should constitute the substance of any critical enquiry in the study of PE, and it is upon this quest that we embark in this work.

In Britain, and elsewhere in recent years, teachers of all kinds and in every sector of schooling have had to contend with a variety of pressures for change, emanating both from outside and within the profession. As Greene (1986, p. 3) has pointed out on the American scene, they have been metaphorically drenched by a 'rain of official and private reports charging schools with "mediocrity" and calling for an ill defined "excellence" for the sake of national defence and increased productivity.' It is as if, says Greene, 'a new form of Kitsch has permeated the school systems and public alike as people all over the country agree that the nation is indeed "at risk", that standards must be raised' (p. 3). As the contributors to this volume point out, teachers in Britain too have been subjected to a similar and vitriolic critique, especially from the highly organized voices of the radical political right (see Davies, 1986; Ball, 1987). These have often come close to attacking any form of educational practice which constrains the ways in which children are imbued with the attitudes of patriotism, traditional masculine dominance and above all competitiveness (Kirk, 1987, p. 19; Evans, 1987). But as is so often the case in public educational debate, the images of PE conveyed bear very little resemblance indeed to what goes on inside schools, the practices which feature in them, or to the concerns, issues and worries of educators over conditions of work, employment prospects, staff development opportunities, levels of resource and so on. PE teachers face a profound contradiction, on the one hand being told by prominent educationalists and politicians (see this volume, Pollard, Chapter 7, Evans and Clark, Chapter 8) that they hold in their hands the nation's future health and wealth, while on the other, inside schools, that they and their subject deserve less time, resource support and recognition than others. They still tend to occupy a marginal status inside schools and this has severe implications for their career opportunities and professional identities.

Attacks on the PE profession have been part of a much more all-embracing onslaught on state schools and teachers in recent years which began most noisily in Britain in the 1960s with the voices of Black Paper writers. Politician educationalists such as Rhodes Boyson, then Head of Highbury Grove School, subsequently junior Minister in several Departments of State, now reconsigned to the Conservative back benches, and Caroline Cox, head of a polytechnic sociology department, nurse education researcher, now Deputy Leader at the House of Lords, mounted an attack on policies of comprehensive schooling, mixed-ability grouping and other organizational and curriculum innovations which were reputed to be examples of a rampant and insidious left-wing anti-professionalism damaging British schools (see CCCS, 1981; Ball, 1984; Evans, 1986a). The charges against the profession then, as now, were falling educational standards, pupil underachievement and the acceptance, even promotion, by teachers of ill discipline and poor pupil control. There is little doubt that these earlier attacks on the teaching profession in Britain, as in the USA (see Apple, 1986), paved the way for the most 'radical' right-wing Conservative government since the war to exploit ruthlessly and expertly what it claims are the failings of the comprehensive system to provide amongst other things a curriculum for a modern technological society, and forms of practice which are sensitive especially to the needs of working-class children. As we see in Chapters 6, 7 and 8, physical educationalists have not escaped this critique. They too have been charged with promoting falling standards in sport performance and positively contributing to Britain's economic decline. All this has paved the way for what is nothing less than a massive piece of social engineering, a level of political intervention in the nature and content of state education provision which makes the comprehensive experiment of earlier years by contrast pale into a deep and irrelevant insignificance. In effect the radical right in Britain has gone where for years others of more liberal and left-wing persuasion have sadly feared to tread. They have gone to the heartlands of schooling, to the curriculum, modes of evaluation, assessment and resource, and they have gone confidently taking the ideology of free-market capitalism, searching for control.

Critical debates about the nature and state of schooling in Britain, needless to say, have had a profound effect not only on the way in which outside 'publics' (parents, employers) think about schools and teachers, but also on the way teachers and pupils think about themselves, how they experience their jobs and schools as places of work. The economic and educational expansion and with it the optimism of the 1960s have now evaporated and given way to a situation of widespread instability, insecurity, uncertainty, unemployment and a contraction in educational provision. Never before, one might claim, has the teacher's lot been such an unhappy one, as they have been inescapably positioned as both the victims and the agents of reform (see Walker and Barton, 1987). Never before have teachers had to contend with such a prolonged and sustained period of upheaval and change or to deal with so many pressures for change from different sources (politicians, industrialists, parents). As one PE teacher in a recent survey commented, 'Why should we have to work all hours when we are continually criticised by all sectors of society, especially by our Secretary of State?' (in Williams, 1988, p. 84).

Teachers such as this have to deal with the heightened and varied expectations placed upon them and with the knowledge that powerful conservative pressure groups outside the profession have designs to redirect, organize and monitor their work (Walker and Barton, 1987). Unsurprisingly teachers feel vulnerable, and often deeply alienated sometimes by the pace and form, at others by the content of a variety of reforms and innovations ranging from GCSE, the proposed national curriculum and bench mark testing, to appraisal of their own performance, which they are expected to understand, participate in and effect and which increasingly emanate from outside the profession. They must also cope with changes emerging from inside their professional groups sometimes as a response to outside pressures and criticism. Innovations in PE, for example, such as Health Related Fitness, new forms of games teaching, and altered examinations and assessment techniques, may be experienced either as resources for teaching or as further inescapable, unwanted and untimely threats to professional identity and current practice, or even future survival.

This is the social and educational context in which PE teachers in Britain have to be placed and against which the studies presented in this reader need to be set. Redundancy, redeployment and early retirement are for an increasing number the order of the day. They are real possibilities being faced by many experienced teachers, while the novitiate is now likely to face the prospect of a long period on the lower pay scales of the career structure, knowing that chances of promotion will be few and far between, that possibilities of 'rising up' the career ladder within PE are limited by their seniors'/elders' declining opportunities to leave the subject for a more obviously pastoral or academic career (PEA, 1987; Bell, 1986; Evans and Williams, 1988). The consequences are well illustrated in the comments of this PE teacher: 'I know PE teachers who have left teaching. I have lost three from my department in the last eight years and part of the fault is my inability to move on to create a promotion for them. I only wish I had the courage to leave and try something new but at my age it's a big risk' (in Williams, 1988, p. 283).

As others too have pointed out (see Ball and Goodson, 1985), the whole conception of a career in teaching has been radically altered in recent years by changes in the control, organization and content of schooling. However, as the contributors to this reader point out, while these changes have affected all teachers, they neither subjectively experience them in a uniform way, nor do they individually or as subject groups possess the same degree of power or resource to confront, challenge, resist or endure the institutional work conditions to which they are subject. Within the current career and occupational structures of the educational work place, competition both between individuals and between subject groups is a fundamental feature of life in school and an inescapable aspect of individual advancement through teaching. While individual teachers may in theory have equal access and opportunities for career advancement, both within the subject and to areas outside PE (anyone can apply for a senior position, etc.), they do not have equal status, social or professional resources to bring to the competitive stakes. Teachers' opportunities for advancement, as we see in this volume, are structured (limited or constrained) by their social class, sex, or by the occupational status of their subject. As others have pointed out (Ball, 1987), there are very clear patterns of advantage and disadvantage in the career opportunities of teachers, and physical educationalists do not feature too well within them. Ball (1987) claims that these patterns are deeply ingrained in our educational system and extend across schools to provide structural advantages for certain groups and disadvantages for others. The most significant of these, in his view, is the organization of and different status imputed to subject departments. This pattern benefits and privileges some teachers and disadvantages others. Drawing on the work of Hilsum and Start (1974), for example, Ball quotes, 'If a headship is the target, then for *teachers of equal experience* the best chances of achieving this goal lie with history, physics, French and maths' (Hilsum and Start, 1974, p. 82). In short, some subjects and the teachers that staff them lack credibility and influence in the eyes of significant others, for example, headteachers, LEA policy-makers, the gatekeepers to career opportunities. This status is reflected both in the type of subject teachers who achieve positions in the senior hierarchy of schools and in the distribution of salary scale points and senior positions within and between subjects.

The table provides further evidence of the low status imputed to PE. PE teachers seem far less likely than others to rise above the level of a scale 3 position within their subject department. While the contributors to this book provide ample evidence of the way in which subject status impacts upon and often limits the innovatory work and career opportunities of PE teachers, they also reveal that this status alone does not account for the difficulties which some teachers experience when seeking promotion, or looking for a job. As will be pointed out (cf. Ball, 1987; Apple, 1986; Deem, 1978; Ozga, 1988a; Evans and Williams, 1988), women are often profoundly disadvantaged in career terms by male dominance in schools, a dominance which features across sectors of schooling and within and between subjects. Even in the primary or elementary sector, where in Britain and the USA women outnumber men, the latter are disproportionately represented in senior positions. In effect the language and structure of schools and the subject departments inside them are often deeply shaped by patriarchy. The gatekeepers to jobs are predominantly men and they, in Physical Education (see Burgess, 1986) as in other subject areas, do not always believe that women are either capable or suitable because of their competing family/work roles for advancement to senior positions. Much more research needs to be undertaken on appointment policies and practices in PE as elsewhere. What little evidence we have suggests that men tend to occupy senior positions in PE departments (PEA, 1987; Scraton, 1985; Evans and Williams, 1988), and receive higher pay scales (Burgess, 1986). Indeed Scraton (1985) has pointed out that these patterns have been exacerbated in recent years as combinations of falling rolls and economic stringency in education have meant that staff have not been replaced or have been replaced with part-time appointments. It has tended to be women who have left their jobs, not from any lack of commitment but because of lack of opportunity. The comments of this female PE teacher clearly express these difficulties: 'There is virtually no chance of a woman being head of department in this school. The Head would never contemplate a female head of department and my only chance of promotion is in pastoral ... or a move to a girls' school. Sex

Table 1.1.   Salary Scale and Subject of Highest Qualification of Teachers in England and Wales, 1982

England and Wales							Percentage
			Full-time teachers				
	Senior posts[1]	Other posts: Salary scale				All	All
		4	3	2	1		
Main subject of highest qualification							(thousands)
English	11	13	16	26	34	100	26.2
Mathematics	10	17	16	25	32	100	21.2
Physical education	4	6	24	32	34	100	19.3
History	13	10	21	26	30	100	18.6
Geography	13	12	22	24	29	100	16.3
Art/craft	3	9	23	31	34	100	15.2
Craft, design and technology	4	12	25	38	21	100	14.3
Home economics	4	4	21	35	36	100	12.8
French	10	12	17	26	35	100	12.5
Biology	7	9	21	26	37	100	12.1
Chemistry	8	16	20	27	29	100	8.9
Music	5	7	30	29	29	100	7.9
Physics	13	20	21	23	23	100	7.3
Religious education	6	8	27	28	31	100	5.8
Other subjects							
Other languages	13	9	23	30	25	100	7.4
Other sciences	11	12	21	28	28	100	6.1
Any other subject	15	11	24	26	24	100	21.7
All subjects	9	11	21	28	31	100	233.6
(thousands)	21.1	25.8	49.6	65.4	71.6	233.6	

Note: [1] Those paid on Burnham scales for headteacher, deputy headteacher or senior teacher

Source: DES (1982) *Statistical Bulletin*, 5/82, March, p. 9.

[Table 1.1] analyses teachers qualified in each subject by salary scale. The columns show the percentage of all teachers with a main qualification in a subject paid on the salary scales for senior posts (defined as those for head teacher, deputy heads and senior teachers), and scales 1 to 4 for other teachers. The percentages in senior posts may be biased downwards slightly by the proportionately large number of these teachers who gave no subject or gave education as their main subject of qualification; this is reflected in the higher than average percentage in this column in the 'any other subject' line. Nevertheless there are marked differences between subjects, with physical education, art/craft, craft, design and technology, home economics and music having a lower proportion of senior posts and Scale 4 posts than the more 'academic' subjects. (DES, 1982, p. 3) equality has not reached this school or many others that I know' (in Williams, 1988).

The contributors to this reader together begin to provide descriptive and illustrative insights into the lives of teachers on the contemporary educational scene, into the problems and the possibilities which many face when trying to realize their hopes and ambitions for themselves and their children. But we still need much more research as to how the opportunities for teachers can be structured by the perspectives and actions of others and how they experience conditions of control over their opportunities, careers and life-styles inside the institutional work place. We also need to explore how these processes both express and help sustain social class and gender inequalities and opportunities. All too often issues of social control in school have been considered and discussed in terms only of control of children. Obviously, to understand how pupils are 'socially controlled' is vitally important in any quest to understand how schools and PE within them impact upon the attitudes of children towards themselves, their bodies and their post-school involvement in physical activity and other forms of leisure. But the point we stress here is that teachers, in common with other workers, are also subject to systems of supervision and control (see Connell, 1985). Never has this been more obviously the case. As central government has sought greater control over the teaching force, it has become increasingly difficult for teachers alone or together to act independently or to claim autonomy. It can appear that the act of teaching is a purely idiosyncratic, autonomous affair, that teachers can shut the gymnasium door on the outside school and wider community. This imagery, always defective, must now be considered as increasingly misleading. Teachers, with renewed edge, carry into their classrooms the expectations and the more formal policy prescriptions of significant others such as parents, politicians and peers, although they may still have some capacity to resist those of their peers (see this volume, Sparkes, Chapter 10).

The Labour Process in Physical Education

In today's economic and political climate the supervision of teachers, the patterns of authority and consent, alliance and cooperation, resistance and opposition that characterize institutions (Connell, 1985) should be high amongst both our professional and research concerns. If nothing else, political intervention in the organization and content of schooling in recent years has re-emphasized and clearly illustrated that teachers are workers, teaching is work and that school is an institutional work place (Whitty, 1985; Connell, 1985; Apple, 1986; Evans and Davies, 1986a). Taking this perspective we can view recent debates about the PE curriculum as part of a broader battle for ownership and control over what is to count as valid educational knowledge, how this is to be produced, distributed and evaluated. In short it is part of a struggle over ownership and control of the labour process of teaching. To consider teaching in this way raises issues of a sort already alluded to in the foregoing discussion concerning the division of labour in schools within and between subjects. It is to ask how power, authority, responsibility and reward are distributed, how teachers and pupils are differently positioned in and through the work of PE, who has influence over what and what are the principles which govern this process (Connell, 1985, p. 82). However, our understanding of the labour process in PE, how knowledge is organized, distributed and evaluated remains even more limited than our understanding of the division of labour in the subject. As we have elsewhere pointed out (Evans and Davies, 1986b) research into teaching Physical Education has long been dominated by a tradition of systematic observation (see also Kirk, 1987). This approach is important and valuable to our understanding of what teachers do in classrooms, gyms and on playing fields. But it is also very limited in its capacity to illustrate why the process of teaching takes a particular, often very limited, form or how it is constructed or framed (limited or facilitated) by the ideas, decisions, values and interests of individuals not only inside the classroom, but also in sites outside (for example, in departmental, faculty, LEA, higher educational contexts). Teaching is a complex and difficult activity. It involves the control and management of pupils, knowledge, time and other resources. But it is crucial to consider that this work, that is, the labour process of teaching, neither begins nor ends in the classroom. What goes on in the classroom, for example, rests among other things upon what teachers bring to it in the form of their professional and personal predispositions, upon how successful they are in securing resources (time, money, staff, etc.), for their department, and on the organizational (timetabling) parameters which are set for them by others within and outside the institution, who have the power to define and set them. The curriculum of PE may also be strongly influenced, if not determined, by others at 'sites of knowledge production' in institutions of higher education (see Evans, 1987; and this volume, Evans and Clark, Chapter 8) suffused with typically new middle-class cultural interests and experienced by teachers variously as de- and re-skilling. As Sparkes also shows (this volume, Chapter 10), timetable space and support for the subject rest importantly on the status imputed to PE by significant others in the broader school context. The hegemony of the academic curriculum in schooling (see Connell, 1985) exerts a powerful influence on this, and on how people think about 'proper learning', valid and useful knowledge. This often ensures that physical educationalists find the task of achieving their desired goals, ambitions and objectives very difficult indeed. Like Schlechty (1976), we too would want to argue that it is necessary to think of teaching as

> the act of inducing pupils to behave in ways that are assumed to lead to
> learning, including *attempts* to induce students to so behave. Whether
> students do in fact behave in a way the teacher attempts to induce
> them to behave is a question for empirical study. Whether the
> behaviour induced by the teacher leads to the intended learning
> outcome, some unintended learning outcome, or no learning at all is a
> question for mental measurement. The results of such measurement
> might be useful to both learning theorists and teaching theorists, but
> measures of mental processes, achievement, and attitude are not the
> alpha and omega of theories of teaching and instruction.
>
> Appropriate questions for teaching theory are questions like:
> What are the conditions under which a particular kind of teacher
> behaviour has the effect of inducing students to behave in ways which
> the teacher expects them to behave? Under what conditions do
> students respond to the behaviour of teachers in ways that are not
> expected by the teacher? What are the effects upon the teacher's
> behaviour of these unanticipated student responses? To what extent is
> the teacher controlled by student behaviour? Is teacher behaviour
> independent of student behaviour or are they woven together in the
> social structure of the school and the classroom in such a way that they
> become interdependent? Can a teacher 'change' his (or her) behaviour
> even if the social system of the classroom is not designed to accommo-
> date that change? More directly, is the social system of the classroom
> largely dependent on the behaviour of the teacher, or are its sources
> more diffuse? To what extent are the social system of the classroom
> and the behaviour of participants therein independent of factors
> outside the classroom and outside the consciousness of individuals in
> the classrooms? To what extent are the social system of the classroom
> and the behaviour of participants shaped by such outside factors as
> reference groups, peer groups, departmental loyalties, and class sched-
> ules? Indeed, to what extent is the classroom a social system?
> (pp. 26–7)

Schlechty's ecological perspective properly emphasizes and highlights the
complex dialectic between individual subjectivity, intention, values and interests, and the structures (institutional, material, ideological) which may facilitate
or constrain their enactment. This interest in the interplay of self, biography
and social structure lies at the heart of the sociological enterprise. But as yet it
has been little directed to the study of teachers and teaching. Specific areas of
interest to us such as the division of labour and the labour process in the
practice of Physical Education are virtually untouched. In this volume we are

concerned to examine how PE is implicated in the process of social and cultural reproduction, and to explore the possibilities within the subject for effecting the arrival of a 'Physical Education for All'. Thus the chapters are both descriptive, sometimes offering detailed accounts of the actions of teachers and pupils at work, and often critical in perspective. Many set out to unpick the social fabric which constitutes the world of PE and schooling in order not to damage but to question, reveal and challenge the often taken-for-granted assumptions, values and principles which guide and direct work within it. These descriptions are modest and inevitably partial, but our hope is that they will nurture the task of appraisal and the development of a knowledge of how PE both contributes toward and contradicts social inequalities (in leisure, work and family life) both inside and outside schools.

The first three chapters concentrate attention on teachers' careers and opportunities and the strategies they may employ towards realizing their ambitions and intentions. In Chapter 2 Sikes draws heavily upon data from both quantitative and qualitative research to investigate the experiences of British secondary school PE teachers and their perceptions of PE as a career within a context of economic and educational contraction. She reveals that for many PE teachers, by contrast with their academic counterparts, age is an important 'determinant' of their career interests and ambitions. Many see sport and PE belonging only to the young and the active. By the age of 30 as they experience the decline of their own sporting prowess, thoughts turn toward getting out of the subject into the less active and more obviously academic areas of the school curriculum. At this age too family commitment can make the job and the degree of investment in terms of time and effort it requires seem more and more unattractive and inappropriate. However, the relatively low status imputed to the subject acts as a substantial barrier to career change. Educational contraction exacerbates this problem, by reducing still further opportunities for teachers to move up the career ladder in PE or out of the subject altogether. As a result some PE teachers feel a deep sense of frustration, even alienation, as a consequence of being 'trapped' in a job which they now have 'outgrown'. In many respects Sikes' chapter nicely sets the scene for the more sharply detailed and ethnographically focused studies provided by Burgess (Chapter 3) and Templin (Chapter 4). Whereas Sikes provides an invaluable overview of the thinking of teachers, Burgess and Templin draw attention to the complex dialectic of self, opportunity and institutional structures within specific school and departmental settings. Drawing on data from a re-study of one large British comprehensive school, Bishop McGregor, Burgess focuses our attention on the perspectives and actions of the head of PE for boys and girls and illustrates the strategies used by the male head of department to secure promotion in the school. He also examines the consequences of this appointment for the curriculum of girls' PE. The chapter raises questions not only about the practice of making appointments in school, how patriarchy infuses this process and the distribution of resources between boys' and girls' PE, but also about the relationship between school and community and how the PE interests, expectations and resource demands of a school, pupil clientele can sometimes conflict with those of a community, adult clientele. Templin, using life history methods, also takes the reader deeply into the thinking of two female mid-career PE teachers, one in a British, the other in an American secondary school. The comparative data are used to explore the influence of critical events in the lives of these British and American teachers and valuably document not only their hopes and ambitions, but also how their actions, perspectives and opportunities for career advancement are differently aided and often constrained by a complex co-mingling of social factors within the institutions in which they work. Despite the massive geographical divide between these teachers, both experience common problems in trying to realize their aims and ambitions. Again we see that this has much to do with the hegemony of the academic curriculum, the status imputed to practical subjects and concomitantly the lack of resources and opportunity for professional development made available to PE teachers. In this respect the very private and personal problems experienced by the teachers in Templin's (as in Sparkes', Burgess', Sikes') study reach out to a general value system in Britain and the USA which encourages theoretical knowledge and undervalues a practical orientation (Evans and Williams, 1988).

The remaining chapters shift the emphasis towards the analysis of teaching and its impact upon the social and educational identities of pupils. However, like the first three chapters, these are still concerned with processes of social and cultural production and reproduction in and through PE. In Chapter 5 Carrington and Williams argue that social inequalities are as deeply entrenched in leisure as in any other spheres of social activity, that patriarchal relations, like class and race relations, are culturally reproduced through leisure and that gender and race continue to act as serious constraints upon opportunities and behaviour. Their study attempts to account for gender and ethnic inequalities by examining their cultural reproduction in and through the symbiotic relationships between school Physical Education and community leisure activities. Drawing on data from their survey of the lives and life-styles of young people of South Asian descent, the authors firstly consider the unequal patterns of participation in leisure activity in the broader school context and they assess the extent to which gender differences are heightened by ethnicity. Secondly, drawing on detailed data from a study of teachers and teaching in one comprehensive school, they document how, despite some teachers' best endeavours to alter and challenge young people's attitudes towards and involvement in physical activity and the adoption of an equal opportunities policy in the PE department and broader school setting, the reproduction of gender and racial inequalities is still achieved despite the best intentions of some of the teachers concerned. The processes they outline are complex, arising from, among other things, the interplay of differentiated practices long established in the lower school PE curriculum, the constraints of the timetable and the conservative attitudes of male PE teachers as well as those of the young people themselves. Crucially, this chapter raises important questions about the policy and the practice of equal opportunities, at the heart of which is the issue of how we can bring children together towards a common culture at the same time as we recognize and remain sensitive to what culturally sets them apart.

In many respects the chapters by Leaman, Pollard, Evans and Clarke, George and Kirk, and Sparkes also take up the theme of equal opportunities in education. They too examine the nature of educational change in the PE curriculum in the primary and the secondary sectors along with its conse-quences for both teachers' and pupils' educational and social identities. Together these authors illustrate that innovations which have featured in the PE curriculum in recent years (such as Health Related Fitness, Teaching Games for Understanding) have caught not only the imagination of teachers in the PE profession but also the critical gaze and even biting scepticism of powerful others. These are areas in which hostile politicians find easy media allies. They are meeting points for the interests of the political radical right, copywriters to corporate capitalism in their sponsorship of the social production of compet-itive individuals, and of PE teachers themselves as they pursue their pedagogic and other professional concerns. By examining both the rhetoric of innovation as it is propounded in what Evans and Clarke (Chapter 8) call the 'official discourse of PE' and the practice of PE in the secondary and primary sectors (see Pollard, Chapter 7), these authors get beneath the surface of recent 'debates' about how PE ought to be, and help us consider the question: are recent innovations in the PE curriculum as radical, as emancipatory or even as widespread as their proponents and opponents would sometimes have us believe?

In Chapter 6 Leaman draws our attention to the 'competition debate' as it has been conducted in Britain in recent years and reveals that PE practices in primary and secondary schools are much more varied than this 'debate' would have us believe. He also contends that in the cause of attracting and keeping children's interest in PE, arriving at a consensus within a department over what is to be taught and how it is to be taught may be a lot more important than any allegiance or otherwise to any single (e.g., competitive) element of the PE curriculum. However, his data suggest that the business of arriving at a consensus in a department is neither unproblematic nor trouble free. The introduction of new ideas into the secondary PE curriculum can be a source not of progress but of tension and conflict between members of staff as their differing ideologies, interests, expectations and conceptions vie for pre-dominance. 'New' and 'old' ideas interact not only to sponsor but also to suppress the process of educational innovation. This is a theme taken up in even greater detail in Chapter 10 as Sparkes documents the process of innovation without change in just one secondary school PE department. But Leaman also raises important questions concerning the important social functions of the 'New PE'. Like others in this reader, he offers the spectre of a PE curriculum helping not to liberate children but to control and channel them towards acceptance of their futures in non-work and leisure. Pollard (Chapter 7) takes up a similar theme. He concentrates attention on PE teachers and teaching in the primary school sector and offers some rich description of activities in one junior school which he calls Hillside. His data document the relationship between classroom practices and broader extra-school political ideologies relating to PE and competition. Focusing on the moral panic created by the national press during the summer of 1985, when a primary school headteacher proposed holding a cooperative rather than a competitive sports day, he goes on to suggest that competition is a powerful force in schools which acts as a constraint on social and educational change because of its 'double articulation'. It offers teachers in the primary sector, who are often very enthusiastic but weakly trained in the art of teaching PE, a means of coping with large class sizes and the problems of management and control which these create especially in the open spaced and 'weakly framed' contexts of activities which feature in PE. It is also a key element of the individualism that underpins free-market capitalism and consumerism. Together these powerful micro- and macro-level interests meet not only to constrain the development of more liberal, child-centred activity but also to help secure the reproduction of gender divisions in and through PE practice.

Evans and Clarke (Chapter 8) also concentrate on the possibilities for educational and social change in and through the PE curriculum. They examine the practices of one highly innovative PE department which in recent years has shown some of the 'dangerous', non-competitive tendencies which helped create the 'moral panic' to which Pollard refers. The discussion focuses on two senior PE teachers teaching Health Related Fitness (HRF), Teaching Games for Understanding (TGFU) and educational gymnastics to two mixed-sex groups of first-year (12-year-old) pupils. They question whether innovations in PE which claim to be 'child-centred' and socially and educationally all-embracing really challenge conventional social (class and gender) and educational (ability) hierarchies or merely serve to reproduce them in different ways. Like Pollard they argue that the ideology of individualism permeates the new PE just as the old and that this may well act as a massive barrier to the development of new initiatives in PE which may indeed have a genuine potential within them for moving the curriculum and pedagogy of PE in the direction of 'a PE for All' (see Evans, 1988). For Evans and Clarke the constraint on educational practices and the process of educational and social change is to be found largely in the 'official' discourse of the new PE as it is produced in educational sites of knowledge production outside the department and broader school context. As this discourse interacts with the limits of a teacher's professional thinking and with teacher uncertainties over how to effect a child-centred pedagogy, so conventional social class and gender categories and hierarchies are announced and reproduced, despite individual best intentions, and the apparent inclusivity of the New PE. George and Kirk also interrogate the perspectives and actions of PE teachers in Brisbane secondary schools, in order to reveal the ideologies which set limits to their thoughts and actions. They argue that the ideologies of healthism, recreationalism and individualism act as substantial barriers to the realization of a form of PE which would help children better understand how the social and physical conditions of their lives and their opportunities to be healthy are constrained by the actions and interests of powerful others.

Sparkes also draws our attention to the way in which new and progressive ideas can be used to create an illusion or appearance of educational innovation without change in the classroom having really taken place. Drawing on data from a case study of a teacher initiated curriculum innovation within a PE department at a large comprehensive school in England, he focuses on the emergent concerns of the teachers in this department as they struggle to come to terms in their curriculum and pedagogy with the innovatory ideas presented to them by a new head of department. Like others in this reader, he argues that the actions of these teachers have to be understood largely as a response to the low status imputed to PE in the broader school setting. He reveals how within this setting they together employ a language strategy of 'rhetorical justification' to legitimize the gap between what they say they do in the educationalist context (see Keddie, 1971) and what actually happens inside the classrooms. The rhetoric or language of innovation functions explicitly to enhance the status of the teacher and his/her subject and to secure resources, whilst requiring little if any change in curriculum content or pedagogy. In Sparkes' view much of this behaviour constitutes a coping strategy, the best means of dealing with the demands and dilemmas of teaching and of exploiting the sometimes limited opportunities available to physical educationalists in the institutional work place. In this process, the curriculum and perhaps the social and ability categories and hierarchies which it tends to support, remain unchanged despite the rhetoric of progress and innovation.

In the final chapter Rosie takes the reader out of the school context into PE in Outdoor Education residential settings. Like others in this volume, he calls on ethnographic data to concentrate attention on the experiences of Youth

Training Scheme (YTS) students some of whom have learning and behavioural difficulties. By offering a comparison of two contrasting approaches to residential experiences, one which is guided by educational aims, the other by the expectations of the industrial managing agents, he is able to document how emergent problems of student control were differently resolved within these settings. Rosie highlights processes of social and cultural reproduction in PE, in this case how pupils with special educational needs are identified, differentiated and labelled.

Finally we stress that while the chapters in this volume are not only descriptive but analytical and critical, they are offered not as definitive statements on the nature of PE teachers' practices but rather as resources. It is to be hoped that they will help raise consciousness about how PE teachers experience their work and its problems, how they construct their teaching and what it does to their own and their pupils' opportunities and identities. We see the business of raising consciousness as a necessary but not sufficient element for effecting social and educational change in egalitarian and emancipatory directions (cf. Kirk, 1988). Our hope is that this book will help practitioners to see more vividly the relations between their

> curricular, pedagogical and evaluative actions and the inequalities in the larger society [a task which] does require something of a wrenching experience, a conscious attempt to step outside our everyday language and commonsense thought. Examining our institutions relationally, seeing them as being constructed in a context that has clear relations of domination and exploitation, is a labour process itself. *It must be worked at* since so many other messages in the media and in our everyday political, economic and cultural discourse deny the reality of such relations. Those involved in critical educational scholarship do have the right to ask the reader to take seriously the complexity of these connections between education and class, gender and race inequalities and hence, the possible complexity of the analysis that uncovering such relations may require. (Apple, 1986, pp. 201–2)

What goes on inside classrooms cannot be explained only with reference to the psychological predispositions (values, attitudes, interests and ambitions) of teachers and pupils. We need also to examine how these are adopted and adapted, conditioned and created as strategic responses to constraints, dilemmas and opportunities that are generated externally at the societal level and productively mediated by institutional structures and processes inside schools, departments and classrooms (Sparkes, 1988). For example, we cannot explain the difficulties experienced by women teachers when trying to gain promotion to senior positions inside schools without reference both to broader societal stereotypes of women within the all-pervading culture of masculinity and patriarchy and to long histories of specific sorts of career productions by individuals within departments, schools and LEAs. The same sort of duality of explanation that does not consign school processes to fatalistic overdetermination would also be required for an understanding of the marginality of PE teachers in general. Without some understanding of how different sorts of activity, the physical and the intellectual, are imputed different statuses and reward in the wider society, we shall not begin to evaluate appropriately the determinative strength of within-system influences. Both are crucially related to the social production of social class, gender and racial categories and hierarchies. In short we cannot and should not, if we are seeking an understanding of PE, separate the private or personal troubles of PE teachers from broader public issues, social patterns or processes (Evans, 1986b). Sadly this reader barely begins to touch the surface of these issues and how they relate to within-school social processes. In the sociological study of PE nearly everything remains to be done.

References

APPLE, M. (1986) *Teachers and Texts*, London, Routledge and Kegan Paul.

BALL, S. (1984) 'Comprehensives in crisis?', in BALL, S. (Ed.), *Comprehensive Schooling: A Reader*, Lewes, Falmer Press, pp. 1–27.

BALL, S. (1987) 'Comprehensive schooling effectiveness and control: An analysis of educational discourse', in SLEE, R. (Ed.), *Education, Disruptive Pupils and Effective Schooling*. London, Methuen.

BALL, S. (1987) *The Micro-Politics of the School*, London, Methuen.

BALL, S. and GOODSON, I. (1985) 'Understanding teachers: Concepts and contexts', in BALL, S. and GOODSON, I. (Eds), *Teachers' Lives and Careers*, Lewes, Falmer Press, pp. 1–27.

BELL, L. (1986) 'Managing to survive in secondary school PE', in EVANS, J. (Ed.), *PE, Sport and Schooling*, Lewes, Falmer Press, pp. 95–117.

BOARD OF EDUCATION (1933) *Syllabus of Physical Training for Schools 1933*, London, His Majesty's Stationery Office.

BURGESS, R. (1986) 'Points and posts: A case study of teacher careers in a comprehensive school', Paper presented to the BERA conference, Comprehensive Education in the 1980s, Kings College, University of London, 21 February 1986.

CENTRE FOR CONTEMPORARY CULTURAL STUDIES (1981) *Unpopular Education: Schooling and Social Democracy in England since 1944*, London, Hutchinson.

CONNELL, R. W. (1985) *Teachers' Work*, London, George Allen and Unwin.

DAVIES, B. (1986) 'Halting progress: Some comments on recent British education policy and practice', in *Journal of Education Policy*, 4, Oct.–Dec., pp. 349–61.

DAVIES, B. and EVANS, J., (1983) 'Bringing teachers back in: Towards a repositioning of the second person on the log', Paper presented at Teachers' Careers and Life Histories Conference at St Hilda's College, Oxford, September 1983.

DEEM, R. (1978) *Women and Schooling*, London, Routledge and Kegan Paul.

DEPARTMENT OF EDUCATION AND SCIENCE (1982) 'The Secondary School Staffing Survey', *Statistical Bulletin*, 5/82, March, London, DES.

DEWAR, A. (1985) 'Curriculum development and teacher's work: The case for Basic Stuff Series in Physical Education', in CARNES, M. (Ed.), *Proceedings of the Fourth Conference on Curriculum Theory in Physical Education*, University of Georgia, Ga., pp. 158–68.

EVANS, J. (1986a) *Teaching in Transition: The Challenge of Mixed Ability Grouping*, Milton Keynes, Open University Press.

EVANS, J. (1986b) 'Introduction: Personal Troubles and Public Issues', in EVANS, J. (Ed.), *Physical Education, Sport and Schooling: Studies in the Sociology of Physical Education*, Lewes, Falmer Press, pp. 1–11.

EVANS, J. (1987) 'Teaching for equality in Physical Education: The limits of progressivism in the New Physical Education', Paper presented to the conference, Ethnography and Inequality, St Hilda's College, Oxford, September 1987.

EVANS, J. (1988) 'Towards a socialist Physical Education', in LAUDER, H. and BROWN, P. (Eds), *Education, In Search of a Future*, Lewes, Falmer Press, forthcoming.

EVANS, J. and DAVIES, B. (1986a) 'Fixing the mix in vocational initiatives', in WALKER, S. and BARTON, L. (Eds), *Changing Policies, Changing Teachers*, Milton Keynes, Open University Press, pp. 96–117.

EVANS, J. AND DAVIES, B. (1986b) 'Sociology, schooling and Physical Education', in EVANS, J. (Ed.), *Physical Education, Sport and Schooling: Studies in the Sociology of Physical Education*, Lewes, Falmer Press, pp. 11–41.

EVANS, J. AND WILLIAMS, T. (1988) 'Moving up and getting out: The classed and gendered career opportunities of PE teachers', in TEMPLIN, T. and SCHEMP, P. (Eds), *Socialisation into Physical Education: Learning to Teach*, Indianapolis, Benchmark Press Inc.

GREENE, M. (1986) 'Teaching as a project: Choice, perspective, and the public scene', in CARNES, M. (Ed.), *Proceedings of the Fourth Conference on Curriculum Theory in Physical Education*, University of Georgia, Ga., pp. 1–13.

HILSUM, S. and START, K.R. (1974) *Promotion and Careers in Teaching*. Windsor, NFER.

KEDDIE, N. (1971) 'Classroom knowledge', in YOUNG, M. F. D. (Ed.), *Knowledge and Control*, London, Macmillan, pp. 133–61.

KIRK, D. (1987) 'The orthodoxy in RT-PE and the research-practice gap: A critique and an alternative view', Unpublished paper, Department of Human Movement Studies, University of Queensland, Australia.

KIRK, D. (1988) *Physical Education and Curriculum Study: A Critical Introduction*, London, Croom Helm.

OZGA, J. (1988a) 'Teachers' work and careers', Unit W1 in EP228, *Frameworks for Teaching*, Milton Keynes, Open University Press.

OZGA, J. (1988b) (Ed.), *Schoolwork: Approaches to the Labour Process of Teaching*, Milton Keynes, Open University Press.

PHYSICAL EDUCATION ASSOCIATION (1987) *Commission of Enquiry into the State and Status of PE (Both Primary and Secondary) in England and Wales*, PEA, The Ling Bookshop, 162 Kings Cross Road, London.

SCHLECHTY, P.C. (1976) *Teaching and Social Behaviour*, Boston, Mass., Allyn and Bacon.

SCRATON, S. (1985) 'Losing ground: The implications for girls of mixed physical education', Paper presented to the BERA Annual Conference, Sheffield, 1985.

SPARKES, A. (1988) 'Culture and ideology in physical education', in TEMPLIN, T. and SCHEMP. P. (Eds), *Socialisation into Physical Education: Learning to Teach*, Indianapolis, Benchmark Press Inc.

WALKER, S. and BARTON, L. (1987) 'Introduction', in WALKER, S. and BARTON, L. (Eds), *Changing Policies, Changing Teachers*, Milton Keynes, Open University Press, pp. 6–8.

WHITTY, G. (1985) *Sociology and School Knowledge*, London, Methuen.

WILLIAMS, T. (1988) 'The Career Opportunities of Physical Education Teachers', MA(Ed) dissertation, University of Southampton, 1988.

2
Growing Old Gracefully? Age, Identity and Physical Education

Patricia J. Sikes

I found that I could work OK right the way through the morning, I could take the lunch time practices, but after that I was getting tired, I was getting bad tempered. It was the only subject a lot of boys came to school for and to have a bad-tempered PE teacher just doesn't work at all. And that was one of the reasons why I thought, well, (at 35) it's time to give way to a younger man. (Male, age 39, Scale 4, Head of House)

I feel quite happy and quite fit enough to teach PE still at 42, I haven't really felt my age, only very slight indications and the fact that I now need to put a little bit more effort into maintaining a certain level of fitness, but the way I feel now, I could put in another 10 years without any problems. (Male, age 42, Scale 2, Second in Boys' PE)

These two quotes demonstrate that, to a large extent, we really are as old as we feel. Getting old and, in particular, the physical consequences of ageing are perhaps of greater significance to PE teachers than they are to teachers of other subjects. No matter what individuals may claim for themselves, physical ability declines with age, and teaching Physical Education tends to be seen to be directly linked with physical ability.

PE in schools is socially constructed (Evans and Davies, 1986, p. 15). What it involves, its relative status and the level of ability, agility and physical enthusiasm required to teach it in what is perceived to be an appropriate and adequate way are also socially defined. This means that, as the various chapters in this book show, the role of the PE teacher varies between and sometimes within different institutions depending on institutional (social and cultural) conceptions of PE.

Setting aside the physical and biological effects (which are not experienced

21

by everyone in exactly the same way), ageing is similarly a social construction. Ideas about what constitutes 'normal' and appropriate behaviour for someone of 40 living in the latter half of the twentieth century are quite different from those applying as recently as the 1950s. My own mother, for example, who is in her 60s, plays bowls, swims regularly and belongs to a Yoga group together with other women of 60, 70 and even 80 plus, yet I remember her mother at the same age as an old lady, who would have been shocked if it had been suggested that she might even put on a leotard. So would her contemporaries because people of that age and from that ('working') class didn't do that sort of thing. This example makes the point that we are as old as we feel it socially acceptable to be, and that if we engage in 'inappropriate behaviour' we may feel socially uncomfortable because we are not presenting the identity we would wish to be known by.

In this chapter the focus is on ways in which some teachers have interpreted, perceived and experienced ageing in relation to their teaching career as PE specialists. How they have done this has implications for the nature and quality of PE in schools and for young people's experiences of it.

Data

The data on which the chapter is based come from two sources: (1) an investigation, conducted in 1987, of seventeen PE and ex-PE teachers' experiences of ageing; in this sample there were nine women and eight men whose ages ranged from 23 to 47; and (2) research into how secondary school teachers were experiencing teaching as a career at a time of contraction. This study involved over 1100 teachers from thirty-one schools throughout England and Wales and in 1981, when it was done, provided a representative sample of the English, Welsh and PE secondary school teacher population. The 'sample' is not homogeneous, but because it is mixed it does provide opportunities for time, space and methodological 'triangulation' (see Denzin, 1970).

With the exception of responses to a questionnaire used in Study 2, data were collected by conversation-interviews which took a life history approach. The advantages of using such an approach to study careers are that: (a) it is holistic and contextualizes careers within the individual's total life experience; (b) it is historical and takes account of developments which influence individuals' career experiences, e.g., the teacher action of the 1980s dramatically limited the extra-curricular activities which have, traditionally, been a major source of job satisfaction and an important part of many PE teachers' jobs; and (c) it relates micro- to macro-theory. As Goodson (1980, p. 74) puts it: 'From the collection of Life histories, we deem what is general within a range of individual studies; links are thereby made with macro-theories but from a base that is clearly grounded in personal biography' (see also Sikes, Measor and Woods, 1985, pp. 13–15).

Age, Occupation and Identity

Ageing is both a unique and universal experience and because of this is an important source of personal and social identity. So, in western societies, is one's occupation (see Havinghurst, 1964; Mulford and Salisbury, 1964; Super, 1981). Ageing, occupational development and identity are inextricably linked. Sofer (1970) suggests that

> the variations in meaning attached to work at different phases of the personal life cycle can be expected to be associated with variations in what the person expects at different phases and what is expected of him. We associate particular ages with particular statuses and with each status go characteristic and legitimate hopes, expectations and duties. Age-status expectations constitute an important link between the personality system of the individual and the social system in which he operates. (pp. 118–19)

These meanings and expectations are likely to be further differentiated, when, as in teaching, there is a hierarchical career structure and 'position mobility follows patterned sequences (and) different motivations ... become appropriate and inappropriate at each stage' (Strauss, 1959).

Research has variously shown that different experiences, attitudes, perceptions, expectations, satisfactions, frustrations and concerns appear to be linked to different phases of teachers' life and career cycles (for example, see Fessler, Burke and Christensen, 1983; Lortie, 1975; Nias, 1984; Petersen, 1964; Sikes, 1985, 1986; Sikes, Measor and Woods, 1985) and specifically to the career of the male PE specialist (MacDonald, 1981; McNair and MacDonald, 1976). All occupations have their own phases (see Glaser, 1968, for examples) but teachers are in the relatively unusual position of always working with children and young people while they themselves are getting older. This makes it difficult for them to avoid recognizing their own mortality and to ignore the fact that, physically at least, their prowess may be declining.

The ways in which individual teachers perceive and experience this aspect of their teaching career vary, as do their perceptions and experiences in other areas of their lives. If 'career' is broadly defined as movement through a number of phases which are sequentially experienced in the direction of some point which is designated, or perceived as, or will prove to be, terminal, then within a lifetime a person can be seen to have a number of careers. For example, a woman may have careers as a daughter, a mother, a girl-friend, a wife, a pupil, a student, a teacher and an athlete, among others. Because they are all part of a whole and influence and interact with each other, it would be meaningless to investigate one without taking account of the others. A two-dimensional approach to the study of careers, as suggested by Hughes (1937), helps to ensure that individual, identifiable careers are not investigated in isolation.

Within this framework careers can be considered: (1) in terms of their objective nature, that is, in terms of the observable, official, ordered stages through which the individual can be publicly seen to pass, and (2) in terms of their subjective nature, that is, as 'the moving perspective in which the person sees his life as a whole and interprets the meaning of his various attributes, actions and the things which happen to him' (Hughes, 1937, pp. 409–10). Inevitably circumstances, including objective career structures, constrain and influence subjective careers but this does not make them any the less the unique experiences and constructions of the individual. In other words, people give their own meanings to their careers. This means that two people in practically identical jobs have quite different subjective experiences of that job because their other careers and life experiences are different and take place in different social and cultural contexts.

Careers structure time (Roth, 1963). They link the individual with the social structure by providing identity and a framework for reference which situates and gives meaning to experiences and which offers a sense of personal continuity and consistency by linking the past, the present and the future. They provide timetables, based on the experiences of those who have already gone through the same or similar careers, against which a person can measure their progress. 'Age asynchronisation' (Cain, 1967), or being 'too' old for, or staying too long at, a particular stage without having an 'acceptable' excuse, usually identifies a person as being in some way deviant.

Studying PE Teachers' Careers

Physiological and biological careers are likely to be of especial importance to PE teachers. Men and women obviously have different physiological and biological careers, which carry different social interpretations and identities, and these result in different male and female careers in PE.

While, as has been mentioned, there have been studies of careers in PE, these have tended to focus exclusively on men. This is not unusual. As Holly (1983) wryly observes, women are not generally considered, and often do not consider themselves, to have careers, they just work and have jobs. This chapter does not do much to redress the balance but, together with other contributions to this volume, it is a start.

The Attraction of PE as a Career

Research suggests that many (from 25 to over 50 per cent of) teachers enter the profession almost by default because they have no clear idea of what else they might do (see, for example, Hanson and Hetherington, 1976; Lomax, 1970; Smithers and Carlisle, 1970). However, all of the PE teachers I talked with had been committed to their career from a relatively early age. They had all wanted to teach and work with young people and they had all enjoyed, been at least reasonably good at, and had spent a considerable amount of their time playing sport.

> I wasn't sort of county standard but I felt that I had the skills to cope with most games and also I very much enjoyed doing it, so that was mainly the basic criteria for choosing PE. (Colin)

> I was very keen on PE and games at school and I thought that it'd be a nice outlet for me to pursue that line and become a PE teacher. (Kieran)

> I wanted to teach and I liked sports so I chose PE. (Andrea)

Teaching offered the opportunity to merge occupational and leisure interests in that the job often gives access to specialist equipment, promotes contact with like-minded others and usually requires that many evenings and weekends are spent in coaching and supervising teams (the teachers' action in the 1980s did, however, have an effect here). Tyro PE teachers are often very attached and committed to their role and what it involves. Goffman (1961) refers to this as 'embracing the role'. As he puts it, 'To embrace a role is to disappear completely into it, to be fully seen in terms of the image and to confirm expressively one's acceptance of it' (p. 106). This is interesting because in some respects the identity associated with the role of the young PE specialist, particularly that of the male, is not necessarily all that attractive to other people.

PE Identities

Male student PE teachers have a reputation for being hard drinking, raucous, vulgar philistines. At the same time they are often seen as vain poseurs, self-styled 'PE Gods', who are chauvinistic womanizers, expecting women to worship them, put up with boorish, insensitive behaviour and make the cricket teas. Particularly, perhaps, in the days of the Certificate of Education, but to some extent still they were, and are regarded as, 'Thick Jocks', with brawn but little in the way of brains. Prowess at sport, or more specifically wishing to make a career out of sport, tends not to be linked with intellectual ability. This perception can have implications when it comes to applying for promotion in that those making appointments seem to be less likely to consider PE teachers as appropriate candidates for posts which have academic and intellectual orientations or connotations, such as head of subject departments/faculties or headships (see Hilsum and Start, 1974). 'Unless you do something to alter the perception yourself, PE teachers are seen as physical people who play sport and are usually good at it and who usually get on well with the kids but who don't have a great deal of nouse. More so for men' (Andrea). While the stereotype of the PE man is of the archetypal macho, 'real', man, PE women who represent and promote vigour and athleticism have placed themselves outside the weak and submissive stereotype of femininity (see Carrington and Leaman, 1986; Leaman, 1984; Scraton, 1984, 1986).

I think sometimes women in PE have to fight quite hard to be taken seriously, both by men and by other women. There's often a perception that somehow these are a fringe group of women who are all sporty and more physically developed than a lot of other women. (Andrea)

I think they think of you as a little bit 'weird', you know, in inverted commas, so keen and so energetic or sports minded. I think a lot of people don't think it's the thing for women. (Linda)

However, there appears to be an alternative female PE teacher stereotype, which is of the:

creative, arty type, [who does] gymnastics and dance. Characteristically, stereotypically they'd be extremely 'feminine' in inverted commas, and the kind of stereotype of a creative person, you know, a little bit dizzy, dead enthusiastic etcetera, etcetera ... the games person is seen as perhaps not so bright. The creative ones are quite bright because they have to express themselves, but the games player is athletic, hearty, perhaps a little bit insensitive. (Helen)

My colleague B, for instance has no problems because dance, which she teaches, is perceived very much as the feminine side, but for me, I'm a games player and an athlete and I'm perceived, I think, as being an unusual woman, let's put it that way. (Andrea)

The influence that these stereotypes have on PE in schools is reflected in the different sorts of activities offered to boys and girls (see Scraton,1986). Furthermore, it seems that male and female PE teachers themselves tend to accept and uphold the stereotypes. A study of option choice and equal opportunities, for instance (Pratt, Bloomfield and Seale, 1984), found that compared to those working in other subject areas a high percentage of PE teachers had 'traditional' attitudes concerning equal opportunities and the differential treatment of the sexes.

Accepting a role means playing it, at least when in the company of one's peers. Male PE specialists in particular tend to form close and supportive groups, both within the occupational/professional context and in wider society where they often belong to sports clubs. These groups have the effect of reinforcing the stereotype in outsiders' minds.

Initial Career Thoughts

All of the PE teachers I talked with had a degree in another subject or had taken two subjects at college. Most of them had always taught in another subject area. While no-one could recall any formal input during their training on career planning or development, some people said that they had been given the impression that it was 'taken for granted' that they would eventually stop teaching PE. Helen, for instance, felt that,

> Basically I accepted the stereotype of the PE teacher finishing around the sort of age of 40. (You picked up this stereotype through) peer group pressure and then teacher pressure as you entered the profession. No-one mentioned it during training. Although you were strongly recommended to take a subsidiary subject because 'You can't always teach PE you know'. So therefore it was accepted in an unwritten way that you'd be atypical if you were still teaching PE at 60. (Helen)

However, even in the light of this unwritten assumption, and even if, as was common, they did not expect to continue teaching PE until they retired, it seems that the majority had no specific career routes or plans in mind. This is not unusual to PE teachers (see Lyons, 1981) and is perhaps not surprising, for at 21 even being 30 seems very remote. As Linda remarked: 'I knew there would be a time when I would have to think of something but at that time going into it as a 21-year-old I didn't give much thought as to what I would do' (Linda). With hindsight and experience views are different:

> When I went into teaching PE it never entered my head to be quite honest, that I would ever get too old to do it ... but I think once you've

started and you look around and you see some people, PE teachers, who you think have p'raps gone on too long, not wishing to be unkind but, you know, there are examples around, and you wonder if they've still got the enthusiasm that they had when they came into the job. (David P)

I've come to think that if I'm doing the job properly, 10 or 12 years will be all I could probably manage in PE because of the actual physical strain it puts you under. (Kieran)

Some women teachers had initially thought that they would be likely to leave teaching to have children, but at the time had not really thought about what sort of job they would return to if they did return. As one teacher remarked: 'I always assumed that I could retrain in something' (Linda).

Initial Involvement

Young PE teachers tend to be strongly committed to their job and role, and (at least in pre-teacher action days) to be heavily involved in extra-curricular activities (see Jenkins, 1974). Most of them have the time and energy to do this because they generally have few family or other commitments. They also find it a lot of fun, if the teachers involved in the study were not exceptional in this respect. One teacher, looking back on his first few years in teaching, commented:

Out of school activities were the most enjoyable time because you didn't have that much of a pupil teacher relationship depending on the basis of being at school and being in lessons. You had with you the kids who were keen and were interested and were prepared to listen and prepared to work hard at whatever they were doing and you didn't have everything else going on around you and the atmosphere was quite informal. It was enjoyable going to a school and meeting other staff and other pupils. The best times I've had really have been, for instance, on a summer's evening with a tennis match. Really enjoyable because there's been no animosity with the kids, a relaxed atmosphere and relationships. (Colin)

Young teachers are close in age to their students and in some schools this enables them to develop relationships which are more like those of an older sibling or a fellow team member (see Sikes, 1985). In addition, regardless of their age, sport is a popular subject which offers teachers the chance to demonstrate their skill and ability, and thereby gain the respect and admiration of some students. These factors facilitate the establishment of what is often a special, relatively close relationship between PE teachers and students (art teachers are in a similar position; see Sikes, 1987). For example:

> I think I've probably got more satisfaction out of the extracurricular activities than the 9 til 4 because sometimes it's a struggle from 9 til 4, well, it depends on what the classes are like. It's not so bad in PE as other subjects. Having taught other subjects I can relate more easily to how good PE is really in that respect, because kids tend to come along and they want to take part. (Young)

Within schools this relationship is frequently assumed to exist, and PE teachers are perceived to be close to, and are identified in association with, young people for whom sport is seen to be an appropriate activity. However, being young involves being attributed less status.

Particularly in the past a school's reputation in the community often had a lot to do with its performance in sport. One teacher even told me: 'If you passed the 11 plus in (Town) you had a choice. If you liked football you went to Roman School because that was the football school, or you went to the Ancient School if you wanted to play rugby and hockey. It's quite true. People made their decision on those grounds' (Phil).

In addition, PE is a core curriculum subject, yet despite these facts in many (maybe the majority of schools) PE has low status in the eyes of both staff and students (see Measor, 1983).

Promotion Prospects

A major consequence of this low status is that PE tends to receive limited resources and fewer promotion points. In many schools, including the majority involved in this research, the post of Head of PE (together with head of practical and craft departments) is at a lower scale than other departmental headships (see Owen, 1970).

All of the male PE and ex-PE teachers I spoke with had initially aimed to become head of a department as soon as possible, and preferably by the age of 30 (this appears to be the aim of the vast majority of new, male, secondary school teachers; see Sikes, 1986). In the late 1960s and early 1970s they were quite likely to achieve this and, compared with other subjects, tended to be promoted to head of department at a relatively early age (see Hilsum and Start, 1974; McNair and McDonald, 1976); further progress was, however, much more difficult.

For women the position was and is different. This is because PE departments tend to be organized with an overall head who is usually a man who also has responsibility for boys' PE. This post will probably be at scale 3 or sometimes 4. Responsibility for girls' PE, generally taken by a woman, is likely to be at scale 2 or 3 and at least one point below that of the overall head of department. Some of the women I spoke with had worked with female heads of PE and one of them had held that position. Stephanie, on the other hand, had never encountered one in a career covering twenty-six years.

Increased consciousness of the need to provide equal career opportunities may have led to some changes but it appears that what Richardson wrote in 1973 is still often applicable:

> Evidently the culture makes it difficult for a woman who teaches PE in a mixed school to accept the risks of professional advancement, even under a headmaster who is willing to give overall responsibility to a woman in (PE). It seems that there is quite powerful collusion at work to maintain the man as the one who shoulders the main administrative burden of managing the department, and to maintain the woman as the one who is protected from this necessity. Yet it is women, working in girls' schools and women's colleges who have taken the lead over the country as a whole in some of the more creative developments in (PE). (Richardson, 1973, p. 308)

Indeed, Helen, who had been overall head of PE before moving into a pastoral post, commented that: 'People did look towards me and say, "Well, there's a woman in a job that shouldn't be done, isn't normally done, by a woman"' (Helen). Falling rolls and contraction have exacerbated the situation for both men and women, and now fewer can hope to reach even head of department level. The following quotes are typical:

> Promotion is very limited in PE due to there being a lack of promotion prospects within the subject, e.g. very few scale 2s. (Male, 36)

> I can see me being stuck on scale 1 for a long time through no fault of my own ... I'm willing to take on extra responsibility for a 2 but there's nothing there for me to take on, 'cus it's a small school all those responsibilities have been delegated, I mean, someone in another department got Outdoor Education years ago. So I can't see there being much promotion here for me. (Kieran)

Research shows that not all teachers (regardless of subject) want promotion (see Bennet, 1985; Sikes, Measor and Woods, 1985), and those who do, want it for different reasons. Some of these reasons do seem to be associated with age (see Sikes, 1986). For example, young people who are setting up homes and starting families may well need the extra money that promotion brings. Also, having taught for two or three years, teachers are likely to feel sufficiently experienced and capable of taking on greater responsibility. They may no longer find their present position as satisfying and challenging as it initially was and feel a sense of frustration because they are not able to use their abilities to the full, or to learn and develop new ones. Many heads of department recognize and appreciate this frustration and do what they can to make it possible for their juniors to gain experience and put their own ideas into practice, but even so they cannot give the money or, more importantly, the status and identity which go with a scale promotion, and it is these which are important to a lot of people.

There are strong social pressures to achieve promotion and there is an implication that there is something wrong with those who are not in posts seen to be appropriate for someone of their age. What constitutes an age-appropriate position is different for men and women. Whereas men would be expected to attain at least scale 3, middle management positions by the (approximate) age of 35, it is much more common and socially acceptable for women to remain in subordinate scale 1 and 2 posts for their entire careers. This is not the place to explore the reasons for this (see Acker, 1983, for a discussion of the issues); suffice it to say that traditional notions of the female role have in various ways contributed to the result that women are underrepresented in senior positions in schools.

The data suggest that men are 'expected' to progress to jobs which have some managerial, administrative, supervisory element. They are not expected to spend the majority of their time on teaching PE and playing games, largely perhaps because they are not thought to be as capable of doing this as a younger person (see Cannon, 1964). Continuing in PE, more or less full-time, can carry the implication that the job is not being done as well as it might be, and even maybe that the teacher concerned is unwilling to accept responsibility, or is incapable of so doing.

Career Moves

MacDonald (1970) found that by their early 30s the majority of male PE teachers were facing and making major career decisions. These decisions usually involved moving out of PE or at least dramatically decreasing the amount of time spent on the subject.

The high level of commitment characteristic of young teachers does, apparently, decline. Such shifts in commitment are not unique to PE teachers; many young teachers of all subjects are initially heavily involved in extra-curricular activities from which they often later withdraw (see Sikes, 1985, Sikes, Measor and Woods, 1985). A major difference is that to some extent extra-curricular activities have traditionally been perceived to be an integral, albeit unpaid, aspect of the PE teacher's job.

A frequent explanation for this change is that family commitments have often increased. One teacher explained how he had balanced his commitments:

> I think you have to be careful on how much (time) you're prepared to put in. I was very very conscious about this, particularly when my two children were little and you had to balance out between your family and your work commitments. My wife wasn't too happy about Saturday mornings, but it didn't last all year. I also used to ration myself to so many nights a week. (Colin)

Another anticipated having to do the same: 'In 10 or 12 years I'll probably have a young family and I won't be able to put the same amount of time in. One has got to change one's priorities somehow' (Kieran). While a female teacher had, not surprisingly, simply found that being a mother, a wife, a housekeeper and a PE teacher was too tiring: 'I found when I came back after having a family I wasn't as committed to all the after-school activities and everything else. Sometimes I was getting home at 7 o'clock and I found that a little bit wearing, as well as being booked up 4 out of 5 lunchtimes and on Saturday mornings' (Linda).

Getting older and finding it physically more difficult to keep up the pace and the level of performance, and suspecting that it will become even harder, are also major considerations for some people. None of them wanted totally to stop their sporting activities; sport is an important part of their lives and their preferred identity. They have just found that they are not going to be able to teach as well as they would like because they are no longer physically capable. For instance: 'When I first started in PE, if I was taking a gym club then I could do a hand spring or a head spring over the box, and I just feel the girls are somewhat missing out when I can't, when I have to say, I'm very honest with them, "I used to be able to do this but I can't now"' (Linda). Not everyone feels like this:

> There are some PE teachers who are still going strong at late fifties and they can compete adequately with the kids in most respects and in most activities. (Colin)

> I don't do cross country and other activities just to prove my point, I do it because I enjoy it and I can do it. I enjoy being with the kids outside and getting wet and things like that, and it gives the kids an incentive. I suspect some people think I'm not physically capable at 46 but I know I am and I know that I'm doing a good job. (Stephanie)

Every PE teacher I have spoken with knows of someone somewhere who is coming up for retirement and is vigorously teaching PE, but they are exceptions. They may, however, have some influence in that they provide alternative role models. For instance, Stephanie (who was 46) told me that she had never thought that age would inevitably cause her to give up teaching PE because as a pupil at school she had had the example of a PE teacher who was in her late 50s and who was still 'going strong'. Similarly I spoke with two men, aged 42 and 39, who were still in PE, had no intention of leaving and who had both started their careers in departments where there were 60-year-old active and competent full-time PE specialists.

It is not necessary to be a brilliant performer to be an excellent teacher and coach, and some teachers felt that they could alter their teaching style and still teach effectively. Yet some teachers, like those quoted earlier, may prefer to be able to demonstrate. However, their reasons for wanting to demonstrate may not necessarily be purely pedagogic, as a 45-year-old head of PE suggested:

> I mean most people who go into PE are good performers in one aspect of PE or the other and when that begins to rub off then they find that they're not as good or they're not as fit or they can't keep it up like they used to, and their enthusiasm goes and then they begin to find reasons not to do this, not to do that, I mean, if you don't like something, fair enough, you stop and do something else. But most of them, I think, basically like what they are doing, and always have done and whatever the reasons there are for leaving it's of their own making rather than the system beating them. I think they think, 'Oh I wish I was able to do that again'. And of course they're pushed gradually into the background, away from the limelight, and p'raps some of them don't like that, p'raps they're not able to cope with it. And there are lots of people in our field who are that way inclined. (Maurice).

This man is saying that some people do not enjoy the identity that goes with being an ageing PE teacher. They do not like the physical implications of being outrun, outbowled and increasingly liable to be 'beaten', nor are they happy with the personal and professional implications. These have already been discussed but are, briefly: at the personal level to do with being considered capable of teaching sport; and at the professional level to do with PE as a low-status subject offering few senior positions, which are in any case usually at a relatively low scale compared with those in other departments.

So, where are these teachers thinking of moving to? 'When I came into teaching I was particularly interested in sport, I wanted to teach PE but my views on that changed. I thought PE was the be-all and end-all of the job and I've since realized that, you know, I attached far too much importance to it' (Prior). When they first start teaching new teachers are very attached to their subject. They enjoy it, it gives them a sense of security because it is an area in which they are 'expert' and it provides them with an identity as subject specialist (see Bernstein, 1971; Lacey, 1977; Sikes, 1985). As time passes and they become more confident as teachers, more mature *vis-à-vis* the students and more aware of the various career possibilities available within teaching, they may begin to think of moving into the pastoral area. This has been a traditional route for PE teachers who are, it seems, often considered by headteachers to have particularly good relationships with students, and, therefore, the expertise required to establish such relationships in the pastoral care context. For example:

> I felt that getting to where I want to be [deputy head] was through the pastoral system. (Ashton)

> I got to scale 4 as acting head of PE, and I was lucky to get the 4 but I realized that I'd gone as far as I could in that route so I shifted sideways and went into pastoral as Head of Year, in order to go up again, which I have since done. (Helen)

Falling rolls and contraction have increased the attractiveness of such jobs and PE teachers often find themselves competing with people with higher-status qualifications in higher-status subject areas. The change in the arrangements of financing in-service training (from a general pool to specific grant-related funding) has also meant that far fewer of them will be able to take advantage of what was the popular strategy of taking a year's secondment to improve their qualifications and their intellectual reputation by obtaining a higher degree such as an MEd, MA or MSc.

Moving into their second subject area is, in promotional terms, unlikely to be successful, again because of their relative lack of qualifications and experience. As one teacher commented: 'My wife often tells me that I should have concentrated on history rather than PE because she feels that maybe history affords a more lifelong process for a teacher, rather than being cut off at a certain age. And the subject seems to have more credibility than PE' (Colin).

In the expansionist days of the 1960s going into teacher training was an alternative route, but this was more or less closed as student teacher numbers were dramatically reduced and training colleges were closed. In any case, college lecturers were still, really, PE teachers, and as such experienced similar difficulties to those of their colleagues in schools.

For women in general and for all but two of those I spoke with, career decisions may be complicated by questions of whether or not to have children, if yes, when, and how long to stay at home. Taking time out often means forfeiting chances of promotion, not only for women having children but also for men who move out of and then try to re-enter the system. Some women feel that their chances of promotion are practically non-existent in any case so they may just as well leave. Thus there are some women who, as Nias (1981) found, do not leave teaching in order to have a baby but who have a baby in order to leave teaching.

Some people decide to move right away from school teaching, but not away from sport, by going into the leisure industry in both the public and private sectors. Health clubs, for example, often advertise that their staff have BEds. Others set up sports shops or go into selling sports equipment, perhaps to their ex-colleagues back in school. Large sports firms even advertise in *The Times Educational Supplement*. Approximately 10 per cent of the male teachers I spoke with said that they were considering or had considered and rejected the idea of a career change. There are opportunists and entrepreneurs in all subject areas but it seems that PE specialists (together with teachers of 'craft' and 'practical' subjects) are more likely to have skills and experiences which they can market.

I did not talk with anyone who said that they had given up hope of eventually being able to move out of PE, though some were beginning to admit to being worried: 'Not being able to move out is a dreaded thought I can tell you, thinking about it. I try not to because, to be honest, it scares me' (Miles), and one man felt very bitter about the position he found himself in:

> I'm 42 and on scale 2 and it doesn't feel very good. It feels as though my teaching career has been a failure, to put it bluntly. Although I know that I'm a good teacher, I've put a lot of time, I've put a lot of effort in, and that the people who had the say over my career have not recognized that. (Colin)

Teachers of all subjects have to come to terms with the fact that they have not achieved the sort of position they had once aspired to. They do this in various ways, some of which may have negative implications for the atmosphere of the school in which they work, and/or the quality of the teaching they provide (see Riseborough, 1981; Sikes, 1984, 1986; Sikes, Measor and Woods, 1985, for illustrations). The situation is perhaps more difficult for ageing PE teachers who may find it increasingly difficult actually to do what is required of them and who cannot summon up the motivation and enthusiasm to go out on the field on a cold and damp winter morning. This was the spectre which haunted some of the teachers I spoke with, that and being a pathetic parody of a sportsperson. In order to avoid this some teachers try to take up more and more teaching in other areas, but at the same salary level. This is not necessarily a situation they are content with—for a man, being on scale 2 and being 55 can be a humiliating experience—but having invested a lifetime in teaching they may not see any alternative.

Conclusions

In teaching, career development is (usually) associated with age and experience.

For PE teachers, whose specialist expertise is based on physical ability, the relationship between age and career is particularly significant, both for the individual and for the children they teach.

The evidence collected for this study suggests that the PE curriculum tends to be 'traditional', in that it has changed very little since I, my parents or even my grandparents were at school. This is in spite of the growth and popularity of 'sport for all' in the outside world. Similarly pedagogy has not altered that much. There are, of course, schools where this is far from true but in general, the picture seems to be one of limited development.

One possible interpretation for this lack of curriculum and pedagogical development concerns age, the 'normal' career pattern followed by PE teachers, men in particular, and the male domination of senior PE positions. Young PE teachers of both sexes generally were good at and enjoyed PE as they experienced it at school; consequently they tend to reproduce their experience, both through their own teaching and later through the departments of which they may become head. They often teach by demonstration because they (a) enjoy the physical activity of participating, (b) enjoy the social aspect of performing to an audience, and (c) have not yet developed their teaching and communication skills — demonstrating is easier for them.

The content that they teach reflects the sorts of activities they enjoy and are good at and which, furthermore, they perceive and interpret to be 'real' PE and sport. Competitive team games, such as hockey, football, netball, rugger, rounders and cricket, are in the first league of 'proper' sport, with the 'masculine' games being well in front of the 'feminine' ones. Swimming, athletics, fishing and aerobics, for instance, trail behind, and this hierarchy is reflected in the amount of time and space given to coverage in the media as much as in the recognition given to them in schools. Thus schools reflect, support and reinforce in a dialectical fashion the social construction of sport.

Headteachers and those on appointment panels are not especially immune to the popular competitive, male-oriented conception of sport, or to the idea that a man is more likely to be a better or more satisfactory head of department than is a woman. Consequently men dominate the senior PE positions and their interpretation of what constitutes an appropriate PE curriculum tends to prevail. Although (throughout the century) women have done a considerable amount of work to develop the PE curriculum, to open it up and make it more attractive and accessible to more students of both sexes, their lack of seniority has meant that their influence has been limited.

Traditionally by the time their teaching confidence and ability are sufficiently developed to allow them to want to experiment with alternative content and pedagogies (see Sikes, 1985, p. 46), and when the physical aspect of the job may become more difficult and less rewarding, men in particular have been looking for a change of direction and for promotion out of an area where they have reached the top. Women may also be seeking a move, or be shifting their commitments from career to family, at least for a time.

An outcome of this youthful, male orientation in PE is limited development which means that students' experience of PE is also limited. As a result the situation tends to reproduce itself with the next generation of PE teachers following a similar model.

In recent years falling rolls have led to a reduction in promotion posts, and competition for all senior jobs has become greater. The social image and identity of PE, in combination with ideas about what are appropriate activities, positions and statuses for people of different ages, can make ageing particularly stressful for PE teachers who wish to move but cannot. The situation is perhaps worse for men who may feel pressure because they are expected to be 'successful' in terms of obtaining promotion. While this applies to teachers of all subjects, the ceiling is perhaps reached earlier in PE.

It may be that, as a group, PE teachers will become on average older (this is happening with teachers in general; see Dennison, 1981; Sikes, 1986). This could have positive implications for PE in schools if, because they are working in the subject longer, teachers have more time to experiment and develop curriculum and pedagogy. The exigencies of age may also cause some to look for alternatives to the demonstration style of teaching. Approaches and content which have tended to be associated with the 'feminine' branch of PE may be brought more to the fore, perhaps improving women's prospects of promotion. A less optimistic scenario is that teachers who want but are unable to move from PE will carry on with reduced enthusiasm, motivation and commitment.

But, to end on a cheerful note, with increased leisure time and more public awareness of health and fitness and with a greater number of 'older' people actively participating in sport, it may be that it will become socially more acceptable and psychologically more comfortable for PE teachers who wish to, to grow old gracefully in their job.

Acknowledgments

I would like to thank the PE teachers who gave me their time, and particularly those whose comments and criticisms, together with those of John Evans and David Sheard, helped me write this paper.

References

ACKER, S. (1983) 'Women and teaching: A semi-detached sociology of a semi-profession', in WALKER, S. and BARTON, L. (Eds), *Gender, Class and Education*, Lewes, Falmer Press, pp. 123–40.

BENNET, C. (1985) 'Paints, plots or promotion: Art teachers' attitudes towards their careers', in BALL, S. J. and GOODSON, I. F. (Eds), *Teachers' Lives and Careers*, Lewes, Falmer Press, pp. 120–37.

BERNSTEIN, B. (1971) 'On the classification and framing of educational knowledge', in YOUNG, M.F.D. (Ed.) *Knowledge and Control*, London, Collier-Macmillan, pp. 47–70.

CAIN, L. D. (1967) 'Life course and social structure', in FARIS, R.E.L. *Handbook of Modern Sociology*, Chicago, Ill., Rand McNally.

CANNON, C. (1964) 'Some variations on the teachers' role', *Education for Teaching*, 64, pp. 29–36.

CARRINGTON, B. and LEAMAN, O. (1986) 'Equal opportunities and Physical Education', in EVANS, J. (Ed.), *Physical Education, Sport and Schooling: Studies in the Sociology of Physical Education*, Lewes, Falmer Press, pp. 215–27.

DENNISON, W. F. (1981) *Education in Jeopardy: Problems and Possibilities of Contraction*, Oxford, Basil Blackwell.

DENZIN, N.K. (1970) *The Research Act in Sociology: A Theoretical Introduction to Sociological Methods*, London, Butterworth.

EVANS, J and DAVIES, B. (1986) 'Sociology, schooling and Physical Education', in EVANS, J. (Ed.), *Physical Education, Sport and Schooling: Studies in the Sociology of Physical Education*, Lewes, Falmer Press, pp. 11–41.

FESSLER, R., BURKE, P. and CHRISTENSEN, J. (1983) *Teacher Career Cycle Model: A Framework for Viewing Teacher Growth Needs*, Paper given at American Research Association Conference.

GOFFMAN, E. (1961) *Role Distance, Encounters: Two Studies in the Sociology of Interaction*, New York, Bobbs-Merrill.

GOODSON, I. (1980) 'Life histories and the study of schooling', *Interchange*, 11, 4, pp. 62–76.

GLASER, B. G. (Ed.) (1968) *Organizational Careers: A Sourcebook for Theory*, Chicago, Ill., Aldine.

HANSON, D. and HETHERINGTON, M. (1976) *From College to Classroom: The Probationary Year*, London, Routledge and Kegan Paul.

HAVINGHURST, R. J. (1964) 'Youth in exploration and man emergent', in BOROW, H. (Ed.), *Man in a World at Work*, Boston, Mass., Houghton Mifflin.

HILSUM, S. and START, K. B. (1974) *Promotion and Careers in Teaching*, Windsor, NFER.

HOLLY, L. (1983) *Why Study Women Teachers' Lives?* Unpublished paper for conference on Teachers' Careers, St Hilda's College, Oxford, September 1983.

HUGHES, E. C. (1937) 'Institutional office and the person', in HUGHES, E. C. (1958), *Men and Their Work*, New York, Free Press.

JENKINS, C. (1974) 'Male careers in PE', *Aspects of Education*, 16, pp. 71–80.

LACEY, C. (1977) *The Socialisation of Teachers*, London, Methuen.

LEAMAN, O. (1984) *Sit on the Sidelines and Watch the Boys Play*, London, Longman.
LOMAX, D. (1970) 'Focus on student teachers', *Higher Education Review*, Autumn, pp. 36–52.
LORTIE, D. (1975) *Schoolteacher: A Sociological Study*, Chicago, Ill. Chicago University Press.
LYONS, G. (1981) *Teachers' Careers and Career Perceptions*, Windsor, NFER Nelson.
MACDONALD, A. (1970) *Career Patterns of Male PE Specialists*, Unpublished MEd thesis, University of Manchester.
MACDONALD, A. (1981) 'Career determinants, and sources of satisfaction and dissatisfaction among Physical Education teachers in secondary schools', Unpublished paper.
MCNAIR, D. and MACDONALD, A. (1976) 'The first four years in Physical Education', *Journal of Psycho-Social Aspects*, Dunfermline College, Dunfermline.
MEASOR, L. (1983) 'Pupil perceptions of subject status', in BALL, S. J. (Ed.), *Defining the Curriculum: Histories and Ethnographies of School Subjects*, Lewes, Falmer Press.
MULFORD, H.A. and SALISBURY, W.W. (1964) 'Self-conceptions in a general population', *Sociological Quarterly*, 5, pp. 35–6.
NIAS, J. (1981) 'Teacher satisfaction and dissatisfaction: Herzberg's "Two-factor" hypothesis revisited', *British Journal of Sociology of Education*, 2, 3, pp. 235–46.
NIAS, J. (1984) 'The definition and maintenance of self in primary teaching', *British Journal of Sociology of Education*, 5, 3, pp. 167–80.
OWEN, J. W. (1970) 'The prospects and training of the man specialist teacher of Physical Education', *Bulletin of Physical Education*, 8, 3, pp. 39–44.
OWEN, J. W. (1973) 'Career prospects in Physical Education and recreation', *Bulletin of Physical Education*, 9, 7, pp. 11–16.
PETERSEN, W. (1964) 'Age, teachers' role and the institutional setting', in BIDDLE, B.J. and ELLENA, W.S. *Contemporary Research in Teacher Effectiveness*, New York, Holt, Rinehart and Winston, pp. 264–315.
PRATT, J., BLOOMFIELD, J. and SEALE, C. (1984) *Option Choice: A Question of Equal Opportunities*, Windsor, NFER-Nelson.
RICHARDSON, E. (1973) *The Teacher, the School and the Task of Management*, London, Heinemann.
RISEBOROUGH, G. (1981) 'Teacher careers and comprehensive schooling: An empirical study', *Sociology*, 15, 3, pp. 352–81.
ROTH, J.A. (1963) *Timetables*, Indianapolis, Ind., Bobbs-Merrill.
SCRATON, S. (1984) 'Losing ground: The implications for girls of mixed physical education', Paper presented to Girl Friendly Schooling Conference, Manchester 1984.
SCRATON, S. (1986) 'Images of femininity and the teaching of girls' Physical Education', in EVANS, J. (Ed.), *Physical Education, Sport and Schooling: Studies in the Sociology of Physical Education*, Lewes, Falmer Press, pp. 71–95.
SIKES, P. J. (1984) 'Teacher careers in the comprehensive school', in BALL, S.J. (Ed.), *Comprehensive Schooling: A Reader*, Lewes, Falmer Press, pp. 247–72.
SIKES, P. J. (1985) 'The life cycle of the teacher', in BALL, S. J. and GOODSON, I. F. (Eds), *Teachers' Lives and Careers*, Lewes, Falmer Press, pp. 27–60.

SIKES, P. J. (1986) *The Mid-Career Teacher: Adaptation and Motivation in a Contracting Secondary School System*, Unpublished PhD thesis, University of Leeds.

SIKES, P. J. (1987) 'A kind of oasis: Art rooms and art teachers in secondary schools', in TICKLE, L. (Ed.), *The Arts in Education: Some Research Studies*, London, Croom Helm, pp. 141–65.

SIKES, P. J., MEASOR, L. and WOODS, P. (1985) *Teacher Careers: Crises and Continuities*, Lewes, Falmer Press.

SMITHERS, A. and CARLISLE, S. (1970) 'Reluctant teachers', *New Society*, 5, March, pp. 391–392.

SOFER, C. (1970) *Men in Mid-Career: A Study of British Managers and Technical Specialists*, Cambridge, Cambridge University Press.

STRAUSS, A. L. (1959) *Mirrors and Masks: The Search for Identity*, Glencoe, Ill., Free Press.

SUPER, D. E. (1981) 'Approaches to occupational choice and career development', in WATTS, A. G., SUPER, D. E. and KIDD, J. (Eds), *Career Development in Britain*, Cambridge, Hobson's Press for CRAC.

3
Promotion and the Physical Education Teacher

Robert G. Burgess

In the 1980s teachers' jobs and teachers' work have attracted much interest among sociologists and educationalists who have begun to analyze the way in which teachers' careers develop and change (cf. Ball and Goodson, 1985; Sikes, Measor and Woods, 1985). However, as Sikes *et al.* (1985) remark, personal change for teachers is not necessarily a smooth development nor is it the result of

> either personal will or external constraints ... Rather the adult career is usually the product of a dialectical relationship between self and circumstances. As the result of meeting new circumstances, certain interests may be reformulated, certain aspects of the self changed, or crystallized and, in consequence, new direction envisaged. (Sikes, Measor and Woods, 1985, p. 2)

As teachers' careers are located within school structures, it is the relationship between the teachers' self and the circumstances in which they are located that will be discussed in this chapter. Here the focus will be upon teachers' careers but in relation to the context of the school in which they are located.

Teachers' careers have been subdivided into a series of age–related phases (Sikes, 1985). However, these phases are often marked by periods of strain when events have occurred that held implications for teachers' careers and identities. These periods that have been termed 'critical incidents' have been discussed by Walker (1976) and by Measor (1985) in relation to teachers' careers. They show that such incidents are key events in individuals' lives. Among the critical incidents that Measor identifies are: entering the teaching profession, the first teaching practice, the early years of teaching and mid–career moves and promotion. It is the last phase with which we shall be concerned in this chapter in relation to two teachers in a Physical Education

Department. But some attempt needs to be made to relate the career phases of the teachers and the related critical incidents to the social context of the school and the departments in which they are located if the dialectical relationship between teachers' selves and circumstances is to be successfully explored.

The Research

During the period 1983–85 I was involved in a re-study of a Roman Catholic coeducational comprehensive school which I called Bishop McGregor School that I had originally studied in the 1970s (Burgess, 1987a; 1983). During 1983 Bishop McGregor School had been designated a community college by the local education authority — a status that had implications for teachers and teachers' jobs. While many schools were contracting in terms of staff numbers as a result of falling rolls, Bishop McGregor staff were facing a period of expansion with many new posts for which they might apply as a consequence of community college status. Among the most common posts for which staff could apply were one- or two-term temporary contracts which provided teachers with an extra salary scale point for investigating an area of work such as courses for the unemployed, distance learning, youth work and so on. In addition, some permanent posts also became available for internal candidates. One of the first key posts to be advertised among McGregor staff was the position of Coordinator of Adult Physical Education and Leisure Activities on a salary of Burnham Scale 4 or its equivalent. The advertisement for this post read as follows:

> A Co-ordinator of Adult Physical Education and Leisure Activities. Salary Burnham Scale 4 or equivalent.
>
> To develop and widen existing programmes of adult physical education, to initiate and conduct research into the needs of the whole community and to bring forward proposals for meeting these needs. The successful applicant will be expected to work in the closest collaboration with the Boys and Girls Physical Education Department of the college in fostering still closer links with all groups within the community.
>
> Applications are invited from persons with suitable experience and qualifications and able to demonstrate a high degree of commitment to the concept of adult formation and leisure pursuits within the whole community.
>
> Letters of application with curriculum vitae and the names of 3 referees should be sent to the Clerk to the Governors, c/o the School,

within 10 days of the appearance of this advertisement. Canvassing disqualifies. Merston is an equal opportunities employer.

While this post was technically open to any member of the McGregor staff, it was only members of the PE Department who submitted applications; a situation that held implications not only for the individuals concerned but also for the boys' and girls' Physical Education Department in which they were located. This chapter therefore focuses on the social processes and social mechanisms that were associated with this appointment.

This research forms part of a broader range of questions about management, staffing and teachers' jobs and careers (cf. Burgess, 1986a, 1987b, 1988a) that it was possible to examine in McGregor School as I had access to governors' meetings, the governors' sub-committee on staffing, teachers' job interviews, staff meetings and departments. Accordingly, my study was developed using a combination of participant observation complemented by tape-recorded conversations with teachers about their work (cf. Woods, 1985; Burgess, 1988b) and the collection of job advertisements, further particulars for posts, letters of application and references for teachers. With these data I can provide an extended case study of problems and patterns of promotion associated with one job appointment in the Physical Education Department at Bishop McGregor School (cf. Van Velsen, 1967; Burgess, 1988a). But we need to consider: what do these data tell us about relationships among teachers within the PE Department and more broadly in Bishop McGregor?

It is important to locate this particular post in the context of the school and college before turning to the PE Department and to a sequence of events associated with the post that I have subdivided into the pre-interview phase, the interview and the post-interview phase (cf. Burgess, 1988a). The ethnographic data relating to the post of Coordinator of Adult Physical Education and Leisure Activities are therefore used to explore the dynamics surrounding a critical incident for the PE Department and for individual teachers' careers.

The Physical Education Department

In common with many secondary schools, Physical Education at Bishop McGregor School was taught in two parallel departments that were segregated on the basis of the pupils' sex (cf. Scraton, 1986). Many writers have pointed to such subdivisions having implications for pupils who are reluctant to share equipment or ideas (cf. Humberstone, 1987). However, at McGregor School this subdivision also held implications for segregated staffing, use of equipment and the timetabling of lessons in the sports hall, the swimming pool and on the playing field. Yet there was also a more fundamental division associated with

Table 2.1. Physical Education Staff at Bishop McGregor School, Summer 1984

Name	Scale post	Responsibility (if any)	Years of teaching	Other information
Terry Dean	3	Head of Boys' PE	11	On secondment for one year to a community college in the authority
Kay Stokes	3	Head of Girls' PE	9	On secondment to a university course
Julia Jones	3	Temporary Head of Girls' PE		Leaving at end of term
Paul Healey	permanent 2 temporary 3	Second in charge of Boys' PE but Head of Department for one year	8	Previously held temporary scale 3 for pastoral care
Roy Cooksley	2	Pastoral Care	8	Seconded in 1985/86
Pat Swift	2		$6\frac{1}{2}$	
Colin Burden	1		4	Temporary scale 2
Jane Whaley	1		1	

staffing and the allocation of scale posts to teachers. In the summer term 1984 the staff members in the Physical Education Department were as shown in Table 2.1. The allocation of posts between the boys' and girls' PE Department was already unequal with a total of four points above the basic Burnham salary having been allocated to the male staff and only two points above the basic salary being allocated to the women staff (i.e., to the head of girls' PE). In addition, temporary scale points above the basic salary had also been allocated to the male staff rather than their counterparts in the girls' PE Department.

In the academic year 1983–84 both heads of departments were on secondment and their posts were filled by temporarily promoting one of the male staff to head of boys' PE and recruiting a full-time woman teacher to be head of girls' PE. It was during this year that McGregor received community college status. Certainly, in all planning meetings, promotional activity and consultation with parents, sport, Physical Education and leisure figured large. It was, therefore, decided to make a permanent appointment that would allow someone to coordinate all adult PE and recreational activities. While the post was advertised internally at scale 4, the idea was that a salary would be 'topped up' so that an existing postholder might move from scale 3 or scale 2 to scale 4. When the post was advertised, it was widely discussed among staff who considered that the only real contenders were the two heads of departments, but Terry Dean was favoured given the experience he had gained while on secondment to another community college. Accordingly, we now turn to examine the way in which this new post helps to highlight the promotion prospects and strategies for the teachers concerned, as well as adding to our knowledge of the way in which key events or critical incidents demonstrate how social processes and sets of social relations operate in the wider structure of the school. We begin by examining the two heads of departments' careers before turning to an analysis of the pre-interview, interview and post-interview phases of the community post.

The Teachers and Their Experience

Both Terry Dean and Kay Stokes had come from similar backgrounds. Both had trained as PE specialists, had always taught in the authority in which McGregor was located and had some experience of community education as they had previously been in other schools that had community college status. Both teachers had previously held scale 2 posts and the head of girls' PE had been a head of department at McGregor for twice the time of her male counterpart. Both teachers were on scale 3 and were of an equivalent status. However, when asked whether the posts were equal Kay Stokes replied:

KS: Yes, equal in terms of status, yes.

RB: Yes.

KS: I don't know. I mean I've been here a lot longer than Terry and I found that I had to bale him out in a heck of a lot of situations. Probably good because we're mates.

RB: Can you give examples?

KS: Well he just didn't realize things were going to happen unless I told him, you know, that this is the time that he should be doing such and this is the time he should, you know.

RB: Yes.

KS: And that kind of thing. I think, I'm not a women's libber, but I think women basically are a lot more well organized than men are. I mean, we've worked very well together for a long time Terry and I, and you know, I respect him. He's got a different approach to me. We've got very different styles, but, you know, I do respect what he does.

The head of girls' PE, therefore, cast some doubt on whether both postholders were equal. In particular, her reference to their differences in style was elaborated upon in terms of the way in which they each interacted with the head and used the time to promote themselves and their departments. She commented:

KS: I very much just get on with my job. I very, very rarely go and

45

see Mr Goddard [the Head] and I don't do myself, or my staff, justice because of that, you know, when my staff are working hard because Mr Goddard doesn't really know that they are because I'm not there telling him all the time.[1]

RB: Yes.

KS: Terry spent a lot more time going to see the Head and, you know, all the rest of it. You see, and I don't respect that, I mean I think my job is to get on with my job and only when I'm in trouble, or you know, whenever I *really* need to see Mr Goddard, well I do so. And even then I would tend to put a note in. ...

RB: Yes.

KS: Rather than actually physically going to see him.

RB: Yes.

KS: I mean when we go into lunch and Mr Goddard is there, Terry's all this, this, this and this and the next, and we've done this, we've done that, that kind of thing, and I don't like that. I can't do that, and I know I don't do my staff justice because I don't do that.

However, she noted that Terry had not only made sure that he had gone to see the head but had also written several papers about going community for the head to see — all strategies that she thought had assisted him to obtain the post.

Certainly, Terry's account of his links with the head bore some similarity. However, Terry explained how just as he had developed a career strategy in moving from scale 1 through to a scale 3 head of department post,[2] so he had thought about the implications of community college status:

TD: Well, again, when I came here I was fairly sure in my own mind what I wanted to do was to make sure that I made a good job of Head of Boys' PE. I didn't set my sights any further than that at the time, and after a couple of years, obviously, then I felt that I'd got fully in control of that particular job. There was talk about community. I was obviously looking, myself, to develop further and the area of community activity. ... I mean the one thing that I'd thought for a long time, was always in holiday times, in the evenings when the school closes down, you've got all these wonderful facilities and nobody can have access to use them and I'd thought, I mean, I'd been thinking and chewing it about for a long, long time ... and of course when the opportunity came to visit community schools I served on a committee. There was a group of four of us that went to visit three schools.

RB: Oh, in April '83?

TD: Probably. Yes, it was that time. We came back and first of all the staff were asked to put forward questions that they would like to ask, you know, because obviously, staff who have not been involved in community education at all want to know what it's all about and so we went away with questions in mind and we came back with some answers and we drafted out a report and reported back to the staff. So that was my first chance to have any say whatsoever in what might happen here ... community, and it was the first chance of getting involved, really, because, career wise I saw that was the way that I wanted to move, and I was in a perfect position with McGregor hoping to become a Community College.

This experience helped Terry to acquire a more detailed knowledge of community education but he also decided to apply for secondment to take up a post of Head of the Faculty of Community Sport at another community college within the Authority. Kay had indicated that Terry maintained close links with the head so I asked Terry about this:

RB: Had you discussed this with Mr Goddard, about what you might do, in terms of going on a year's secondment to another school? or to ...

TD: Well, yes, but it was difficult discussing it [laughs]. My aim was ... I mean I could see 12 months ahead that they would need someone to coordinate community physical activities, here [McGregor School]. I mean it was obvious that was going to come about. If I could gain the experience, I would be in a very strong position to apply for that post. So, yes, I discussed it with Mr Goddard, but I couldn't, not in such a way as to say 'well hold the matter back Mr Goddard, you'll see me all right' ... [laughs]. I mean obviously I couldn't do that.

RB: Did he not indicate anything from his point of view?

TD: [laughs] A leading question! He couldn't ... I don't think ... he couldn't say anything positive, but there were ... I suppose there must have been odd things that were said that made me, encouraged me, let's put it that way.

The Pre-Interview Period

When Kay Stokes went to follow a university postgraduate course, Terry Dean went to a temporary community college post. Both teachers were learning about management but Kay Stokes' studies were theoretical, while Terry Dean was learning about the management of Physical Education in a community setting which involved practical experience at organizing classes, financial management, and making links with the community through a community association. He was, therefore, acquiring the background experience that was essential for the McGregor post.

Terry Dean kept the head informed of his progress at the other community college and the head kept him informed of developments at McGregor as he remarked:

> *TD:* He [the Head] notified me of the change that was going on to keep me involved, because my job was at McGregor and not at Huxley [the other college], that was a temporary appointment, and obviously he tried to keep me in touch with the developments community-wise. I asked him to let me know, I wanted to know what was going on and didn't want to be left in the dark. I was out in the sticks at Huxley so not knowing what was going on, and so we had two, two quite long chats about things and he told me more or less, this was in about April time, the first meeting, I think. No it must have been, that was when the second one was, it must have been earlier than that when he informed me that there was more or less certain to be a coordinator of adult physical recreation in September. I thought it would be advertised much earlier than it was. He couldn't make any promises, and didn't. I didn't expect them.

While no promises were made to Terry, Kay Stokes believed the job was 'set up' for him as she found that prior to the job being advertised Terry's timetable had been established on the assumption he would obtain the post. Kay explained.

> *KS:* Before the job was even advertised, I came in to see the timetable and the Deputy Head was very reluctant to give it to me and I said, 'Look, you know, I've got to get something sorted out. I've got to let my staff know what they're teaching and what have you and I want to see the timetable you know', and in the end he gave it to me and said, 'Well don't look at this section of the timetable', which was where the boys' PE was, and of course I did! He gave it to me and I looked at it, you know. And Terry had only been timetabled for something like 12 periods of PE, before the job had even been advertised. And I went to see Mr Goddard about it in the end and he said, 'Well, I understood you weren't interested and that; you wanted to go into pastoral work' and I said, 'Well, you know, when I did come to see you

about it, I said', and I distinctly remember saying 'I wanted to keep my options open' because I was at an age where I don't want to go on teaching PE, you know, forever, that sort of thing. ...

RB: No.

KS: You know, I've got to be thinking in terms of moving some-where else, you know. Having been on this course, I felt, perhaps I ought to capitalize on it now, because in two or three years' time the effect of the course will have diminished.

RB: Yes.

KS: But of course the posts aren't really there at the moment, you know, I mean I basically said to him, 'I want to keep my options open'. ...

RB: Yes, yes.

KS: ... 'Will you back me in whatever I decide to do?' He said, 'Yes'. So I certainly didn't say that I wasn't interested in the com-munity post, but I also didn't say that's the 'be all and end all' of it. I mean, I think, Terry is probably the better person to do the job. I don't ... I don't dispute that. I mean he's got more time than I've got because he's a man. But I also felt very hurt because, I mean, I've been here for eight years and I've done ... the PE department here when I came wasn't very good at all. And I'd given a heck of a lot of time and energy.

As far as Kay was concerned, the head and his deputy had already worked on the assumption that Terry would be appointed to the new post. On this basis she did not apply, but she did concede that Terry was the most suitable person for the job.

The Interview

Only the boys' PE staff applied for the post of Coordinator of Adult Physical Education and Leisure Activities. The governors had decided that they would all be interviewed and therefore Terry Dean was in competition with two of his staff: one who held a permanent scale 2 post and another who had a temporary scale 2 post. With those three staff members in competition for the post, Terry regarded himself as the 'favourite', as he remarked:

TD: I mean, I knew that when I came along that morning I was favoured for the job. There was no doubt about that. I mean that was obvious.

Certainly, among the members of the interviewing panel this view was shared as Terry was told he had given them an excellent interview — what the head had described as 'more like in-service education for governors'. However, as Terry remarked:

> TD: I was obviously quite elated really, having got the job and also having had a good interview ... I mean if I had got the job on a bad interview now, that wouldn't have pleased me very much, if that had happened, which might have happened. I might not have gone through the interview very well at all, but still been offered the job because the fact that they knew me, and that maybe everything shouldn't be based on interview when you know somebody really quite well. So it could have worked out that way. It didn't do, ... so I was pleased. Yes.

The interview demonstrated the way in which the job advantaged Terry and also Terry's ability for the post. At the start of the interview the head introduced the candidates who were to be seen as:

> Terry Dean who has been at Huxley College doing an excellent job on secondment. Colin Burden who has been on a temporary scale two for community work and who has done an excellent job and Roy Cooksley who has a permanent scale two and wishes to make it up to a three.

With this introduction the third candidate was already at a disadvantage, while the positive remarks about the first two teachers gave Terry Dean a positive advantage as he held a permanent scale 3 post compared with Colin Burden's temporary scale 2.

Having introduced the candidates, the head was then asked by the LEA adviser on the panel if a job description was available. He replied by indicating that it was all in his head and covered himself by saying, 'It probably said in the initial notice that anyone who wished to discuss the post with the head is free to do so.' However, he continued by explaining that this post was for a coordinator between the school and the community who would encourage people in physical fitness. In particular, the head cited courses for the young unemployed, rock climbing, martial arts and the development of a users' group as being his priorities. With this job description, Terry Dean was again put in an advantageous position as he had held the post of coordinator for community sport at Huxley Community College and the interview panel were able to ask him about the way in which he had carried out this temporary one-year post and how he would develop courses for the unemployed and establish a users' group at McGregor School. It was on the basis of the answers that Terry provided that members of the interview panel were able to go into further detail with the other two candidates. However, at the end of the three interviews, the Chairman of governors suggested that Terry was the most suitable candidate for the post and without any discussion he was called back to be offered the post. But this promotion for Terry Dean had implications, not only for the development of community sport, but also for the school PE programme in the following term, which I describe as the post-interview period.

The Post-Interview Period

As Terry Dean was on secondment, his post did not take effect until the autumn term. It was at this time that his appointment to this new position highlighted differences between boys' and girls' PE and also between school and community-based activities. Terry defined his new post in the following terms:

> TD: Well I see my job as being to set up physical activities in as broad as possible way as we can to as many different people, in terms of age, sex, whether employed, unemployed and to try and put on a programme which tries to achieve a balance between the type of person that comes in, whether it's during the day or in the evenings, and also the sort of programme that we can put on bearing in mind the cost, whether something is going to be run, just from the point of making sure that we break even, or whether something's going to be run in terms of making a profit.

Such a definition highlighted the relationship (or lack of it) between the school and the community. As far as Terry was concerned, he was attempting to bring together school-based and community-based activities; an ideal expressed by those engaged in community education (cf. Hargreaves, 1982; Burgess, 1986b). Terry explained,

> TD: What we're trying to do is to bring the two together [school and community], as best we can, in terms of continuity for the pupils who are at school at the moment. First of all continuity in several ways. First of all that when they leave school, they've got something that they can continue doing. For example, we've set up the community basket ball team, and that's made up of about five of the current fifth year basket ball team that plays in school. So that when they leave, we will be into the league next year and they can continue playing their basket ball

without a break, so we try and bridge the gap so it's ... but where we can bring them together, and have a sort of a 'carry on through' from like school to community, then obviously that's what we're trying to do well ... and obviously because a lot of the pupils at the moment are involved in community activities, but it also is of course in terms of time, because the majority of things that we do community sports wise, takes place in the evenings so the school operates in the day time, community in the evenings, so there's an obvious cut-off from the point of time. The day-time activities that we put on are aimed at members of the community who are not here as members of the school.

However, such developments meant that Terry was not only involved in organizing boys' and men's Physical Education, but also Physical Education for women in the community. As far as Terry was concerned this did not create any problems but this view was not shared by Kay Stokes who considered that 'going community' should have no direct effect on the girls' PE programme. However, she remarked:

KS: What I do find is different is the attitudes of staff who are very much involved in the community side of things and I've particularly noticed it with the head of boys' PE who is, you know, sort of my counterpart, because he's taken on the community side of everything and I find that now we're not working towards the same ends because my priority is still with the education of the kids in the school, whereas his is now more sort of geared towards community and when we discuss things, he seems to be thinking of everything in terms of the community and he's putting, I think, far too much emphasis on that side to the detriment of the Physical Education Department. I mean if you just look at the timetable that we've now got, we've got two blocks left completely free for community use. Now, logically, that really didn't have to happen.

It was in the area of timetabling and resourcing of the PE programme that the heads of girls' and boys' PE held different views. Terry explained that in order to establish the community programme he had needed to create space on the timetable:

TD: You see, one problem that immediately springs to mind, that is ... I wanted to create time on the timetable or daytime activities. ... Immediately there are constraints because there was a full timetable and what I did was to double up with two different year groups on at the same time and that poses problems about the use of facilities which means that some groups are missing out on some activities that they've done in the past to make way for the space for the community and that's something that we had to iron out. That was a problem in ... by the mere fact that I ended up with the job with a week to go before the end of term — it was done without any consultation.

RB: Mmm.

TD: ... and that's obviously not the best way to go about things. It's best to consult people first and then make a decision. But, I made the decision myself without consulting anyone, because I didn't have the chance to and that created a little bit of friction.

RB: With whom?

TD: Well, mainly to begin with, it was with the girls' side because I'd had a chance to chat it through with the men but unfortunately it was a matter of informing the women's PE that this is what I'd done and we'd have to do this, that and the other, and of course, it's not always readily accepted.

It was this lack of consultation with the women PE staff that resulted in the girls having less access to the sports facilities and equipment as Kay Stokes explained:

KS: Tuesday 1 and 2 and Wednesday 5 and 6 are left completely free for community use. Now that means that at other times of the day, we've got second years and first years on together and the same here and the same here [pointing to the timetable]. There's three occasions where that happens, or we've got a fifth year games group on. Now this puts real pressure on the facilities. And it means that on Friday morning, these two lessons, my first years don't get a balls skills lesson which really is essential to their basic education, you know, physical education ... .

RB: Yes.

KS: Now you see that is where the community has been put before the pupils in this school. I mean these kids have to go ... will have to go outside every morning. Every Friday morning throughout the winter. They will not get a chance to go in the sports centre, which, you know, as first years they really need to do a lot of basic skills. I mean I do think it's criminal to see facilities left idle and I've always said, you know, the school should open up in the evening and their facilities should be used. I mean to leave a sports hall and the swimming pool and the gymnasia empty, you know, when people are crying out to use them, I think it's criminal. But I don't think the community should be put before the education of the kids because primarily that's what we're here for.

On this basis Terry's appointment raised a series of critical questions about the relationship between school and community, and about the dual use of facilities in Physical Education by adults and by pupils. In addition, questions were raised about staff resources, as it was argued by Kay Stokes that the girls' PE staff could not engage in any further teaching as all their timetabled time was filled with other subject work, but the boys' PE staff would be able to contribute to the community sports programme given the time that was available to them, especially the head of boys' PE.

Thus the appointment of Terry to the scale 4 post had not only been a critical incident in his career, but had also shaped the relationship between school and community, and between boys' and girls' PE in Bishop McGregor School.

Conclusion

In this chapter we have provided a detailed ethnographic account of a period of promotion for the head of boys' PE in Bishop McGregor School. Such periods in teachers' careers have been termed 'critical incidents' by Sikes *et al.* (1985). However, their use of the term is confined to an analysis of teachers' jobs and careers. Here, we have attempted to set the critical incident in a broader context, as in event analysis (cf. Gluckman, 1942; Mitchell, 1956, 1987, pp. 1–33; Van Velsen, 1967) so as to trace the relationship between changes in the individual's career biography and changes in the institution in which the career biography is located. By taking a promotion in PE as our example we have examined how the new post was established in Physical Education as a consequence of the school being given community college status. Furthermore, we have explored the ways in which this critical incident in the career of the head of boys' PE can also help us to examine the relationship between boys' and girls' PE in Bishop McGregor School, the relationship between school and community and the implications of community education for resources and staffing within a department in a comprehensive school.

This study of teachers' careers and career strategies also highlights aspects of inequality between men and women teachers (cf. Burgess, 1988a). In particular, attention has been drawn to implicit and explicit sexism towards women teachers, given the expectations of those members of the senior management team in McGregor School. This also had implications for power relations between men and women within the PE Department and more generally in the structure of the school.

Such situations need to be carefully considered by school governors, local authority advisers and members of the senior management team of schools when engaged in teacher appointments. Decisions concerning appointments may, at first sight, appear to be isolated incidents in the career of particular departments and of particular teachers. However, the decisions that are made can influence patterns of power, patterns of innovation and change and the model of a particular subject area that is portrayed to all school students. Teachers' careers, promotion possibilities and appointments, therefore, not only need to be the subject of investigation by researchers, but also need to be monitored by those practitioners and policy-makers who are involved in these decisions.

Acknowledgments

The data on which this chapter is based were obtained during a re-study of Bishop McGregor School. The fieldwork for this study was supported by grants from the University of Warwick Research and Innovations Fund and the Nuffield Foundation to whom I am most grateful. I would also like to thank John Evans for his editorial support and Hilary Bayliss for typing and retyping this chapter.

Notes

1 For a similar view, where links with the head influenced the standing and status of a PE Department, see Bell (1986).
2 For a discussion of male careers in PE see Glew, (1981).

References

BALL, S.J. and GOODSON, I.F. (Eds) (1985) *Teachers' Lives and Careers*, Lewes, Falmer Press.
BELL, L. (1986) 'Managing to survive in secondary school physical education', in EVANS, J. (Ed.), *Physical Education, Sport and Schooling: Studies in the Sociology of Physical Education*, Lewes, Falmer Press, pp. 95–117.
BURGESS, R.G. (1983) *Experiencing Comprehensive Education: A Study of Bishop McGregor School*, London, Methuen.

BURGESS, R.G. (1986a) 'Going for a job: An ethnographic study of teachers' interviews in a comprehensive school', Paper prepared for the annual conference of the British Educational Research Association, University of Bristol, September.

BURGESS, R.G. (1986b) 'School and community: It's so close together you can't see the join', *Journal of Community Education*, 5, 3, pp. 5–8.

BURGESS, R.G. (1987a) 'Studying and restudying Bishop McGregor School', in WALFORD, G. (Ed.), *Doing Sociology of Education*, Lewes, Falmer Press, pp. 67–94.

BURGESS, R.G. (1987b) 'Something you learn to live with? Gender and inequality in a comprehensive school', Papers prepared for the Ethnography of Inequality Conference, St Hilda's College, Oxford, September.

BURGESS, R.G. (1988a) 'Points and posts: A case study of teachers' careers in a comprehensive school', in GREEN, A. and BALL, S.J. (Eds), *Comprehensive Education in the 1980s*, London, Croom Helm.

BURGESS, R.G. (1988b) 'Conversations with a purpose: The ethnographic interview in educational research', in BURGESS, R.G. (Ed.), *Conducting Qualitative Research*, New York, JAI Press.

GLEW, P. (1981) 'P. E. as a career for men', *British Journal of Physical Education*, 12, 3, p. 79.

GLUCKMAN, M. (1942) *An Analysis of a Social Situation in Modern Zululand*, Rhodes-Livingstone Paper no. 28.

HARGREAVES, D.H. (1982) *The Challenge for the Comprehensive School*, London, Routledge and Kegan Paul.

HUMBERSTONE, B. (1987) 'Gender and inequality in physical education and outdoor education: A transformation of pupils' conventional concepts of femininity and masculinity', Paper prepared for the Ethnography of Inequality Conference, St Hilda's College, Oxford, September.

MEASOR, L. (1985) 'Critical incidents in the classroom: Identities, choices and careers', in BALL, S.J. and GOODSON, I.F. (Eds), *Teachers' Lives and Careers*, Lewes, Falmer Press, pp. 61–78.

MITCHELL, J.C. (1956) *The Kalela Dance*, Rhodes-Livingstone Paper no. 27.

MITCHELL, J.C. (1987) *Cities, Society and Social Perception*, Oxford, Clarendon Press.

SCRATON, S.J. (1986) 'Images of femininity and the teaching of girls' physical education', in EVANS, J. (Ed.), *Physical Education, Sport and Schooling: Studies in the Sociology of Physical Education*, Lewes, Falmer Press, pp. 71–95.

SIKES, P.J. (1985) 'The life cycle of the teacher', in BALL, S.J. and GOODSON, I.F. (Eds), *Teachers' Lives and Careers*, Lewes, Falmer Press, pp. 27–61.

SIKES, P.J., MEASOR, L. and WOODS, P. (1985) *Teacher Careers: Crises and Continuities*, Lewes, Falmer Press.

VAN VELSEN, J. (1967) 'The extended case method and situational analysis', in EPSTEIN, A.L. (Ed.), *The Craft of Social Anthropology*, London, Tavistock.

WALKER, R. (1976) *Innovation, the School and the Teacher (1)*, Open University Course E203, Unit 27, Milton Keynes, Open University Press.

WOODS, P. (1985) 'Conversations with teachers', *British Educational Research Journal*, 11, 1, pp. 13–26.

4
Settling Down: An Examination of Two Women Physical Education Teachers

Thomas. J. Templin with assistance from Kevin Bruce and Linda Hart

I'm moving across very nicely which is what I want. The magical figure 40 looms — I made the decision when I first started teaching that there was no way I was just going to be a PE teacher at the age of 40 because I had seen too often, women and men become stuck. I think there are people in our department that are becoming stuck and there was no way that I was going to be. That's why I started going towards the pastoral system. That's why I worked through that and now I'm doing the second part of my plan which is the other subject areas and then a deputy headship. (Kate, English, age 38)

It seems the longer you stay in the fight the more dissatisfied you get and you can see the handwriting on the wall. Where I am right now — it's like I told you 7 years and I'm out — I'm going to try to get into something else. I've been in the game 14 years and all my associates who have been in it 30 years keep telling me it's getting worse not better ... if I were allowed to teach, I would not be thinking about 7 years and out — devoting a life long commitment to it, but it's so frustrating that you have to deal with your inner self. I don't want to lose any more self respect and dignity because of it. (Sarah, American, age 40)

Levinson and his associates (1978) write of the course and seasons of a person's life and suggest that there exists a certain flow over time, 'the patterning of specific events, relationships, achievements, failures, and aspirations that are the stuff of life' (p. 6). They continue by stating that each season of one's life cycle 'has its own time; it is important in its own right and needs to be understood in its own terms. ... Each has its necessary place and contributes its special character to the whole' (p. 7).

This chapter examines, in part, the lives and seasons of the two, mid-career Physical Education teachers quoted above. It examines various aspects of each woman's career by focusing on their perceptions of role in their teaching careers, their relationships, their commitments, their satisfactions, their struggles and their aspirations. The impetus for this study stems from a desire to learn more about the uniqueness of the occupation of teaching from the teacher's viewpoint. As a result of observing and talking with PE teachers from both England and the US, I was able to formulate a comparative frame of reference about Physical Education and teachers in two school settings within different countries. It is hoped that pre-service and in-service teachers alike will gain some insight into their own lives and careers as they compare them with those of the teachers Kate and Sarah, who are the subjects of this study.

Careers: Conceptual and Methodological Framework

The study of teacher careers has received significant attention both in the US (Becker, 1976; Lortie, 1975) and in England (Ball and Goodson, 1985; Lacey, 1977, 1987; Lyons, 1981; Sikes, Measor and Woods, 1985). Unfortunately, there have been few studies on the lives and careers of PE teachers (Evans, 1986; Locke, Griffin and Templin, 1986; Sikes, 1986). The definition of career has been interpreted in many ways, but typically is defined in terms of (1) occupational mobility through a series of related positions, and (2) participation and commitment to a line of work. These two characteristics may be united or viewed separately. That is, the normative view of career is typically seen in terms of individual advancement, but this is limiting in that some may be concerned with both advancement and commitment. In contrast, an individual may not be all concerned with advancement, but with a commitment to one's objectives in his or her work (i.e., student learning).

This study moves beyond the traditional conception of career by viewing the concept more broadly. Specifically, the concept of career is grounded in a whole-life perspective and as 'the product of the dialectical relationship between self and circumstance' (Sikes, Measor and Woods, 1985, p. 2). As Sikes (1985) suggests within her chapter, 'career' is characterized in various ways:

1. It is subjective. The structure and content of a career depends on how the person concerned sees it. This in turn involves considerations of a person's interests.
2. It takes a whole life view. Careers are seen within the entire longitudinal perspective of life.
3. It takes a whole personal world view. That is to say it considers all

of a person's interests and activities, in, for example, job, family, hobby, or alternative job.

4. It is concerned with on-going development.
5. It is concerned with a person's identity. (pp. 2–3)

While our study focuses on the mid-career experiences of two PE teachers, Sikes' characteristics of career helped us frame the research. The study utilized interactionist principles in the analysis of the teachers' perceptions and reactions to everyday circumstance within their teaching experiences.

The Settling Down Period

The developmental model of Levinson *et al.* (1978) fits neatly within the whole-life career perspective. Although the model is based on the study of males, the authors suggest that there is evidence 'that women go through the same development as men ... but in partially different ways that reflect the differences in biology and social circumstance' (p. 9).

The model addresses the various eras and stages which adults move through in shaping their lives and careers. For example, the two teachers in this study were in the settling down period of early adulthood. This period is characteristic of individuals aged 30 to 40 in mid-life who seek to establish a niche in society and work at advancement (Levinson *et al.*, 1978, p. 140). The settling down period is the stage in which individuals seek self-identity or 'becoming one's own man' or woman by making it in their personal and professional lives. One should note, however, that within this period all is not always rosy. One's journey through this period may reflect both stability and instability, success and failure, and advancement or a life that remains in flux. In essence, 'marker events' or events which have notable impact on one's life may occur within this period and it is the description of some of those events as disclosed by the teachers studied which will be examined here.

The Life History Method

One form of ethnographic research used to study the concept of career is the life history method. Through a series of interviews of an individual over time, 'life histories often try to construct subjects' "careers emphasizing the role of organizations, crucial events, and significant others in shaping" subjects' evolving definitions of self and their perspectives on life' (Bogdan and Biklen, 1982, p. 61).

The life history method is grounded in the pursuit of personal truth and it is important to understand the wider socio-historical context to which the individual's perceptions may be linked. Certainly, it serves as a useful method for studying the occupation of teaching.

The use of the life history method here falls in line with four basic assumptions about the method (Goodson, 1983, p. 142).

1. that the teacher's previous careers and life experience shape his/her view of teachers and the way he/she sets about it.
2. that the teacher's life outside school, his/her latent identities and cultures, may have an important impact on his/her work as a teacher.
3. that the teacher's career is a vitally important research focus.
4. Life histories of schools, subjects, and the teaching profession provide vital contextual information.

In essence, through a series of (five, one-hour) interviews with each teacher we hoped to document the experiences of the two teachers and how they interpret, understand and respond to their lives as teachers. We believe, as does Goodson (1980), that 'in understanding something so intensely personal as teaching, it is critical that we know about the person the teacher is' (p. 69). The following contributes to such an understanding.

Two Teachers

Kate

Kate, aged 38, has taught girls' Physical Education for sixteen years in a large comprehensive secondary school (1900 pupils, ages 11–19) in a small country town in south-east England. She is one of nine PE staff members (five males and four females). A scale 4 teacher, Kate also serves in a pastoral role as the head of one of four houses within the school. In addition to teaching PE and her pastoral duty, Kate teaches community studies and a careers course. She has coached throughout her career and earns £12,000. Kate is in her second marriage and has no children.

Although her childhood participation in sport served as a natural springboard into PE, Kate looked back upon her entry into teacher training and PE itself with some misgivings.

> I think in hindsight, probably because I didn't get a great deal of careers advice and if I think back I don't know whether I would have done it [enter PE]. I think I would have gone into teaching, whether I would have gone into PE I don't know. ... I think there is so much

more to offer. ... I think possibly I may have gone on and done geography, which I've always enjoyed and maybe do PE as a subset.

Kate's decision to enter a three-year certification course at a college of education after attending a secondary modern and grammar school was influenced by her former teachers and coaches.

Mr and Mrs Smith who I have remained in contact with were very influential in my formative years. They were teachers and they'd say, hey, look you have got a brain, forget this bit that you've failed (the eleven plus exam) and you're here, get on and work and use it. The female PE teacher was absolutely useless, but the guy was great and he took a couple of us and really trained us very hard. It was he and the Smiths who sort of said, you ought to go on to higher education, you ought to continue this (sport involvement, teaching games).

Kate was not unlike many other entry teachers who, as Sikes points out in this reader (see Chapter 2), have little idea of what else to do. Although Kate considered entering the forces, she decided to enter teaching as if by default. She was an accomplished athlete, was recognized as such, and was encouraged to maintain her association with sport through Physical Education.

In the Beginning

It is difficult to embody in words alone the mad pace of Kate's daily existence. From the time she came to Smith School from another school, where she taught for one year, Kate has taken on a very demanding work load. Like most beginning PE teachers, Kate taught PE during the day and was responsible for coaching a variety of teams after school throughout the school year. It was this additional role of coaching which was most demanding:

At first, it was hard in that there were huge demands on me. I did one year at another school and then transferred here, I've been here since. The demands at that stage were such that I had very little free time. Very few free preparation periods. It was expected I would work after school taking teams to matches. It was expected that I'd do things on Saturdays. Take kids to games and things like that. It was very tiring.

The strain of her heavy teaching and coaching schedule was compounded by personal problems early in her teaching career. During Kate's fourth year of teaching she went through a divorce which affected her job significantly.

I was married in '72 and divorced in '76. That was fairly traumatic, fairly upsetting and therefore teaching did become a job and was lower on my list of priorities at that point, my social life was more important and trying to seek happiness for myself was all important ... it was awful because I wasn't prepared for my lessons ... my own confidence took a great knock because of a relationship that went totally rotten ... I came through it 'cause I was a survivor. That's my nature. I can take knocks, but I can usually find ways of coming back.

Part of Kate's coping strategy through this tough period was to become totally immersed in her school work.

As I started to come through the upset and started the need to fill my life, it was very easy to fill my life totally with school. I could then go home utterly exhausted and just collapse in a heap and forget about myself and having to survive and be happy.

Beyond throwing herself into her work, Kate attributed her 'coming through the upset' and surviving to the development of a new relationship which resulted in her second marriage. So important was this relationship to her present duties that Kate suggested:

I can honestly say to you that I couldn't cope with my job without my husband. He's very very good to me. He has a canny knack of knowing when to let me sleep ... the good thing is we both appreciate the fact that we're both working.

Since marrying again, Kate stated that she has been able to 'get on with her home life and her school life. Life's been very good since [meeting her husband].'

The Daily Grind

While the school timetable ran from 8.50 a.m. to 3.45 p.m. each day, Kate's school day began at 8.00 and usually ended between 5.00 and 5.30 each evening. Within a fifty-eight period (one period = fifty minutes) timetable per week, Kate taught five periods of community studies, nine periods of social-vocational career preparation, twenty-seven periods of PE, and had seventeen hours of free periods which she devoted to her pastoral role. In addition, Kate, like every teacher in the school, assumed a tutorial duty twice a day for fifteen minutes for the purpose of checking attendance and providing tutorial care. In essence, Kate was a very busy person moving in and out of various roles.

Although Kate saw the interpersonal nature of teaching and coaching as 'a positive springboard' into her pastoral role, she claimed the association ended there in relation to the time demands of her house role. Furthermore, she suggested how the recent teacher industrial action had helped resolve the conflict and tension over how she should distribute her limited time. It had meant a decreasing coaching involvement.

It's [head of house role] not a job that lends 100% to linking with PE because I still try to put some time in over there. Although following industrial action it's nowhere near what it used to be. There is a conflict of role and conflict of time. I have to try to justify priorities. The house has to come first.

Preparation time for teaching also worked into the formula of load conflict for Kate. Such preparation, however, was directed toward her classroom and house duties rather than towards her PE teaching.

I have a file sitting here full of lesson plans from previous years and I've been doing an awful lot of dipping in and thinking I ought to be doing the next follow on. I've got less [PE teaching] which helps. Last year I had a lot of switching to Smith which was difficult. However, it means I've done a lot of planning in previous years and I call upon that. I've had to because I've got a bad load in the classroom and that work load is all very new. ... I've got to spend a lot of time preparing notes. These are the other subject areas. I know I can teach PE. I know that I can probably teach PE better now if I spend more time planning it, but I don't have the time.

In addition to the time needed to prepare her classroom responsibilities, Kate's house role called for her to carry out various pastoral responsibilities. Kate prepared written reports about students, she had to contact and meet with parents about their children, and she conducted and attended meetings with school administrators (the headmaster and deputy heads), other house administrators and her own house staff. Equally, she met with the PTA once a month. Beyond these roles Kate also perceived the need to help facilitate staff development and the teacher appraisal process in her school: 'I also want to get involved in the staff development committee which is looking at staff appraisals. I feel it's an area that we have neglected for a long time.'

What did these multiple roles mean to Kate? While she saw her time commitment to be greater than others in the school this does not bother Kate. What concerned Kate was her work load and the load of other teachers which constrained innovation and quality instruction.

Innovation, I feel, in many areas at the moment is being halted because of the sheer multiplicity of people's roles and also through the sheer lack of time — not through lack of interest, not through lack of motivation, not through lack of desirability and being aware of national trends. It's all there, people are aware of it, but they haven't got the time and the energy with which to do it.

Such a heavy load negatively affected the quality of Kate's teaching, especially in PE.

I don't like teaching a lesson off the top of my head. I have to admit it, I do it more and more as time goes on, but I don't like doing it. I find my teaching isn't as good. I know if I'm not sufficiently prepared, then it's not stretching and challenging for them. They're not going to enjoy it, they're not going to respond well, so I'm not going to enjoy it. Unfortunately, this is the way it is.

Promotion

It was the multiplicity of roles that motivated Kate to examine the direction of her career. It was clear Kate wished to move into more classroom teaching and then advance to deputy headship. Kate was confident that her desire to decrease her teaching load in PE was a sound career decision which would facilitate her ambitions. However, at this stage of her career, Kate stated, 'I would not want to eliminate PE totally from my timetable, because I greatly enjoy it ... but I will say I don't want it all the time now. I'm quite happy with the balance and the change to go into the classroom.'

Ultimately, Kate did foresee a change. First, she suggested the importance of moving primarily to classroom and house duties.

I firmly believe that in 10 years' time, I don't want to be permanently on games. I've started now to teach other areas. ... I am very happy with my timetable. I've been trying for four years to be mainly on site, to have quite a big classroom proportioned for my time ... I'm moving across very nicely which is what I want ... I'm happy with my classroom teaching and I know that I'm making progress and I also know that I've got the capabilities if I want to make a career in the classroom. Plus I've got my administration position here.

Secondly, she believed that in order to achieve her goal of becoming a deputy head, she must begin the application process now.

I've got to make the next stage within the next 3 or 4 years because otherwise I'm going to get stuck as a head of house. ... The next stage is the deputy head, but I haven't got a degree which is a problem. So I may well have to do a year of something to get a degree.

Even without pursuing a master's degree, Kate felt that she had a chance to be considered for a deputy headship based on her own experience and what she felt are expanding opportunities for women.

> It is slightly easier [to advance] on the feminine side than it is on the masculine side. ... Because there are a limited number of women pursuing careers to this level, that makes it slightly easier. It's more of a possibility.

Hence, as Sikes suggested, Kate is not unlike other PE teachers who have moved into the pastoral system. Certainly, her aspiration to move into a deputy headship will be difficult as she competes with teachers (perhaps especially males) from other subject areas with higher qualifications. Yet Kate believed that her gender and her movement into other (non-PE) subject areas as well as her pastoral experience would assist her in obtaining a senior position. This, as others in this reader point out, may well be a naive view of promotion and of the difficulties which women in particular experience when trying to advance their careers; but for Kate the next step was to apply for deputy headships in various schools.

Beyond Kate's heavy work load, she saw few problems standing in her way toward career satisfaction and advancement. Below I examine how she perceived her relationships with others, staff development issues and PE as a subject area in relation to her present status and her future in the educational system.

Relationship with Others

Students. Kate felt that her relationship with students was very positive, and that this was fostered by her PE teaching, her own personality and particularly by her house role.

> One important point is because of the very nature of PE; that is, it is on a more relaxed basis than a structured classroom situation. That actually helps a little in how I am able to relate to a number of youngsters. Because of my personality, because of the way I like to talk to and interact with kids, because I enjoy their company. I feel that comes over in the house duty and that assists.

She felt that her relationship with students had grown stronger over the years and that her standing in the school eliminated the kind of discipline problems that she had previously encountered in her earlier career as a teacher.

> I can honestly say, I don't have any discipline problems at all because

I'm lucky and I've risen to a respected position in the house system as well. There are a few who you fear and dread before you walk in. I wouldn't ever want to use that and exploit that, but it does help.

Consequently, she felt comfortable with her students, they provided no grounds for her to be dissatisfied with her work as a teacher.

PE Teaching Colleagues and the PE Department and Status. Kate had an amiable relationship with her PE teaching colleagues. It was apparent that the members of the PE teaching staff related positively with one another and Kate was accepted as an important member of the department. Her colleagues were quick to cover for Kate when she had to attend to emergency house duties that arose. Kate, however, felt that the PE staff lacked leadership and that certain individuals were 'stuck' and needed to improve their teaching or move into other areas of responsibility within the school or leave teaching altogether. For example, Kate offered the following about one colleague relative to her own career:

> ... I don't think he enjoys his PE. He doesn't stick to the syllabus. He does it his own way. He undermines what the department's trying to do. It's a very negative influence, but it comes back to the County and the fact they don't foresee the need and the priority for training at a later stage in a career. I've seen these things going on and this is why I've made my move. ...

She was particularly critical when addressing the leadership provided by the department head.

> I think he as head of department has lost direction, he's lost initiative and the driving force. He's receded into a hell. ... He is a different person to the person I'm used to in terms of leadership qualities, motivating people, and communicating. He's not prepared to get up and battle. ... Most departments have regular meetings. We're not meeting these days.

Although other non-PE teachers and the head of school perceived and stated that the PE department was a valuable part of the curriculum, it was also seen as the most troubled subject within the school. Unfortunately, it received few signs of significant support or attention in solving personnel and curriculum problems. This brings about suspicion as to the actual versus espoused status of PE in the school. Kate stated:

> I know that the deputy head has the perception that the department with the most problems in the whole school is the PE department. I've talked to the head about it and he perceives that as a problem, I

actually think in the widest context that the head is weak on staff discipline. If you actually are critical of the departmental situation like, who should be active, it should be the head. I don't think the head is that sort of guy. He doesn't like to get in that sort of area. ... He values many of the individuals in the department, but he should be a little more critical and say now what's this functional departmental unit like. Forget the individual people, what's the unit like. ... I think you've got to put some of the responsibility on the head.

In Kate's view PE was a troubled department, it lacked leadership and direction and the support of significant seniors within the school. This appraisal of the PE situation had an important bearing on how Kate viewed her career as a teacher, the careers of her colleagues and PE as a subject area.

Staff Development

Early in her teaching career Kate attended courses related to instruction in a number of physical activities which she found stimulating and beneficial to her instruction. She continued to attend such courses periodically, but perceived the need for more structured and frequent on-site in-service activities for the entire teaching staff. Unfortunately, the timetables of the majority of staff left little time for such activity and those responsible for initiating such activity had not done so. Kate believed staff development should become a contractual right of teachers: 'I think there should be a certain number of days we are contracted to be in school to engage in in-service training.'

Although one staff member was specifically responsible for the coordination of staff development, opportunities were still absent. Kate stated:

... she's too busy, tied up with too many other things. She almost needs not to be teaching at all. She needs to have a lot of other administrative work taken off her plate and she needs to address her time to staff development.

Kate had suggested to the head of school that the faculty responsible for teaching the Personal Life Skills Program (PLSP), which she coordinates, needed additional in-service training:

I saw her at a parent teacher social on Friday. After a couple of glasses of wine, I took her to one side and I said to her how worried I was about PLSP and about how there is insufficient staff training. ... She actually said, I understand, but what am I going to do.

Staff development was a real source of concern for Kate, but one which appeared to receive little attention. Each faculty had to be responsible for his/her own development and could not depend on the wider school system to provide such opportunity. As a result, Kate engaged in self-initiated development activities to advance her career.

Sarah

Sarah, aged 40, has taught high school Physical Education and Health for fourteen years in a large mid-western US city in which she was born and raised. The PE staff has six teachers, three males and three females. She teaches in the same high school which she attended in her adolescence. Sarah has coached throughout her career. She is single and lives with her parents. Sarah has first and higher degrees in Physical Education and earns around $30,000. She is an active equestrienne and softball player.

Entry into Teaching

Sarah's entry into PE was delayed. After graduating from high school Sarah was employed in a music shop filling a variety of roles. She had been active in the high school band and orchestra and the job was a natural choice. Yet, after five years in this position, a close friend of Sarah encouraged her to continue her education and pursue Sarah's desire to develop a career more closely aligned with helping others.

> It [music job] wasn't people-oriented enough and as a little kid I always felt I wanted to go into something that was humanity-oriented with people. ... I decided after 5 years of working there that there had to be something better suited for me. In the back of my mind I always perceived as what I was going to do (teach) and what I needed to do to fill my own expectations.

So Sarah entered a state university to become an elementary teacher. After beginning her training Sarah realized that, through her involvement in residence hall intra-mural sport, classroom teaching would not be satisfactory and that teaching Physical Education would fill her career needs. Her love of sport, her need to be active and her desire to help others see the benefit of physical action led to her final decision to enter PE.

> I was too active for that [teaching in an elementary classroom] and I've always been an active individual and I couldn't imagine myself in that kind of environment. ... I felt an opportunity in PE for people to learn

more about themselves. I thought that in some way if I could have an impact on an individual, trying to get them realizing the importance of the physical aspect of their being ... perhaps they could enjoy life a bit more because I had enjoyed finding the fellowship through physical activity and sport.

In addition to support from a close friend in her decision to enter teaching, after Sarah enrolled in the PE department she gained the support of a member of university faculty in PE.

As I got involved with some of the people in the PE department, they were very influential and very supportive. There was one individual who was a very strong role model. She was an older Professor. She was really involved and enthusiastic in sport and in people. She was probably my driving force. ... She was the individual I looked to for support, as a role model, and for suggestions.

Sarah's parents were supportive of her decision.

They thought it was very good that I finally got the puzzle put together. They knew that I was feeling around trying to figure out where I was going. ... I talked with them about it and they said if I wanted to go to school they would be very supportive and they were.

Finally, Sarah felt that she had made the right decision to enter PE.

I felt very confident and I was very pleased with the decision that I had made and I threw myself into it 120% ... I had a lot of support from the people within the department. I was involved in a lot of activities. I knew when I made the right decision that all the indicators were positive.

She felt very well suited to teaching and considered that she had the necessary characteristics for a career in the profession.

Dedication, drive and commitment. I have an innate ability to perceive things, to evaluate. ... I could look at a sport movement or a sport skill and make some suggestions to help that individual improve.

Initial Career

Sarah felt well suited to enter PE and looked forward to her career. She was excited about returning to her home town and to the very school in which she had received her secondary education. In her view she had returned to one of the premiere schools in the state and cherished the fact that this would also mean being with her family.

> When I was hired in I felt very very good about my career. I felt I was very successful in what I had set out to do. I was proud of the fact that I was good enough to be selected as a member of the school corporation. ... I really wanted to stay close to home because I'm a home-oriented person. When I had the opportunity to interview and they offered me the job, I jumped on it.

The importance of being close to her family is reflected in Sarah's personal value system.

> I'm a family person. My family is important to me and I'm old fashioned. I guess I'm a freak in times when things aren't supposed to be that way. A lot of people my age have split and gone everywhere to seek employment. Employment careers have always been important to me, but family has always been important to me.

Sarah was in a unique position for employment having been a former student of the school and having done her practice teaching in a local junior high. She well understood the advantage she held relative to other applicants.

> They had seen me in action because I did my student teaching at one of the junior highs and at that time I was also involved in athletic training and I was the first female graduate from Ball State with an athletic training certificate. I was the first female to be involved in athletic training at Jeff. So I have a lot of firsts. They knew my capabilities, they knew my philosophy, and I was a native, I had an interest in the community and they are going to be more accepting with an individual they feel comfortable with than with an outsider they know very little about. All those things combined probably made me a good candidate in their eyes.

Early Preparation

Sarah thus felt well prepared in terms of the technical/methodological demands of teaching.

> When I started I was fairly well prepared. I knew from my schooling how to build a progression, a sequence. What you had to do, the drills that went into developing this specific skill. All I had to do was sort out the basic skills that were specific to that age group and what was needed in the sequencing of their skill levels. ... I didn't have a whole

lot of preparation to do because it was so ingrained in my undergraduate training that it was a natural for me. It was easy for me to see where we had to move and what had to be done and the manner in which I was going to do it. So the preparation in the early years was basically an evaluation type and hand out information to the students.

However, this commitment had become more and more difficult for her to maintain. Sarah looked back on her career and suggested how the idealism fostered in her training was quickly altered upon her entry into teaching.

Whenever you come out of a university program, you have high expectations of idealistic objectives and the realism hits you the first day of school because nothing ever works the way it's supposed to or rarely does it work the way it's supposed to. The expectation was that you have kids that are coming to you to learn and the realization is that that's not always the case. As the years have gone on our society has become so complex and so different with its needs that I perceive education as being irrelevant to a lot of kids.

The Teaching Role

In contrast with Kate, Sarah felt frustrated by her students' attitude to learning. In her view they saw education as largely irrelevant. She felt that her own role was largely that of a manager or supervisor and not that of a teacher and facilitator of learning.

I see myself as more of a manager than a teacher and the pros are you can get through the day and you can service a lot of students. That's getting people through the program and that's satisfying requirements, but when it comes down to teaching, the real value of what's supposed to happen, then there's the trade off. You don't get that. You can't.

Sarah was unhappy and frustrated with her role, particularly in relation to the complacency of the majority of her colleagues in PE who appeared to be satisfied with the 'management' role and just getting through each school day.

It seems like I'm the freak in the system. That I feel my responsibility is to teach, not to manage and sometimes I feel I'm the only one that feels teaching is important. Everybody else says, just get through, just manage it.

In essence, Sarah wanted to be a competent and accountable PE teacher. She did not want merely to roll out a ball, let kids play and manage on their own.

For Sarah the battle was to resist any movement away from her version of competent teaching.

> There's fear too that I'm going to have to adjust to the management situation and I don't like that at all. So there's an inner conflict battle within myself knowing that I'm a teacher and what I've been hired to do and it disgusts me to see that kind of thing happening in other people and disgusts me to think even more that I may become one of those people. So there's a real inner conflict going on with me. ... I think that's what has made me so unhappy because I can't give in to the roll out the ball syndrome, play syndrome. Play is good, but I think in an educational setting at the level we're at, some interaction, feedback, information, transfer has to take place.

One strategy used to cope with such internal conflict was Sarah's insistence that she maintain her role as a Health teacher. She reviewed her schedule:

> I have a split schedule, I teach PE and Health. I have 3 PE classes and 2 Health. Next fall they were going to put me in a straight PE and I said wow wait because there are basically 3 of us in Health that have developed a new program where we have adopted new textbooks. We're really excited about the textbook and what we can do with it. Then they say they're going to put me in straight PE and I said I have to have a relief from that situation and so the Health has let me do that. It's a good setting because it's more of an academic setting where the kids we're dealing with have to know information.

Workload

The pace and routine of Sarah's work load, like that of Kate's, made for a very exhausting existence.

> From the time I hit the door there's no time to relax, unwind, interact with your associates. The bells ring and the students come. The bells ring and the students leave and another group comes in and it's so regimented all day long and by the time you get done with 7 periods you're whipped. ... During the prep period you found yourself running a lot to get stuff organized, visual aids, printed material, computer stuff and I just found myself just spinning my wheels not getting too much done. Just totally being worn out 'cause of the pace you have to go at.

Also, I found myself getting more and more frustrated because there's no time to interact, to sit down and work on things.

Her teaching responsibilities particularly in terms of preparation were extended to after-school hours and to periods during her summer holidays. Sarah felt that more time should be structured during the school day to allow for such responsibilities.

I upgrade and change every two years all my handouts and tests because things change and I always upgrade and change and this is the year for me to do that. I find I'm doing computer work, I'm doing programs, I'm looking at programs to integrate with PE and Health. So this is a big year and I have computer time scheduled, I have library time, but I don't get paid for any of this and I find myself really getting upset that I don't have time during the school year to do this that I'm not getting paid for. It's expected of me, but they [school administrators] don't give me the time to do it.

Sarah was also able to look at her schedule in terms of her good days and bad days. She did so by looking at the receptivity of her students to her lessons which appears to depend on the day of the week or having adequate teaching/practice areas.

I think it boils down to kids and their receptiveness. I perceive most of our kids, not all of them, but most of our kids being turned off by school and it seems to be Tuesday and Wednesday are the good days. Monday they come in and they're tired from the weekend. Tuesday and Wednesday you can catch them pretty good. Thursday they start partying and Friday school's out. So we get 2 days as I perceive it of good instructional setting and I know how bushed I am after 7 periods. It's rigorous, you walk in, boom boom boom boom boom and you walk out. There's not much interaction, there's not much fun. Everybody has their own direction that they're going.

On the bad days Sarah felt down because of the lack of control in her own teaching area; it affected her self-image.

That frustrates me and it frustrates them and I feel like I have no control over what's happening. The kids know that and they look at me as though, oh boy, don't you have any control over anything. So in turn I have a low image of myself 'cause I can't get done what I've set out to do. Then my patience gets very short. The kids are out of sync with the program. They're a little more irritable or out of control.

Relationships

Teaching Colleagues. Sarah liked the people with whom she worked. She had a cordial relationship with her fellow PE teachers and found it easy to interact with them. At the same time, however, she was frustrated by the fact that the majority of her PE colleagues did not share her high commitment to teaching, and suggested that this also applied to colleagues in the wider school setting.

> Sometimes I feel I'm the only one that feels teaching is important. Most everybody else says, just get through, just manage it. There's a definite conflict in our philosophies and that makes the relationship and the working condition a little uneasy, but I'm not the only one who has that. I would feel bad about feeling that way if I were the only one who felt it, but there are teachers who are outside the discipline that feel the same way. We have our differences and we get them out on the table and we talk about them. ... We plan and we all say yes, this is what we're going to do, but when it comes down to running it in the class, I'm not sure what transpires. ... There may be times in there when they do teach, but it's not on a day to day basis.

This presented a problem for Sarah when students came to her lessons from other PE teachers' classes. It was difficult for students to understand that Sarah prioritized teaching and learning over just playing and it brought about the impression that some of her PE colleagues held their own subject area in low esteem. 'Different philosophies from another individual and you have to change the kids' philosophy. ... It's a philosophy that comes down through the whole system of PE. ... That it isn't important, it doesn't count. ...'

Sarah's concern with her own self-image led her to question her values, commitment and behaviour as she analyzed the program and actions of her colleagues. 'Well I wonder, I've got all these people around me who don't agree with me or don't seem to hold the same ideal. I get to thinking, boy, I'm in the wrong place because I'm like a weird puzzle part that doesn't fit.' Fortunately for Sarah another colleague who was in the initial stage of her career served as a source of support. But, with the exception of this one teaching colleague, Sarah was frustrated by the lack of a shared commitment to the teaching/learning process among the other PE teachers. The department head provided little leadership and appeared to do little himself in modelling teacher effectiveness. In this context Sarah wondered if her commitment was worth the struggle.

Students. Although Sarah perceived education 'as being irrelevant to a lot of kids', her motivation to stay in teaching is linked to her desire to interact with adolescents and help them become physically educated. She commented on her relationship: 'I think the kids have helped me stay younger. I have no problems dealing with the kids. ... The things that frustrate me aren't the kids, it's the adults.' She described her relationship with her students as amiable yet did not lose sight of the fact that she expected them to meet her demands.

> I think you're there to teach, that's your major responsibility. You're there to present material and you're there to guide the student along a path. Once you've established your credibility here, warmth will come. ... I think the respect and the warmth comes by the end of the semester. ... I feel that and they start to show that. I'll go out and the kids are all doing what they're supposed to be doing. ... They understand that's the expectation of them.

Sarah was very concerned about those students who needed special attention and assistance and believed that her PE and Health classes have great relevance to these children.

Thus Sarah's relationship with her students was businesslike, yet caring. A positive relationship grew from the students' ability to meet Sarah's expectations. She loved the challenge of educating the students and worried what might happen to them if she were to leave teaching.

Administrators. Sarah's perception of the school's administration was similar to her perception of her teaching colleagues. She perceived she was respected in her work, but remains frustrated by their view of Physical Education and the lack of accountability within the system. Furthermore, Sarah believed she has had to adjust her own work ethic to cope with her frustrations.

> I feel that they know what kind of job I'm doing and they respect me for that. It hasn't always been easy to deal with liking someone or working with someone when they are so far off of what you believed in. ... I've changed. ... I've had to overlook some of the things that are not right to get through. ...

One thing that Sarah had difficulty in overlooking was the adversarial relationship which existed between teachers and administrators, particularly during contract negotiations. She was very critical of the school superintendent.

> I think he does everything in his power to frustrate the teachers, to divide and want the teachers to be conquered. ... He has given us the impression that he really doesn't care about the school corporation and the kids in the community. All he cares about is breaking up a teacher group so that he has power and he has control.

This characterization was linked to Sarah's school principal as well: 'A comment made to me by the principal was that one of the things that he felt was that teachers were very spoiled and that they needed to be taken down a notch or two.' In Sarah's view both her principal and department head were likeable individuals, but not great supporters or promoters of the PE program or the development of the teaching staff.

Hence the very thing that is linked to school and teacher effectiveness — administrative support — was a characteristic missing within Sarah's teaching. It was a characteristic that contributed to Sarah's desire to leave teaching in the future.

PE as a Subject Area

Sarah is not unlike many PE teachers who believe that PE is of marginal importance within the school curriculum. She based her claim on changing values in society, curricular priorities and the attitudes of physical educators themselves.

> I think that Physical Education is perceived as not as important as reading, writing, and arithmetic per se because it doesn't have anything to do with making money. It has to do with taking care of oneself to live a happier life. To a lot of people the only thing that's valued in life is the money. So it's a value system and it's whatever your priorities are. Some people prioritize money as being the number one thing and health is clearly down here.

Sarah suggested that the PE facility itself was subject to takeover at any time for the purpose of other school activities.

> Everybody uses the facilities so there's no specialness about what we do. ... We have the music people come in and use the gym and our classes aren't there and so on and so forth. Then it also projects the idea that this is not important. This PE class is not important because other things take priority.

In Sarah's view incompetent teaching had contributed to the marginal status which PE held in the school.

> I think if we as physical educators had said, hey we're going to do this right and this is what it's all about, then it would be different, but we've gone through so much of roll out the ball ... that it is going to be difficult to change.

Thus the lack of administrative support, low commitment on the part of her colleagues and the low status of PE combined to make it very difficult for

Sarah to maintain a responsible attitude towards her teaching. Again she found herself wondering if it was worth the effort and as a consequence saw herself moving out of teaching: 'It seems the longer you stay in the fight the more dissatisfied you get and you can see the handwriting on the wall ... the hassles you go through and the lack of respect, you lose your self-respect. You see yourself losing ground.' Sarah saw herself moving on to another PE-related occupation. Not unlike many excellent school teachers, Sarah has considered going on for a doctoral degree in teacher education within Physical Education, and then into a position in teacher education at a college or university. This would allow her to stay connected with adolescents.

> I could see myself doing something like that, teacher education. I don't want to sever my relationship with the age group I'm working with 'cause I think that it's vital that they have people who are caring and understanding and who are trying to show them a way to reach their goals.

Sarah believed that there is a place for her after she retires from teaching, be it in teacher education, business, or as a PE coordinator for a school system. She believed she could contribute positively to the future. Thus, after years of teaching and coaching, Sarah now sees the end in sight. Her dilemma was that she found herself in a job which she was quite competent in, yet a job that had little status and where 'non-teaching' was implicitly condoned and favoured. Sarah wanted to be valued and treated as a professional, but wasn't.

Summary

The profiles of Kate and Sarah provide for interesting comparisons. Both commonalities and differences appeared to exist as I analyzed their careers. For example, Kate seemed less committed or certain about her entry into PE than did Sarah. Both possessed athletic skill, yet Kate's entry appeared to be more by default, occurring with the encouragement of others rather than through a process of self-selection. In contrast, after delayed entry Sarah was quite certain that PE was the subject area for her.

Both Kate and Sarah assumed a variety of roles through their careers, many of which were conducted simultaneously (teaching and coaching or teaching in different subject areas). They worked long hours for very different compensation and, while they enjoyed the interaction with their students, they have recognized that quality instruction in PE is not a major expectation within the school curriculum. Kate realized the quality of her instruction in PE was less than perfect, yet did not fret about it. Sarah was concerned about quality instruction, yet perceived herself as moving toward the norm of the 'non-teaching' teacher due to various constraints.

Kate and Sarah perceived the status of PE similarly and they felt that there was little leadership within their departments or schools to enhance PE within the curriculum or facilitate staff development. Equally they perceived that few of their colleagues contributed towards the improvement of the curriculum.

Finally, Kate and Sarah were unlike some female teachers who made their 'occupational career secondary to their career as a wife and mother' (Sikes, Measor and Woods, 1985, p. 46). Being single (in Sarah's case) and without children and having a partner willing to enter into a supportive and symmetrical relationship (in Kate's case) differentiated these women from those female teachers for whom the structures of family life and the ideologies which support them serve as barriers toward the pursuit of professional careers. They did not see their work as an interim engagement (Lortie, 1975). However frustrating their jobs seemed, they worked hard in their positions and saw education as life-long endeavour in one form or another (i.e., teaching, administration, teacher education). It was the form which further differentiated Kate from Sarah; making it or finding a niche were very different for each person.

Kate was similar to many male teachers who have sought to leave teaching for pastoral or administrative duties. Kate suggested that 'being stuck in PE' or 'being stuck in her pastoral role' were not part of her career ambitions and that making it meant one more move into the role of deputy head. She did not belittle either of her current roles and was satisfied with her movement to date, but again feared being stuck. Although many would argue that her gender, her lack of qualifications and her association with PE stack the odds against Kate's employment as a deputy head, she believed she would make it. Time will tell.

In contrast, Sarah did not bring meaning to her career by seeking upward mobility (though these ambitions were now being forced on her). In one way Sarah was very much like the women in Biklen's (1986) study who had a very strong commitment to teaching and whose careers have great meaning. They, like Sarah, were quite content to make their contribution in the classroom.

Sarah's entire career had centred on teaching and coaching (she had no administrative ambitions), yet her commitment has wavered like that of so many other teachers who struggle to remain satisfied and realize their ideals in difficult circumstances. She is faced with the prospect of leaving teaching because she is tired of working in a system where there are few shared goals and few colleagues with a genuine concern for PE. She is tired of feeling abnormal and wondering whether or not she should compromise her own values. Sarah wants to make it as a teacher and she knows she has the skills to do it, but is frustrated by a system which has made it increasingly difficult, if not impossible, for her to do so. Although she was not concerned with mobility, it is ironic that the limitations of her work have forced her to consider moving into roles which often are defined as advanced.

Settling Down

It is clear that 'settling down' may be interpreted differently for Kate and Sarah. Sarah wanted firmly to anchor her position as a valued teacher who was able to practise her craft while maintaining close ties to her family. She was concerned about the future welfare of her pupils and wondered what might happen to them if she left teaching. Sarah wanted to be understood and appreciated, yet had a difficult time achieving these goals. She copes through substitution; that is, through her family, her friends and involvement with equestrian events and softball.

Kate worked hard toward advancement and progressed. Her occupational life and overall life structure have been strengthened through her marriage. She sought to advance higher and become a senior member of the education enterprise and break from PE — a move that may enhance her opportunity to advance still further.

Hence, while Kate's niche appeared to be career mobility, Sarah wanted to be satisfied and supported in her role as a PE teacher. Although there was no doubt that Kate served her occupation well, the occupation had served Kate as well and she hoped that it would continue to do so through an appointment to a deputy headship. Sarah's career had centred on serving her occupation and the content of teaching through the service of adolescents. A concern for the quality of teaching had overridden a concern for teaching as a facilitator for other occupational choices. Unfortunately, the occupation had not consistently served Sarah well in meeting her goals and needs. Once satisfied, Sarah hoped to find a new niche in teacher education after six more years of teaching.

Kate's and Sarah's experiences seemed to mirror two of the sequences described by Levinson *et al.* (1978). Kate's career appeared to emulate sequence A wherein life has proceeded according to expectations (i.e., advancement). She had experienced suffering and hardship, but survived her difficulties and moved steadfastly toward advancement. She perceived that further mobility would mean a disassociation with PE, association with other subject areas and short-term service in her pastoral role. She had a strong sense of self and has confidently progressed. She had what she wanted to this point and hoped to get more — the deputy headship. However, given her subject-matter 'roots' and her gender, a struggle seems inevitable.

Sarah's settling down period was quite different and more characteristic of sequence C. She had succeeded throughout her career and had been quite satisfied with the accomplishment of her goals (successful teaching). Yet she felt she had become a bureaucratic functionary. She found her work situation to be increasingly oppressive and felt compelled to break out. She was estranged from her work (Webb, 1985). Teaching had required her to be someone she has difficulty accepting and to take on ambitions, ironically, that she did not desire. She had tolerated her situation and coped through 'substitution' or involvement in outside activities and through the support of a few colleagues, her family and friends.

Sarah was confronted by the predicament of deciding her career direction. Although she had considered moving into teacher education, there were no guarantees that such a shift would meet her needs. Levinson *at al.* (1978) emphasize the significance of this dilemma: '... staying put may lead to a kind of living death (suicide); breaking out may be destructive ... and not bring the better life she craves' (p. 159). It is curious that in very different ways both Kate and Sarah were confronted by the possibility that without further advancement or movement into new roles the living death to which Levinson referred may be a reality.

Final Thoughts

This study has revealed the idiosyncratic nature of the biographies of two mid-career female teachers. Little has been highlighted as to major differences between American and English systems of Physical Education relative to these cases because little was discerned. Certainly some differences emerged when I examined curricular offerings, facilities, financial resources and the emphasis on interscholastic sport; but such contextual differences did not appear to influence either woman significantly.

What was of significance to both was the marginality of PE (Hendry, 1975) as a subject and the consequences of this marginality on career direction (Kate's desire to break from PE in order to advance and Sarah's desire to break due to lack of commitment by others to the subject). Both teachers work in cultures which undervalued the physical relative to its place within the school curriculum, and by association the activities and status of PE teachers. Indeed much of what has been said and described here could/would apply equally well to male PE teachers, although, as others in this reader point out, their opportunities to escape the difficult conditions of the work place may be somewhat greater than those experienced by women.

It is interesting to note that marginality is a concept that not only translates into how external agents attach status to PE or PE teachers. PE teachers themselves may perceive PE or PE teachers as marginal in terms of contributing to pupils or to their own life and occupational experience and career development. As a consequence they help sustain the low status and support, that are given to the subject.

One's personal and occupational life presents opportunities, challenges and rewards as well as constraints, frustration and failure. These are some of the characteristics which describe the lives and careers of the women studied here. They both have had their own unique seasons to their lives. It is these seasons and those of other PE teachers which we must further describe, understand and learn from if we are better to understand and ultimately begin to alter and improve the conditions of educational practice for both teachers and pupils.

References

BALL, S. and GOODSON, I. (1985) *Teachers' Lives and Careers*, Lewes, Falmer Press.

BECKER, H.S. (1976) 'The career of the Chicago public school teacher', in HAMMERSLEY, M. and WOODS, P. (Eds), *The Process of Schooling*, London, Routledge and Kegan Paul, pp. 75–81.

BIKLEN, S. (1986) 'I have always worked: Elementary school teaching as a career', *Phi Delta Kappan*, 67, pp. 504–8.

BOGDAN, R. and BIKLEN, S. (1982) *Qualitative Research for Education: An Introduction to Theory and Methods*, Boston, Mass., Allyn and Bacon.

EVANS, J. (1986) *Physical Education, Sport and Schooling: Studies in the Sociology of Physical Education*, Lewes, Falmer Press.

GOODSON, I. (1980) 'Life histories and the study of schooling', *Interchange*, 11, 4, pp. 62–76.

GOODSON, I. (1983) 'The use of life histories in the study of teaching', in HAMMERSLEY, M. (Ed.), *The Ethnography of Schooling*, Driffield, Nafferton Books, pp. 129–55.

HENDRY, L. (1975) 'Survival in a marginal role: The professional identity of the physical education teacher', *British Journal of Sociology*, 26, pp. 465–76.

LACEY, C. (1977) *The Socialization of Teachers*, London, Methuen.

LACEY, C. (1987) 'Professional socialization of teachers', in DUNKIN, M. (Ed.), *The International Encyclopedia of Teaching and Teacher Education*, Oxford, Pergamon, pp. 634–44.

LEVINSON, D.J. *et al.* (1978) *The Seasons of a Man's Life*, New York, Knopf.

LOCKE, L., GRIFFIN, P. and TEMPLIN, T. (Eds) (1986) 'Profiles of struggle', *Journal of Physical Education, Recreation and Dance*, 57, 4, pp. 32–63.

LORTIE, D. (1975) *School Teacher*, Chicago, Ill., University of Chicago Press.

LYONS, G. (1981) *Teacher Careers and Career Perceptions*, Windsor, NFER-Nelson.

SIKES, P. (1986) 'The mid-career teacher: Adaptation and motivation in a contracting secondary school system', Unpublished doctoral dissertation, University of Leeds.

SIKES, P., MEASOR, L. and WOODS, P. (1985) *Teacher Careers: Crises and Continuities*, Lewes, Falmer Press.

WEBB, R. (1985) 'Teacher status panic: Moving up the down escalator', in BALL, S. and GOODSON, I. (Eds), *Teachers' Lives and Careers*, Lewes, Falmer Press, pp. 78–89.

5
Patriarchy and Ethnicity: The Link between School Physical Education and Community Leisure Activities

Bruce Carrington and Trevor Williams

In 1985, prompted by a concern with the formation and implementation of policies to promote greater gender and ethnic equality in sport and physical recreation, we embarked upon an investigation into factors influencing the leisure opportunities and behaviour of young people of South Asian descent (Carrington, Williams and Chivers, 1987). This research, which aimed to explore the extent to which gender differences may be heightened by ethnicity, was undertaken in a northern city in England where ethnic minority groups formed less than 5 per cent of the overall population. Our sample comprised 114 young people (50 males and 64 females aged between 11 and 24 years) and consisted mainly of Muslims whose families had originated from Pakistan and some Sikhs and Hindus largely of Indian descent. On the basis of structured interviews with these young people and members of their families (most of which were administered by a male and female South Asian assistant) we found the following. The out-of-home activities of the males were generally much more extensive than those of the females. In the case of sport and physical recreation South Asian males regularly participated in football (52%), rugby (12%), cricket (24%), weight-lifting (32%), badminton (14%) and the martial arts (14%). Their attitude towards sport and physical recreation appeared to be as positive as that of their peers from other ethnic backgrounds (cf. DES, 1983). Female participation, on the other hand, was only minimal and restricted to a few activities: badminton (5%), tennis (5%), swimming (2%) and roller-skating (2%). Gender differences within this group were especially pronounced.

It was evident that ethnicity accentuated the high participation rates of males and the low participation rates of females. In accounting for the differences we suggested that sport and other physical recreation activities were perceived as quintessentially masculine in this as in other cultures (Leaman, 1984; Glyptis, 1985). Several factors were identified as contributing to this outcome. First, females were subjected to much greater parental control than males and they appeared to attach greater importance to 'izzat' (the need to uphold the family's status and honour). Parents were generally apprehensive about any out-of-home activity, including sport, in which their daughters were unsupervised or which would bring them into direct contact with members of the opposite sex. Second, the leisure time of the young women was often appropriated by members of their family; as with other groups (e.g., Hendry *et al.*, 1984) their domestic commitments often left them with few opportunities for out-of-home leisure pursuits. Their opportunities for home-based leisure were also more circumscribed than those of their male peers. Third, experiences of racism at school, work and 'on the streets' served to heighten parents' anxieties about their daughters' out-of-home leisure activities. Fourth, the lack of appropriate provision in sport and physical recreation may have contributed to the low participation rates in this sphere among females; single-sex provision, for example, was rare. Fifth, these gender inequalities were in part influenced by the female respondents' lack of confidence in their physical abilities and skills.

This last finding suggested that questions could raised about the quality and effectiveness of Physical Education and in particular about the adequacy of institutional responses to cultural diversity in this area of the curriculum. Physical Education has been a source of conflict between South Asian parents (especially Muslims but including Sikhs) and schools for some years. The Swann Committee (DES, 1985; p. 342), among others, alluded to this when it stated:

> Asian pupils can be placed under very strong pressures in being torn between on the one hand their obedience to their parents, their adherence to their faith and their allegiance to their community, and on the other hand their desire to comply with the normal practices of the school and the instructions of their teachers.

It urged schools to be 'sensitive to the pressures on children' and to show 'tolerance of and respect for cultural difference' but pointed out that such a position may 'be in marked contrast to the perhaps more rigid cultural stance adopted in the home' (DES, 1985, p. 342). In our view Physical Education staff should take full account of the values and beliefs of both Muslim girls and their parents when appraising their pedagogical, organizational and curricular strategies. Unless staff treat seriously the religious and moral objections which Muslims level against the subject, then it is impossible to see how Physical Education can ever be reconciled with egalitarian concerns.

Many of the young people approached in our survey were, or had been, pupils at Arkwright High School (pseudonyms are used throughout the chapter). For this reason a case study of Physical Education at that particular school seemed the appropriate step to take in developing the previous research. The case study, which is the subject of this chapter, was primarily concerned to identify the dilemmas and constraints facing PE staff when implementing an equal opportunities policy and to assess the strategies they employed. Specifically we wanted to examine the extent to which the gender inequalities found in our leisure survey were reinforced or challenged by the school. The fieldwork was conducted in the summer of 1987 and consisted of unstructured interviews with the headteacher; with teachers with particular responsibilities for anti-racist, multicultural education and home-school links; and with members of both the boys' and girls' PE departments. Accepting Lather's (1986) conception of collaborative research as a 'dialogic enterprise' (i.e., an educative process), we regarded the interviews as providing a forum in which teachers and researchers alike might reflect upon and critically appraise pedagogical, organizational and curricular strategies in the school to promote ethnic and gender equality. Eschewing the traditional (asymmetrical) division of labour between researcher and researched, we aimed to be as open and frank as possible with our subjects. Every effort was made to explain the purposes of the research prior to each interview. To provide a focal point for these discussions, the main findings of our previous work were summarized in a preamble. Subjects were then invited to comment on their own and the school's responses to equal opportunities in general and to identify any constraints upon innovation in this sphere.

The School and Physical Education

Although not socially homogeneous, Arkwright is located in a predominantly 'respectable' working-class area. At the time of the research it had in the region of 1500 pupils aged between 11 and 18, of whom nearly a third were from ethnic minority backgrounds. About 20 per cent of the school's population were Muslims, 4 per cent were Sikhs and 2 per cent were Hindus. The latter groups were described by one teacher, Steve Bennet, as 'more upwardly mobile' than the Muslims and more likely to withdraw their children from Arkwright and send them to fee-paying schools. As well as these pupils of South Asian background, about 3 per cent of those attending the school were of Chinese or Vietnamese descent.

Although there was some coeducational provision, like most secondary schools in the United Kingdom (cf. PEA, 1987) the bulk of the teaching of Physical Education at Arkwright occurred in single-sex groups; boys received tuition in football, rugby, cricket, basketball, softball, athletics and fitness training, while girls received tuition in gymnastics, dance, hockey, netball, rounders, tennis and athletics. There was, however, some coeducational PE; swimming was part of the core curriculum for both sexes and it was taught in mixed classes from the first year onwards, while in the fourth and fifth years pupils could opt for a programme of coeducational leisure activities. In the latter they could choose to do ten-pin bowling, squash, tennis, table tennis, badminton, aerobics, fitness training, weight-lifting, cricket, rounders, athletics and photography or, as an alternative to this programme, they could elect to undertake community service.

The PE programme, then, was fairly traditional but the effects of patriarchy were quite noticeable to some members of staff. Sheila Hargreaves, for example, a younger member of the girls' PE staff, was especially critical of her male colleagues for excluding gymnastics and dance from the boys' curriculum. She was also associated with extra-curricular clubs in each of these activities and in volleyball. Whereas both sexes were encouraged to participate in all of the activities, girls tended to opt for dance and gymnastics, and boys for volleyball. Sheila believed that the stereotyped choices of the pupils were due in large part to what she perceived as the imbalances within the boys' PE curriculum; boys, she maintained, rejected gymnastics 'because it was not included in their PE programme.' She had offered to provide coeducational dance lessons but, while this proposal had received the ostensible support of Tony Short, the headteacher, it had been resisted by her male colleagues. 'Boys', she observed, 'don't have the opportunity to take gym or dance — this is the *real* problem.' In general, though, the rest of the PE staff were less concerned than Mrs Hargreaves, and certainly less vociferous, about male disadvantage in Physical Education. They recognized the necessity of single-sex provision in a school with a significant proportion of South Asians and their concern was to work within the guidelines of the school's policy on racial and ethnic equality.

The school, in common with others in the LEA, was implementing an anti-racist, multicultural education policy. Among other things staff were expected to report incidents of 'direct or suspected racism' to the Deputy Head and various steps have been taken to counter institutionalized and personal racism and make the curriculum less ethnocentric. The school's commitment to make a broadly-based equal opportunities policy was made unequivocally in its booklet for parents which stated: '... everyone matters, everyone is different and everyone is of equal value. We are committed to taking positive steps to ensure that children achieve their full social, aesthetic and academic potential regardless of their sex, colour or background.'

The staff we approached seemed to be favourably disposed towards the policy and in this respect had much in common with multiracial schools elsewhere (cf. Troyna and Ball, 1985). Particular steps had been taken to improve communication between the school and ethnic minority parents. For example, a Multicultural Working Party had been established which comprised teaching staff, parents (from various ethnic backgrounds) and representatives of the Community Relations Council. In addition to a vigorous pastoral and outreach scheme the school was extending its community languages provision and senior staff were at pains to stress that they were making every attempt to combat racism and ethnocentrism in their organizational, curricular and pedagogical practices. One particular concern of the Working Party had been Physical Education and members had devoted considerable time to the discussion of South Asian parents' anxieties. Parents expressed concern about both their sons' and daughters' involvement; extra-curricular activities often clashed with Supplementary School and during Ramadan certain curricular activities were proscribed. Dress and the issue of girls being seen in a deshabillée state by males had also prompted considerable discussion.

Differential Responses of Pupils to Physical Education and Leisure

The Working Party had contended that Physical Education must be taught using the guidelines set out in the school's policy on anti-racist, multicultural education. The implementation of that policy, however, was complicated by several factors. The most salient were the attitude of many girls (South Asian and white alike) to PE, the especially low status of Physical Education in South Asian culture and the institutional restraints on staff.

The ambivalence or even hostility shown by many of the adolescent girls towards involvement in sport and physical recreation gave cause for concern among all the PE staff. The activities were often perceived as antipathetical to prevailing notions of femininity (cf. Carrington and Leaman, 1986; Evans *et al.*, 1987; Moir, 1977) and Brenda Rogers, the head of girls' PE, believed that female resistance to the subject could not be explained by the facilities available or by the nature of the activities on offer. Girls, she noted, enjoyed PE (especially indoor activities) in the first and second years, but during the third year this interest often 'tailed off'. When asked to account for this decline in interest she replied, 'They just want to go home and watch television.' Even activities which could be more readily reconciled with the culture of femininity were eschewed. Mrs Hargreaves, recounting how members of the third year dance club had 'suddenly stopped coming', noted: 'There's a lot going on in the city and keeping friends is important to the girls. If their friends go out, they'll go along with them. This is a problem with all clubs; the girls just don't turn up.'

As found in other research (Taylor and Hegarty, 1985; DES, 1983) such gender differences in response to sport and physical recreation were particularly pronounced among South Asians. South Asian boys responded positively to various activities. Geoff Evans, head of boys' PE, felt that they were overrepresented in the school cricket teams. In common with PE teachers elsewhere (e.g., Carrington, 1983), he rationalized this particular difference in biologistic terms, claiming: 'ethnic minority kids are more useful at cricket — their body-type is more conducive to this activity.' He went on to note that 'tennis was enjoyed by the immigrant [sic] lads' and that many were enthusiastic about weight-training. In relation to this he remarked, somewhat cryptically, that the group were 'preoccupied with their physiques' and that weight-training may have been useful in 'self-defence'. The responses of South Asian males to both curricular and extra-curricular Physical Education activities, then, were generally favourable and this despite the fact that many parents did not share their sons' enthusiasm. According to Steve Bennet, the coordinator of the School's Multicultural Working Party, 'the status of PE in the ethnic minority communities is not the same as in the general community. I think that, from the minorities' point of view, education is to get a better job; the value of sport is lost on them.' Haleena Hussain (a teacher of English as a Second Language with a responsibility for home-school liaison) concurred with this view. She noted that South Asian parents 'placed much more value on academic work' but looked upon PE as 'just playing around'. Among girls this was especially pronounced for in Arkwright, as elsewhere (Taylor and Hegarty, 1985), cultural and religious differences, family and home pressures and a lack of single-sex provision in *some* activities had resulted in the withdrawal of many South Asian girls (particularly Muslims) from Physical Education.

Another factor complicating the implementation of the equal opportunities policy was the institutional constraints under which PE staff had to work. One important issue centred on the provision of swimming. In view of the 'deep-rooted reservation', to use Taylor and Hegarty's phrase, which many South Asian parents have about their daughters' participation in this activity and, despite the ostensible commitment of the PE staff to the goal of equal opportunity, the following question arose. Why was swimming taught in coeducational classes when the remainder of the *core* PE curriculum classes was taught in single-sex groups? Mr Bennet, among others, explained that the introduction of a block timetable presented a major constraint to innovation in this sphere. He stated:

> The timetable is regulating something it shouldn't be regulating. I think that the timetable should start with (i.e., be predicated upon the principle of) single-sex swimming for everyone. The problem is the number you can get through the baths — we've got too many kids for

the baths. I don't know the ins and outs of the timetable, but it seems to me that the way to get a lot of classes through is to have them mixed — that's the constraint. To do single-sex swimming you've got to have another subject going on at the same time. It used to be music. So at one time you'd have two classes of girls doing swimming and two classes of boys doing music, and then they'd swap ... but we moved to block timetables.

The PE staff had tried to accommodate the resistance of both South Asian parents and their daughters. They had attempted to arrive at workable solutions to these dilemmas which faced them in their day-to-day working lives and several of these attempts are of interest in our clarification of the school's contribution to the cultural reproduction of gender and ethnic inequalities in leisure.

Implementing an Equal Opportunities Policy in Physical Education

Various strategies — pedagogical, curricular and organizational — were employed by PE staff to promote equal opportunities, obviate girls' resistance (both South Asian and white) and respond to the particular needs of South Asian pupils and their parents. Let us now consider each of these strategies in turn.

Pedagogical Strategies

In an attempt to secure cooperation and compliance from disaffected (and potentially disaffected) female pupils irrespective of ethnicity, they had opted for what Leaman (1984) has described as a 'strategy of compromise' and a number of concessions had been made. For example, showers were no longer compulsory (but available if required) and few restrictions were placed on dress. As Mrs Rogers explained:

Girls are loathe to change their clothes. I'm sure if we didn't insist on changing, more would take part. We find children coming to the lesson already in their kit; they walk around the school in their tracksuits. The Asian girls cannot show their legs, so they bring leisure suits in all kinds of colours. Mrs Hargreaves doesn't mind this — she thinks it adds to the aesthetic value of the lesson. So we can't make the white children stick to regulation colours if the coloured [sic] children don't. We're really lax, but do insist they change.

This is a fairly common and general solution in the gymnasium and on playing fields to the moral objections to South Asian females being seen by males in a state of deshabillée (DES, 1985). Cognizant of this, Mrs Rogers and other members of staff recognized that the introduction of coeducational swimming at the school would not only be a source of parental disquiet but would also be antipathetical to the goal of equal opportunity. She was extremely critical of coeducational swimming because it would invariably result in non-participation among South Asian girls and she suggested to Mr Short (the headteacher) that if the timetabling constraint was insurmountable then South Asian girls should be encouraged to wear pyjamas or leotards at the pool (cf. Glyptis, 1985; DES, 1985). Mr Short, however, did not agree for that would have meant giving one group of pupils favourable treatment over other groups and Mrs Rogers was left to face — and attempt to resolve — what Bullivant (1981) has referred to as the pluralists' dilemma, i.e., how to recognize and celebrate cultural diversity whilst concomitantly transmitting a common universalistic culture. She noted:

> I want every child to have the chance to learn to swim. It may save its life one day. ... It's not fair that religion should not let children have this opportunity. The parents might say that we should provide single-sex swimming. But we haven't the space on the timetable. I feel they're being rather awkward and they probably feel that we're being awkward, but a kiddie's life could be at stake. This is more important than any religion.

Another area in which similar pedagogical problems arose was in the implementation of the anti-racist facet of the policy. Mr Bennet, for example, made this observation about how practice might be improved:

> We need some advice on what to do when things go wrong. Alright, we monitor a racial incident, but how do we actually handle it? We're told to report it; we're told to do something about it, but what? How do you handle it? I think with many of these anti-racist policies the people who are trying to train others don't know the answers themselves.

This illustrates the sense of helplessness that many teachers experience when faced with the problem of translating generalized, and often ambiguous, policy prescriptions into workable strategies for action (e.g., Banks, 1986; Richards, 1986). Most of the time PE staff 'muddled through', learning by direct experience how to deal with actual or potential racial incidents. Mr Evans, for example, admitted that he made 'mistakes' from time to time. He had stopped allowing boys to select their own teams during games lessons because invariably they made 'in-group' choices. On occasions wholly, or almost wholly, white or South Asian teams had been selected because he had been unable to persuade male pupils to make choices on the basis of achievement rather than ascription. Another member of the boys' PE staff, James Brown, had encountered similar difficulties when dealing with racial incidents involving the football team at away matches. Racism, he felt, was more likely to surface at 'all-white' schools and usually took the form of verbal abuse directed against one of Arkwright's South Asian team members. Sometimes the remarks made were more innocuous. Mr Brown gave this example: 'Look at the *size* of that black lad!'

Curricular Strategies

The school's Multicultural Working Party had given much consideration to Physical Education and in particular to swimming. They had recommended, for example, that during Ramadan, Muslim pupils should be permitted to take Islamic studies instead of swimming. The recommendation had been implemented although apparently with only limited institutional support. According to Mr Bennet, 'The head was in favour of the proposal but made no special provision for it. In other words, it was done by staff giving up their time during free periods.'

Because of Muslim and to a lesser extent Sikh parents' attitudes to coeducational swimming, South Asian girls at Arkwright were not compelled to participate in this curricular activity. Parents were notified by letter about these arrangements and invited to withdraw their daughters from the activity if they wished. The PE staff, as we have seen, were critical of this de facto inequality, and had made an effort to circumvent the constraints imposed by the block timetable. They had mounted a course of extra-curricular, single-sex swimming lessons before school, but despite the enthusiasm of staff the strategy was not successful. The initial response of the girls had been very positive but their interest soon began to wane because, according to Mrs Hussain, the activity was perceived as marginal because it occurred outside the normal timetable. She noted, 'Girls ask, "Is it worth doing?", and grumble because they have to come out earlier.'

On another front the optional leisure programme offered in the fourth and fifth years had been introduced in an attempt to promote greater gender equality and overcome the girls' resistance to Physical Education. But staff recognized that this initiative too had its limitations. Among other things it attracted very few South Asian girls, most of whom elected to do 'community service'. Several staff lamented the relatively high levels of absenteeism among white girls enrolled on the programme. An examination of the department's attendance records corroborated these observations. In accounting for this response Mrs Rogers noted that although some girls may have been deterred by the high cost of the activities (e.g., £2.50 per week for horse-riding, 50 pence for squash and 70 pence for bowling), their withdrawal from the programme was largely prompted by other factors. She alluded to the effects of patriarchy on the life styles of the girls in question when she remarked: 'Leisure doesn't matter — the parents, the home are not supportive. The girls go home and help mum (with the chores). Girls *work* during the leisure sessions.'

In addition to this optional programme for older pupils the staff had attempted to package the core curriculum of the lower school in a way that appealed to girls. Considerable stress was placed upon the development of aesthetic and expressive skills, that is, skills which are generally seen as congruent with conventional images of femininity. However, the policy of 'catching them young' had largely failed to overcome the girls' mounting resistance to Physical Education from the third year onwards. As Mrs Hargreaves observed: 'In the first and second years, there's lots of gym and dance, with an emphasis on choreography and composition. The interest is there and there's no skiving. Skiving is a third year thing.' The introduction of the coeducational leisure programme in the fourth year did little to prevent this skiving, or to extend the recreational repertoires of those girls who choose to participate. Many continued to make largely gender-specific choices. For example, aerobics, rounders and horse-riding attracted only girls, and weight-training, squash, cricket and football remained male bastions. However, neuter activities such as athletics, ten-pin bowling, tennis, table-tennis and badminton were equally appealing to both sexes.

Organizational Strategies

Recognizing, however, that part of the solution to the problem of non-participation might lie with parents, the staff had taken various steps to liaise with the home. They tried several strategies in an attempt to extend participation among both autochthonous and South Asian girls. For example, when a girl suddenly dropped out of extra-curricular activities, her parents would be contacted by letter in the hope that they would facilitate a change of mind. This approach was often in itself insufficient, as Mrs Rogers pointed out: 'We send letters home asking their parents if they can come and their parents say "No".' The 'personal touch', however, proved to be a much more effective strategy. As other schools have found (Taylor and Hegarty, 1985), especially with South Asian parents, home visits establish trust and allow mutual adjustment to develop. In the case of Arkwright this has been effectively translated into practice by the PE staff through door-to-door transport provision after matches and clubs. Such provision helped to allay the anxieties of parents about their daughters' safety and well-being whilst encouraging a measure of well-deserved confidence in the teaching staff. Some teachers, though, believed that communication between Arkwright and South Asian parents could be improved further, both in Physical Education and in other areas. According to Mr Bennet:

> We need to talk (directly) to parents about the school system and its values. We should go out to them and not expect them to come to us and ask questions. It must be a very daunting prospect if you don't know the system, have a working-class background and don't have the communication skills needed to come into a big school like ours.

The following example was provided to illustrate the point:

> On occasions, when we've had, for example, lads good at football and they cannot turn up on a Saturday because they're going to Mosque school, I've had a word with their parents and tried to get them to allow their kids to exploit their talents. It seems the best way of doing things is personal contact. Letters, even if translated, don't have much effect.

Often, though, the conflict between the home and school was just *too* great. Mrs Hargreaves summed up the difficulties facing the PE staff at Arkwright when invited to comment on her role as a teacher in a multiracial school: this, she stated, was 'to provide equal opportunities for those who want it', but added, 'many Muslim parents reject what is offered.'

Conclusion

Despite the apparent commitment of many PE staff to a broadly-based equal opportunities policy, it is unlikely that their pedagogical, curricular and organizational strategies resulted in any significant increase in girls' overall participation, or did much to ensure that all pupils, irrespective of gender, were provided with similar chances to realize their potential in a diverse range of activities (for an analysis of the concept of equal opportunities in PE see Carrington and Leaman, 1986). Girls' antipathy towards PE appeared to increase with age, and predictably this resistance was especially pronounced among Muslim pupils.

It would appear that the PE curriculum at Arkwright School did little to counter the stereotypical conceptions of gender held by many pupils. The existence of separate male and female enclaves in the lower school, and correspondingly a traditional, differentiated curriculum, may have legitimated the popular view that girls are 'naturally suited' to activities involving grace, balance and aesthetic movement, as opposed to those involving strength, stamina and aggression. Although members of the Girls' Department were cognizant of this limitation and had taken steps to persuade their male counterparts to extend the boys' curriculum to include activities such as educational dance and gymnastics, their efforts had been to no avail.

Arguably the more broadly-based but optional coeducational Leisure Programme came too late in the pupils' educational careers to undermine any gender differences in attitude to sport and physical recreation already established by the core curriculum in PE or by other socialization influences such as the peer group, family or media. As a curricular strategy to enhance girls' participation, the programme may also be criticized on other grounds. First, insofar as it was not compulsory it may have been perceived by many pupils as peripheral and inconsequential. It is ironic that disaffected white girls truanted from the programme (which ostensibly sought to challenge the status quo between the sexes) to undertake domestic chores at home. It could be said that by rejecting this aspect of schooling and by allowing their families to appropriate their leisure-time the girls were preparing themselves — albeit unwittingly — for future positions of marginality and subordination in the home and other contexts. Second, the programme, which was premised upon the tenet of 'non-discrimination' (Carrington and Leaman, 1986; p. 221), took no account of physical differences between boys and girls or, more importantly, of the socially conditioned differences between them in attitude, motivation and skill. Pupils, therefore, when confronted by a coeducational programme which comprised masculine activities (e.g., football, weight-training), feminine activities (e.g., aerobics, rounders) and neuter activities (e.g., tennis, badminton) tended to make safe choices (i.e., own gender or neuter). Perhaps such gender differentiation would have been less marked if some single-sex provision had been made available in the programme, thus reducing the pressures on pupils to conform to traditional male and female roles. Indeed, such provision may have helped to obviate the resistance of South Asian girls to the programme.

Although various positive steps had been taken to accommodate South Asian pupils and their parents in PE (e.g., concessions to girls over dress, door-to-door transport after matches, extra-curricular single-sex swimming), the *curricular* arrangements for swimming continued to be a cause for concern. The response of the school (as opposed to individual members of the PE staff) to anxieties expressed within the South Asian communities about this activity was essentially pragmatic and expedient, and premised upon an untenable, relativistic approach to the curriculum. By allowing Muslim and Sikh parents to withdraw their daughters from coeducational swimming and by failing to provide appropriate alternative provision, the school was in effect prepared to sanction a 'watered-down' curriculum for this section of the population.

Certainly Mrs Rogers recognized the limitations of this well intentioned, but flaccid form of non-partisanship when she defended the place of swimming in the core curriculum for *every* pupil. Together with other PE staff she appeared to accept Lynch's dictum that schools ought to foster 'a critico-rational acceptance of cultural diversity and the creative affirmation of individual and group differences with a *common humanity*' (Lynch, 1983, p. 17, emphasis added). The block timetable not only militated against this type of universalism but the PE staff, possibly because of their relatively low status in the school hierarchy, were unable to surmount this institutional constraint. Their 'solution' to the dilemma (single-sex swimming lessons outside the normal timetable) had little impact because South Asian girls seemed to regard swimming, together with other aspects of PE, as an activity relegated to the peripheries by their parents and the school alike.

As we have argued elsewhere (Carrington, Williams and Chivers, 1987), patriarchal relations are culturally reproduced through leisure (especially recreational sport) and gender differences, both in opportunity and behaviour, may be accentuated within South Asian culture. The implementation of the equal opportunities policy at Arkwright School did little to interrupt this process of socio-cultural reproduction.

References

BANKS, J. (1986) 'Multicultural education and its critics: Britain and the United States', in MODGIL, S. and C. *et al.* (Eds), *Multicultural Education: the Interminable Debate*, Lewes, Falmer Press, pp. 221–31.

BRAH, A.K. (1978) 'South Asian teenagers in Southall: Their perceptions of marriage, family and ethnic identity', *New Community*, 6, 3, pp. 197–206.

BULLIVANT, B. (1981) *The Pluralists' Dilemma in Education*, London, George Allen and Unwin.

CARRINGTON, B. (1983) 'Sport as a side-track: An analysis of West Indian involvement in extra-curricular sport', in BARTON, L. and WALKER, S. (Eds), *Race, Class and Education*, London, Croom Helm, pp. 40–65.

CARRINGTON, B. and LEAMAN, O. (1986) 'Equal opportunities and physical education', in EVANS, J. (Ed.), *Physical Education, Sport and Schooling*, Lewes, Falmer Press, pp. 215–27.

CARRINGTON, B., WILLIAMS, T. and CHIVERS, T. (1987) 'Gender, leisure and sport: A case-study of young people of South Asian descent', in *Leisure Studies*, 6, 3, pp. 265–79.

DES (1983) *Young People in the 80's: A Survey*, London, HMSO.

DES (1985) *Education for All* (Swann Report), London, HMSO.

EVANS, J., DUNCAN, M., LOPEZ, S. and EVANS, M. (1987) 'Some thoughts on the political and pedagogical implications of mixed sex grouping in the Physical Education curriculum', *British Educational Research Journal*, 3, pp. 59–71.

GLYPTIS, S. (1985) 'Women as a target group: The views of the staff of action sport — West Midlands', *Leisure Studies*, 4, pp. 347–62.

HENDRY, L.B., RAYMOND, M. and STEWART, C. (1984) 'Unemployment, school and leisure: An adolescent study', *Leisure Studies*, 3, pp. 175–87.

LATHER, P. (1986) 'Research as praxis', *Harvard Educational Review*, 56, 3, pp. 257–77.

LEAMAN, O. (1984) *Sit on the Sidelines and Watch the Boys Play*, London, Longmans.

LYNCH, J. (1983) *The Multicultural Curriculum*, London, Batsford.

MOIR, E. (1977) *Female Participation in Physical Activities*, Dunfermline College of Physical Education.

PEA, (1987) *PE in Schools: Report of a Commission of Inquiry*, London, PEA.

RICHARDS, C. (1986) 'Antiracist initiatives', *Screen*, 27, 5, pp. 74–9.

TAYLOR, M.J. and HEGARTY, S. (1985) *The Best of Both Worlds ...?*, Windsor, NFER-Nelson.

TROYNA, B. and BALL, W. (1985) 'View from the chalkface: School responses to an LEA's policy on multicultural education', in *Policy Paper 1*, Coventry, Centre for Research in Ethnic Relations.

6
Competition, Cooperation and Control

Oliver Leaman

1986 and 1987 were unusual years for the Physical Education profession in Britain. Physical Education had become controversial, and newspapers frequently expressed concern at what they took to be recent developments in the discipline. To a certain extent this onslaught was part of the strategy of identifying unpopular policies with the 'Loony Left', and clearly played a part in the preparations for the general election. There was also a move to attack bodies such as the Inner London Education Authority (an authority explicitly progressive in its intentions to challenge sexism and racism in and through the school curriculum; see Baylis, 1984) and the relative autonomy of teachers and schools in general, with the subtle implication that education would run far more smoothly given a heavy dose of central government control. Physical Education had a simple role to play in this strategy. There is an accepted and generally acknowledged commonsense role for Physical Education in the curriculum, and that is represented by competitive sport. In most adults' experience of school the identification of Physical Education with sport is a strong one, and any change in this relationship might seem eccentric. The message that the media were pushing suggested that extremists in schools who were opposed to competition on political grounds had gone to the ridiculous lengths of even trying to eradicate competition from Physical Education, which seems to be an attack upon the institution of sport in British society.

It is worth examining the media campaign briefly before looking at some of the implications which different approaches to competition have for schools. *The Times* newspaper (now a 'respectable' purveyor of a Conservative political line) throughout 1986 was particularly scathing about the decline in competitive sports teaching in the state sector, arguing, as one might expect, that the spirit of competitiveness is a valuable social instrument. In a second leader called 'A Question of Sport' on 17 November 1986 the newspaper reported agreement by both the Conservative and Labour Parties on the importance of competitive sport. Within that context the leader writer argues 'that teachers of all kinds, from those who run the egg and spoon race to PE instructors who might have it in their power to groom young men for sporting glory, should urgently re-assess the dafter social theories now around.' The reference to the egg and spoon race (as others in this reader point out) relates to a Bristol teacher who tried to introduce this activity into that traditional event, the annual sports day, in order to underplay its competitive thrust. This led to a huge outcry in the popular press, which was grimly echoed in both *The Times* and *The Independent*. In the latter a leader appeared on 18 November 1986 which firmly set its face against any dilution of the 'games' element in Physical Education. It suggested that 'PE teachers (and those who train them in the colleges) have tried to raise their status by making their subject more academic. In doing so, they have fallen for the trendy sociologists' view that competitive sport is bad for children and that it is better to set personal targets for individuals to beat. This is patent nonsense.' The message which came across was that a significant change was taking place in Physical Education, and that the 'extremists' on the left were challenging the traditional structure of competitive activities. In doing so they were at the same time challenging the commonsense interpretation of what Physical Education is about, and how it should be pursued.

The acme of this debate was perhaps reached at the time of a *Panorama* programme on BBC 1, on 9 March 1987. This programme suggested that many PE teachers were critical of team games and were more interested in pupil participation in a range of physical activities which they could cope with at varying degrees of skill. Indeed, this approach was blamed for a relative lack of fitness of recruits in the Army. British children were represented as an increasingly sedentary population who were being let down by their teachers' low expectations of what they are physically capable of doing. This was not entirely due to a distrust of team games and an attack on élitism in sport, though. The teachers' dispute was acknowledged as a significant explanation for the decline of team sports, especially where these take place at weekends and after school. Additionally, the legal requirement that local authorities dispose of surplus land has had a serious effect on the stock of playing fields available for team games. The relatively high costs of maintaining sports fields in good order had also encouraged some local authorities to get rid of them often by selling them off for property development. This point had been emphasized repeatedly by Peter Lawson of the Central Council of Physical Recreation (CCPR), a fervent adherent of team games and competitive sport. Although the CCPR often seems to be an organization in search of a role, as there is no obvious rationale for its existence separate from the Sports Council, since its inception it has been an important mechanism for 'state intervention' in the nature and content of community physical recreation and Physical

Education in schools (see Hargreaves, 1986). In recent years it has taken up the cause of promoting a more 'traditional', (skill-based, competitive games-oriented) notion of sport and Physical Education.

It was not just the approaching election which set the agenda for the debate on Physical Education. Sport in Britain as a whole had been firmly on the political mat for much of the 1980s. The Conservative Government had been heavily interventionist with regard to sport (see Hargreaves, 1986), from its early discouragement of British athletes from participating in the Moscow Olympic Games to the Popplewell Enquiry with its linking of crowd violence at Birmingham and the Bradford fire. The Heysel disaster contributed to the general feeling that all was not well with British sport. Not only was the Government intervening heavily in sport, it was also seeking just as strenuously to participate and transform the school curriculum. One of its slogans in the latter campaign was to return the curriculum to the control of parents and the 'sensible' majority of citizens who were concerned at the way in which schools were apparently on occasion becoming disengaged from the normal expectations of British society. One of the successful aspects of the Government's campaign was the gulf which had emerged between what teachers said they were trying to do and the memories which parents had of their own school days. Their Physical Education had been in many cases a simple matter of games with some gymnastics (see Whitehead and Hendry, 1976), built around the production of teams and winning inter-school competitions. Although many adults have unhappy memories of school sport, especially if they were not themselves part of the successful élite of team players, they might well think that what they had to put up with was good for them in some way. We shall see later that there is some evidence to support such a feeling among many adults.

The New Physical Education

What is the 'new PE' which has sparked off such controversy? One can point to various features which mark a significant departure from past practices. Firstly, there is a concern that every pupil in the group taught should benefit in some way from the PE lesson, however physically limited initially and regardless of their lack of enthusiasm for the subject. The importance of exercise and the benefits it can bring are emphasized. There is a stress on pupils' understanding what they are doing, rather than just repeating drill and routine exercises (see, for example, the *Bulletin of Physical Education*, 1983). There is an increase in the theoretical content of the subject due to the development of the Health Related Fitness approach, and for some in the profession a growing importance of the place of examinations in PE. To a certain extent these developments reflect the changing content of teacher training courses validated by universities and the Council for National Academic Awards (CNAA) and their encouragement of a more theoretical and intellectual approach to Physical Education. Since PE teachers now have degrees rather than certificates they are expected to master a non-practical subject-matter like everyone else on degree courses, and this has had an effect on the content of the curriculum in school. Finally, some schools have taken on board an equal opportunities policy (see Baylis, 1984; Leaman, 1984; Evans *et al.*, 1987), and this has implications for the teaching and structure of Physical Education, ranging from whether coeducational schools maintain separate departments for girls and boys, to mixed activities, and a different approach to children coming from ethnic minorities. As we shall see, there is some evidence that the rapid change in the nature of Physical Education has had some dispiriting influences on the morale and confidence of the profession.

PE in the Primary Sector

In 1986 I interviewed seventeen teachers in both infant and junior schools who had some responsibility for Physical Education. In my choice of schools I tried to establish a reasonable mix of 'progressive' and 'traditional' schools, and these were located in a variety of geographical regions. In all of these schools, irrespective of age range or geographical location, there was a high degree of congruence in the attitude held by teachers towards competition. Very few thought that competition was an important part of their curriculum or lesson structure. Those primary schools which did participate in inter-school leagues valued their successes in such competitions, but the teachers involved were, almost uniformly, unexcited by their competitive nature, even though in some cases they recognized that competitive success was useful for their standing in the school and an aid to promotion. For the most part, however, teachers were sceptical of the benefits of such competition in the educational development of their pupils, and were determined to make a sharp distinction between being a teacher and acting as a coach. The latter role or activity was often seen as more appropriately taken or carried out by someone else in out-of-school time. Two comments, however, need to be made here. One is that in the local communities which feed junior schools (7–11 or 13 years of age) the sorts of competition which are prestigious almost exclusively took the form of boys' sports and games. This has the effect of segregating to a degree the physical activities of boys and girls inside schools, and quite early in their school career. For example, extra-curricular PE in this sector tended very often to take the form of provision, by male teachers and male parents, of football for boys. Many teachers questioned the desirability of this process. Secondly, there is a widespread lack of confidence amongst many junior teachers in their ability to teach Physical Education. They often stressed their inability to extend their teaching from a rather limited and unexciting repertoire of activities to something better organized and more interesting. While there was a great deal of interest expressed in introducing more work on dance and gymnastics into lessons, most had little knowledge or understanding of how that might be achieved.

This point is worth exploring in more depth. The ideology of the primary and infants' school teacher is often very different from that of the Physical Education specialist in the secondary school (see Asquith, 1987). All my interviewees expressed their adherence to the notion of 'teaching children' as opposed to 'teaching subject'; most were explicitly 'child-centred' in their philosophy and classroom practice, and they explained their suspicion of and opposition to competitive Physical Education with reference to this commitment. A competitive approach was assumed to exclude and deny more pupils opportunity for enjoyment or even participation in the activities of PE. But this commitment to child-centred teaching was rarely expressed in their PE teaching. The content of these lessons was often very limited indeed (cf., Asquith, 1987) and this was acknowledged by the teachers themselves, who felt badly undertrained in PE and lacking in appropriate skills and techniques to develop more interesting, stimulating and 'child-centred' PE. Without such skills many had fallen back upon the traditional competitive sports as the basis of their work, with most of their attention being upon the better players, while others avoided those sports in favour of a rather diluted movement curriculum. Few of the teachers interviewed were happy or satisfied with their approach to Physical Education, and they often stressed that their curriculum had been arrived at through reflection on what they could do, as opposed to what they would have liked to do. For them the teaching of team games and a limited form of movement education was a 'coping strategy' (see Hargreaves, 1978; Pollard, this volume, Chapter 7), the best they could offer given the limitations of their professional training.

PE in the Secondary School

I interviewed Physical Education staff in nine secondary schools, four in London and the south-east, three in the north-west and two in the Midlands. The schools were all mixed comprehensives, but in other respects differed widely. Three of the schools had adopted a very critical policy towards competition in Physical Education, three were agnostic and the other three were wildly keen on competition. These last were completely untouched by the apparent controversy over competition. Most of the Physical Education

staff were in the Professional Association of Teachers, they seemed 'conservative' in their outlook, keen to preserve the traditional practices of PE, and
during the period of teacher action (over pay and conditions of work) they did
not engage in strike action with the enthusiasm of their colleagues. Contrary to
union policy these teachers frequently supported after-school games sessions
in the week and on Saturdays, and held team meetings during lunch times. In
the perspectives of these teachers the dispute interfered with the smooth
running of their schools' sport, but no long-term effects were expected. In their
curriculum both boys and girls were encouraged to join teams and they catered
for a wide range of ability. Prominent positions in the building were reserved
to display the cups which had been won. The headteacher often spent a lot of
time speaking in morning assembly about the prowess of the school teams, and
the Physical Education staff felt valued and important members of the teaching
community. The use of the term 'community' is important here, since many
staff from other subject areas were involved in school sport especially in
coaching team games. However, although in all three schools girls' sports and
teams were well supported both in terms of resources (human and physical)
and time, the emphasis was clearly upon the boys' activities. A strict regime
predominated during Physical Education lessons. Children without proper kit
were obliged to participate in underwear, and relatively unskilled pupils were
allowed to do the minimum as long as they satisfied the staff that they had
made a reasonable attempt at mastering the activities offered.

In these schools the Physical Education staff could not understand what
people who were critical of competition were worried about. They had not had
problems in their departments in inspiring high levels of enthusiasm for what
they had to offer. They had met resistance to their work, but they felt that this
was no more likely or apparent in their subject than in any other, and they
believed that there are always some pupils who do not want to become
involved in what the school wants them to do. All three schools drew on
pupils from a wide mixture of socio-economic areas, and in each no serious
problems of control and discipline had been experienced. Indeed, the staff
referred approvingly to the ease with which they managed to control their
pupils within the traditional curriculum which they offered, because (as I was
frequently told), 'everyone knows where they stand.' There was strong
support from parents for what the school was trying to do in Physical
Education, and the parents I spoke to on parents' evenings clearly identified the
school's policy with what they had experienced when they were at school.
Both staff and parents had a highly positive attitude towards competition in all
aspects of the curriculum, and this was so even amongst those parents who
freely admitted that they had not enjoyed Physical Education when they as
pupils had been subjected to it. In fact, this latter group sometimes appeared to
be even more enthusiastic about school sport than those who had been

proficient when younger. They seemed to hope and believe that their children could succeed where they had previously failed.

By contrast the three schools I have called 'agnostic' did participate in competitive sport, but only to a rather limited extent. There was little interest in the school as a whole in such activities, cups were not displayed in a prominent position and the headteachers rarely referred to school teams. There was very limited participation in coaching and training by other than PE staff, and the latter did not spend much time outside official hours on their work with teams. Moreover, PE staff were divided in their attitudes towards what should constitute a 'proper PE'. The relatively older teachers were adherents of traditional games, while their younger colleagues very often were more interested in a 'sport for all' approach. The status of the PE departments in these schools was not high, and the lessons I observed were not especially well structured or interesting at least to the outside observer. The pupils interviewed and observed often seemed to find it difficult to work out what it was that the PE staff required of them, since different teachers had different objectives in mind. The teachers' dispute had led to a considerable drop in morale and commitment which was reflected both in the content of the lessons and in the organization of out-of-school fixtures. The infighting in the department had brought about additional strains, and the control of pupils was clearly a problem. In the lessons I observed pupils seemed to be responding to a lack of confidence in the PE staff by testing and trying their patience, and truancy from physical education sessions was high. There was not a concerted effort to challenge this level of truancy, and in one of these schools staff seemed relieved when a third of the class was missing from their PE lesson. This state of affairs contrasted sharply with the situation in the schools which were keen on competitive games, where any pupil absent was pursued until a satisfactory explanation was provided.

The PE departments in the three 'agnostic' schools had divided up into warring camps, and each sought support for their views from other teachers, especially those in the hierarchy, and from parents and governors. It would be wrong, however, to give the impression that in all such cases the teachers involved felt animosity towards each other; on occasions a 'debate' was conducted at quite an impersonal level but dispute over teaching PE was far from being the most important matter on most of these teachers' minds. But there did exist a lot of jockeying for position in terms of the pro or contra competition campaign. Many of the older teachers reacted aggressively towards curriculum change because they felt that there was far too much of it, especially in Physical Education. Many felt that they could not keep up with the many changes being advocated in the profession, they seemed threatened and alienated by the innovations proposed. As a result they retreated to their commitments to competition and tradition in the hope that the 'debate' would soon play itself out. In adopting this strategy they were far better placed than younger staff to gain the support of the parents and pupils. Their lessons were more popular with many of the children who often seemed confused by the lessons which were oriented more towards health-related fitness and teaching for understanding which did not in their view constitute 'proper PE'.

The three schools which were critical of competition possessed much happier PE departments. Their accounts of how their policy on competition developed suggested that they had not started off with any particular ideological attitude towards competition, but just found it progressively harder to organize their lessons in terms of competitive sport. All these schools are in the Inner London Education Authority (ILEA) and they had been encouraged to review and develop a wider notion of Physical Education by the local PE inspectorate. This concern to revise and rethink PE was an expression of the absence of appropriate facilities and a widespread drop-out rate from the previous more traditional skill-based games approach to PE. In the 'new PE' of the Authority, all games were taught to mixed-sex groups, and a very wide range of physical activities was provided. The emphasis seemed to be on providing access to a wide range of physical activities and experiences rather than on achieving expertise and high-level performance in any one of them. There is little inter-school team sport and Saturday mornings are generally free from working obligations for staff. All the staff I spoke to were in favour of this approach and they believed that the school as a body supported them. Teachers felt that the new approach had brought a dramatic change in atmosphere when teaching PE and they experienced satisfaction at having moved away from a programme which in their view had overconcentrated upon an élite to the detriment of most of the pupils. If any pupil wished to become involved in competitive sport he or she was pointed in the direction of an appropriate club. All the staff interviewed felt that this way of organizing Physical Education had resulted in a far better atmosphere in lessons, less truancy and the prospect of a greater participation in sport when the children become older.

However, the 'new PE' in these schools did not herald the disappearance of competitive team games. All the staff thought that sport was an important part of Physical Education, and sport is by its very nature competitive. Rather, in their view it was the atmosphere and ideology within which the traditional activities were carried out which differentiated their schools' curriculum from the more traditional PE as, for example, it was represented in the three competitive schools described above. Pupils were encouraged to see the competitive aspect of sport as an enjoyable and non-threatening feature of games, and when competition took place it involved peers against peers, rather than very skilled pupils against poor performers. My observations suggested that standards of performance were generally better in these schools than in the other two types of PE departments, and that weaker pupils in particular were encouraged to do well and improve. On the other hand, it was also my impression that pupils in the three ILEA schools were less likely to achieve the high levels of performance which some pupils did achieve in the other sorts of schools. The staff themselves were aware of this, and did not regard it as a criticism of what they are doing. They argued that if one spends a disproportionate amount of time and effort on just a few pupils (in PE or elsewhere) then it is only to be expected that a higher level of performance will be achieved; but in their view such an allocation of resources is basically unfair and to be avoided in a school.

These teachers stressed too that parents had not been antagonistic to this sort of approach to Physical Education and argued that this was due to the way in which the PE departments had approached parents and governors and made very clear what they intended to do and the reasons behind it. In addition, both the school and the local authority were stoutly behind the policy and were prepared to back their PE staff in case of dispute. Many of the staff did wonder, though, whether it would have been quite so easy to 'sell' their policy in an area with a strong tradition of a particular sport, and of parental involvement in it. This was not felt to be a problem in ILEA, with a rapidly changing school population of a very varied ethnic background and with many one-parent families. Several staff told me that in their opinion 'sport was the last thing in parents' minds' when it came to worrying about what was going on in school. In many respects these teachers came closest to adopting the sort of approach to Physical Education which teachers in junior schools would like to have implemented. But unlike their PE counterparts in the primary sector as specialist teachers they felt proficient and confident in their ability to devise an interesting, progressive 'child-centred' package of physical activities for their pupils.

Discussion

The arguments for and against competition in Physical Education took an interesting variety of forms in the schools I visited. Those broadly in favour of an emphasis upon competition argued that sport is essentially competitive, and so this is the element to be stressed in the PE curriculum. Those critical of competition argued that sport is essentially competitive, but that this should not play a large part in Physical Education, and where it does take place winners and losers should not feel that there is an enormous gap between them, or that their success or failure should influence how they are valued as persons. In particular these teachers felt that no single sport or group of children should be allowed to dominate the PE programme in school. Boys and girls should both be given the opportunity to win and lose at a whole variety of activities, and thus acquire the ability to cope with the discovery of different levels of attainment and learn from those experiences. Some teachers, however, particularly those in the competitive schools and the older teachers in the agnostic schools, thought that it was important for pupils to learn to be competitive in sport because competition is a feature of life outside school and coming to terms with it was an important prerequisite to taking one's place in the adult world. It was frequently pointed out that in public schools there is a far greater emphasis upon competitive sport than in state schools, with far superior provision and teaching resources, and this must be for a reason. Successful parents who send their children at considerable expense to such schools obviously expect that the atmosphere of competition and high achievement will help their children be successful. Against this the emphasis on cooperation and a downgrading of competition in the state secondary sector might be seen as part of a process of preparing children for their future as less successful participants in the struggle for more prestigious jobs and incomes in adult society. The notion that 'nice guys finish last' was one which worried even some of the teachers who were critical of competitive sport.

My observations suggested that staff found it much easier to control their pupils if the department and school as a whole were giving out the same message, irrespective of whether this message is for competition or largely against it. Pupils found it difficult to know where they were in the schools which embodied a variety of often conflicting commitments and approaches to Physical Education. This was not necessarily because the lessons themselves were less well prepared or devised, but because the context within which those lessons took place was unstable. In some ways this is a dispiriting observation, since it would be attractive to think that a mixture of emphasis on competition and non-competition in a Physical Education curriculum would be desirable in at least an experimental sense. Different teachers could try different approaches with different groups of children in such a situation. In the three 'agnostic' schools, however, differences sometimes verging on conflict between the staff had contributed to severe control problems, and a rather unhappy role for Physical Education in the school. It may well be that the practice of mixing methods and curriculum contents (some competitive, others not so) is both possible and desirable, but if it is to be achieved it has to be founded upon unifying principles and some agreement within a department and amongst teachers over values, aims and objectives for the subject. Where this is absent, innovation, whatever its form, can be a highly problematical affair (see Evans *et al.*, 1987).

The stereotype of the radical anti-competitive PE teacher which the *Panorama* programme (and the popular press) tried to portray as the norm in PE remains a rare bird indeed in the United Kingdom. The situation still is much more complex and varied. The claim that PE teachers are even mildly to the 'political left' caused much amusement in staffrooms up and down the country after the programme was shown. The data presented here, however, suggest that the old stereotype of the uncritical enthusiast for competitive team games is also becoming rarer. Teachers in primary and secondary schools have begun to question their practices, have begun to examine why there is so much apathy and indifference amongst their pupils towards in- and out-of-school Physical Education and sport. The profession is going through a period of change, and some teachers are attempting to redefine what Physical Education is about. The debate on competition is only part of the process. It remains to be seen how that debate will be resolved.

References

ASQUITH, A. (1987) 'An Investigation into Games Teaching in the Primary School: A Participant Observation Study of an Innovatory Teaching Programme,' Unpublished MA (Ed) dissertation, University of Southampton.

BAYLIS, T. (1984) *Providing Equal Opportunities for Girls and Boys in Physical Education*, London, ILEA College of Physical Education.

BRITISH ASSOCIATION OF ADVISORS AND LECTURERS IN PHYSICAL EDUCATION (1983) 'Games teaching revisited', *Bulletin of Physical Education*, 19, 1.

EVANS, J. *et al.* (1987) 'Some thoughts on the political and pedagogical implications of mixed sex grouping,' *British Educational Research Journal*, 13, 1, pp. 59–71.

HARGREAVES, A. (1978) 'The significance of classroom coping strategies', in BARTON, L. and MEIGHAN, L. (Eds), *Sociological Interpretations of Schools and Classrooms: A Reappraisal*, Driffield, Nafferton Books, pp. 73–96.

HARGREAVES, J. (1986) *Sport, Power and Culture*, Cambridge, Polity Press.

HOWARTH, K. (1987) 'Initial training in primary schools', *British Journal of Physical Education*, 18, 4, pp. 152–4.

LEAMAN, O. (1984) *Sit on the Sidelines and Watch the Boys Play: Sex Differentiation in PE*, London, Longmans (for Schools Council).

The Independent (1986) 18 November, p. 32.

The Times (1986) 'A Question of Sport', 17 November, p. 17.

WHITEHEAD, N. and HENDRY, L.B. (1976) *Teaching Physical Education in England*, London, Lepus Books.

7
Physical Education, Competition and Control in Primary Education

Andrew Pollard

In the summer of 1986 the staff of a Bristol infant school serving a large estate of public housing and many disadvantaged families decided to organize a non-competitive sports day for their children. Seeing one of their main responsibilities as being to nurture the self-concept of each child, they aimed to avoid having 'losers'. There would be a range of activities and opportunities for each child to succeed. To their extreme surprise and dismay the event hit the local and then the national headlines. It thus became an 'exhibit', and was used to illustrate arguments within a fast moving, and sometimes acrimonious, debate on the place of competitive sports in schools. It was alleged, as we shall see, that 'trendy' teachers were undermining the nation's ability to compete in football, cricket and other sports, that the 'natural' competitive instincts of children were being thwarted and that the basis of our industrial future was at risk.

In a primary school on the other side of Bristol the topic was also prominent in staffroom conversation. This school was located in an affluent and fashionable suburb and many of the pupils were sent to private schools by their parents at the end of their primary school career. Most of the staff were committed to the traditional sports day that provided an important event in the summer term calendar. Parents and governors would attend and 'houses' would compete against each other in an afternoon of races. A minority of staff, mostly in the infant department of the school, opposed the sports day. They argued partly on grounds of the worthwhileness and difficulty of requiring very young children to sit and watch other children racing for long periods of time (for the infants had but two races in which to compete), and also at a more fundamental level on the principle of competitive activities itself. It was felt that it was more appropriate for each child to be challenged by personal targets so that they could all achieve successes in their own terms. Despite these misgivings the sports day went ahead. There was some tension in the staffroom over this period. For instance, a newspaper editorial condemning 'lefties' for undermining competitive sports at school mysteriously appeared on the staff noticeboard. Perhaps it was posted because it stated, with no equivocation, some things which could not be said directly. The tracksuited, male football-team coach was suspected but, as the concern to restore staffroom relationships reasserted itself, the issue gradually passed into the category of 'things which we don't discuss'.

So what was going on? What are the issues and social forces which underlie such events? In this chapter I have employed a number of sociological concepts to analyze the links between teacher practices and national concerns with regard, in particular, to competitive team sports. I shall argue that competition in Physical Education has endured and is likely to persist because of a double articulation which supports it. At the face-to-face classroom level, particularly with older children, competition is often used as a means of control — a means of managing large groups of children. It thus makes practical sense, and to question its educational worthwhileness is to threaten an important teacher coping strategy. At the macro-level of national policy, culture and development, competition is seen by influential groups as a source of industrial survival, personal character and shared tradition. The case I shall make highlights these linkages using the concept of hegemony. A provocative twist in the tail of the paper is a brief consideration of the extent to which competition in school sport should be seen as a gender issue.

This study is analytical but it is offered to illustrate a line of sociological reasoning rather than as a 'proven' research report. Although the study is informed by work in schools over many years and supported by documentary analysis, PE lessons were observed and teachers interviewed in only two junior schools (7–11) over a period of one term. This was carried out as part of a school experience programme involving Bachelor of Education (BEd) second-year students for whom I had supportive and supervisory responsibilities. These students had previously experienced twenty-five hours of coursework on PE as part of their course — a not untypical amount for initial teacher education courses.

Here I have drawn on one of the schools in particular — a school which I shall call Hillside Junior, which occupied a cramped city site with no on-site playing field but nevertheless with a consistent record of success in inter-city sports. Football had provided a particularly rich vein. To such cases I have applied sociological concepts which have been constructed in a number of other case studies (e.g., Cohen, 1972; Pollard, 1985).

As with many forms of ethnographic work, the value of such analysis may be seen in terms of generating theoretical propositions with regard to taken-for-granted practices. This chapter is offered as a conceptualization of some of the issues involved in PE and competition and as a medium for reflective professional discussion.

The Macro-Level: Competition and the 'Moral Panic' of 1986

Here I aim to trace the course of the public furore and debate about the place of competition in school sports which began in the summer of 1986. I shall use the concept of 'moral panic' and I therefore begin by discussing both that concept and the theoretical approach from which it is derived.

The concept of moral panic stems from interactionist studies of the ways in which conformity is maintained in society. Another way of putting that is to say that it originates from studies of the ways in which deviant behaviour is identified and controlled. A starting point for this approach is Becker's often quoted statement that 'social groups create deviance by making the rules whose infraction constitutes deviance' (1963, p. 9). At a wider, societal level this proposition becomes extended to suggest that certain forms of behaviour are identified as being deviant only when they are publicly identified as such. The recurring patterns of such processes of societal reaction are revealed by the concept of 'moral panic'.

Moral panics in the public domain tend to follow a similar sequence (Cohen, 1980). Initially perhaps, there is a gradually developing form of popular culture or even, as in the case here, a form of professional practice. This becomes more widely apparent when it is highlighted by a dramatic event which shocks some people. This is followed by expressions of public disquiet. Gradually a sense of 'moral outrage' is generated as 'true values and cultural traditions' are asserted by certain interest groups — perhaps amplified by the media. This finally leads to a mobilization of a control culture so that those now identified as 'deviants' are isolated and are either pressurized into conformity or ostracized so that they no longer constitute a 'threat to the social fabric'. Among the more important sociological studies which document such processes of moral panic are those of Becker (1963) on marijuana use in the USA, Cohen (1972) on Mods and Rockers and Hall *et al.* (1978) on the 1972–73 mugging panic and its relationship to the economic and political crisis.

The panic of 1986 about competition in schools essentially followed the familiar pattern, though what was noticeable about it was that it was a form of professional practice which came under the spotlight. As others in this collection point out, this fact can be connected with the general attacks on the teaching profession and on educational standards which have characterized the 1980s in Britain and elsewhere.

For some years there had been trends, particularly within secondary schools, towards a broadening of pupil involvement in sport. This had involved moves away from traditional team games and had spawned concepts such as 'Teaching Games for Understanding', 'Health Related Fitness' and 'Sport for All' (Spackman, 1983, 1984). Despite the worthy intentions and thoughtful professionalism with which these new approaches had been introduced (see the discussions in the *British Journal of Physical Education*), there was always some concern about the perceived reduction of competition. In March 1986 the Health Education Council (HEC) and the Physical Education Association (PEA) addressed this issue in their joint newsletter from their Health and Physical Education Project (HEC/PEA, 1986). There, speeches by specialist HMI and the HMI document on 'The Organisation and Content of the 5–16 Curriculum' were cited favourably as supporting further development of a broadened and more relevant form of PE. To reinforce this, the most prominent article identified and questioned the underlying assumptions of the 'competitive mythology' — that competition is character-building, produces excellence and is a preparation for life (Sparkes, 1986). The profession seemed unaware of the extent and nature of the public furore and moral panic which were about to engulf them.

The 'dramatic event' which precipitated the uproar is attributable to Mrs Carol Rowbotham, senior PE inspector of the Inner London Education Authority. In June she was reported as stating that, in order to facilitate the maximum involvement of all pupils in PE, competitive team sports should not be played during school hours. Of course, ILEA was at the time a favourite source of sensational press stories and it did not take long for news of this latest 'excess' to hit the tabloid headlines.

Even leader writers of 'quality' newspapers, normally more restrained, joined the chorus. For instance, the leading article in *The Times Educational Supplement* of 11 July asked:

> So what is to be made of the 1960-ish ideology which prompts ageing PE organisers to decry traditional forms of sporting competition on the basis of value-judgments which are wildly at odds with the society the schools exist to serve? Last weekend, London TV viewers were treated to a comprehensive school where pupils engaged in stool-ball, a primitive fore-runner of cricket played with a soft ball which, ... (it was said) ... 'allows both sexes to play and is not competitive'. Viewers must have reflected that one thing is fairly certain: the West Indian pace attack was not reared on stool-ball and stool-ball is not going to help England find a quick bowler.

Here the major initial source of the public groundswell is clearly revealed, for the indignation quickly became enmeshed with questions about the performance of English players in World Cup football, in the Edgbaston test match and at Wimbledon. Were both national pride and the public's main source of leisure interest to be undermined by a few trendy teachers?

In the face of such flamboyant expressions of public disquiet a number of strategic withdrawals, clarifications and attempts at diversion were made. ILEA announced a plan for a 'Junior Olympics' and political parties, including Labour, were quick to state their commitment to competitive sport. Several teacher unions (NUT, NAS/UWT, NAHT and PAT) met with the Central Council for Physical Recreation and called for the government to bolster competitive sports in state schools. Whilst 'rejecting entirely the claims that have been flying about' (David Hart, NAHT), the unions tried to broaden the debate to cover resource issues by pointing out the voluntary nature of much of teachers' involvement in team sport and the extent of recent sales of playing fields by rate-capped local authorities. The media interest continued, catching up the Bristol infant school cited in my introduction and confronting them with the 'irresponsibility' of subverting children's 'true instincts' before casting the school once more into relative obscurity.

By the Autumn a wide range of bodies had had their say, including the organizing bodies of specialist team sports, the headteachers of public schools and a number of industrialists. The Football Association set up an 'Enquiry' which was paralleled by enquiries on behalf of organizations such as the Secondary Headteachers Association and the British Sports and Allied Industries Federation Ltd. The interest from industry represented, I would suggest, the point when the phase of asserting the 'moral enterprise' began to pass and the 'control culture' began to be mobilized. Manufacturers of sports equipment had expressed their views earlier in the summer, but now the nature of the contributions began to change. It was our national economic survival which was now, it seemed, at stake. For instance, Prince Philip lectured to the British Institute of Management on 26 November and advised them that:

> There are those in education who, in the name of freedom and equality are trying to do away with competitive sports. ... This negative attitude is doing untold damage to the morale of all those engaged in industry and commerce. ... The process of education and training for life in an industrial community is being corrupted and, consequently, the national economy as a whole suffers. (Reported in *The Daily Telegraph*, 27 November 1986)

On the same day a joint seminar was held by the Department of the Environment and the Department of Education and Science at which the issue was debated. The seminar, chaired by the Sports Minister, Mr Tracey, was attended by over ninety representatives of sports' governing bodies and by physical educationalists. In a statement to the press afterwards Mr Tracey was at pains to stress 'that no-one at the seminar had questioned the value of competition in sport' (*The Times*, 27 November 1986), but, nevertheless, he immediately set up a joint DOE/DES study to investigate further.

The Executive Committee of the PE Association published a bitter statement in the November/December edition of their journal (PEA, 1986). This noted the ill-informed attacks and misrepresentations produced by the media and castigated those who had taken the opportunity to 'make political capital and exploit [the] situation for personal gain' — many of whom 'should have known better'. They presented a detailed statement of the PEA position on the subject. The first clause indicated that:

> opportunities should be made available for all pupils, regardless of ability, interest or sex, to experience the benefits of a balanced physical education programme which would normally include involvement in a wide range of competitive sports.

The statement has a very different tenor from that of the March journal. Dignity is maintained but the equivocation — or clarification — regarding competitive sport is a testament to the battering which the Association had suffered since the spring.

It is very hard to draw precise conclusions about the results of such events. The issue has continued to run (for instance, a BBC *Panorama* programme in March 1987 reported on the Secondary Headteachers' enquiry and extrapolated the issue to suggest declining standards of fitness among schoolchildren) but the panic has subsided. Perhaps the job has been done, for there can be few teachers who are now unaware that to challenge competitive sports is highly contentious and perhaps even fewer headteachers who are prepared to risk their schools becoming the subject of media hysteria over the issue. Now it is 'known' that 'society' expects such things — for they are entwined into our moral, symbolic and economic fabric. In such ways is control exercised and the spread of deviance circumscribed.

In another way, though, the spread of the 'sport for all' philosophy had a quite different source of resistance to overcome: that of teachers who find traditional forms of competition convenient and helpful as a means of structuring PE sessions and controlling the physical activity of large numbers of children. To investigate this we must turn to the 'micro'-level, to the concerns and situation of teachers as they work with their classes in school. In this second part of the chapter I refer mainly to junior school teachers.

The Micro-Level: Competition and Class Control

The apparatus lesson was well organized, but they did have to be stopped a few times because of the noise level ... and Sharon was sent off the apparatus for shouting and screaming half-way through the lesson. I don't know what it was about, but Martin and his friends seemed to become much more aggressive than usual as soon as they were let loose on the apparatus. (BEd student)

Perhaps we would expect student experience of Physical Education lessons to reflect some disruption of the sort illustrated above, and yet I believe that a great many teachers are nervous about taking Physical Education lessons which require them to teach their children outside the confines of their classroom. Apart from the time limitations on initial teacher education courses which seriously restrict the professional preparation of non-specialist teachers for teaching Physical Education, there are a number of reasons why even experienced teachers may approach Physical Education activities cautiously.

The first points to make are of a general nature and relate to the fact that the control of large numbers of children in classrooms is inherently difficult. There are constraints of resources, time and activity. There are pressures from a variety of sources for numerous kinds of educational output. It is no wonder that many teachers feel stressed by the situation in which they work (Dunham, 1984). The job is challenging and personal fulfilment can only come from finding ways of balancing the demands of the role with the sense of self of each teacher and with their values and commitments (Nias, 1984).

People in any walk of life try to overcome or avoid situations in which they feel vulnerable and, as I have argued elsewhere (Pollard, 1982, 1985), in classroom circumstances teachers develop coping strategies as a means of overcoming the potential threat to their control and thus to their self. One example of such a coping strategy is 'routinization' — the use of routines in classroom activities which reduce the managerial and organizational pressures which would otherwise have to be faced. Of course, individual children in classrooms face a somewhat similar position to teachers and also develop coping strategies. These tend to mesh into those of the teacher. For instance, the strategy of 'drifting' is commonly to be found in association with routinization.

The outcome of the negotiation and strategic interaction which takes place between teachers and children is usually some form of working consensus; taken-for-granted understandings about classroom life come to be established and then provide a framework for social interaction. The concept of working consensus thus represents a technical expression of what many primary school teachers refer to as a 'good relationship'. As it develops the class feels as if it is 'settling down' and the sparring, which often makes the start of a school year so strenuous, becomes more infrequent.

The emergence of a working consensus requires that certain classroom rules are understood and for the most part accepted. These usually embrace topics like noise levels, types of movement, styles of address and quantity and quality of work. Further, they take on specific meanings and have particular force in particular situations. This variation in the strength of classroom rules can be analyzed using the concept of 'rule-frame'. When rule-frame is strong then children's actions are clearly defined and circumscribed, but if the rule-frame is weak children have much more scope for choice. Another way of putting that, perhaps from a teacher perspective, is to say that they may begin to 'get out of control'.

I would suggest that the threat of weakly rule-framed situations is commonly associated with Physical Education lessons. Of course, there is no reason why teachers should not anticipate potential difficulties but there are circumstances, associated with organizing physical activity in schools, which seem to make such anticipation particularly important. I will identify three. The first concerns the transition from classroom sessions to Physical Education sessions. This is likely to involve children in changing their clothes and the complexities with infants of buttons, laces, zips, what is 'the right way round' and 'where do we put our things?' are often replaced with juniors by a fascination with what other boys or girls have 'got on underneath' plus pre-pubescent sensitivity and anxiety. At the more technical level a class of children usually completes their changing over the span of several minutes leaving the quick-changers waiting for the more reluctant or diverted. Having travelled (hopefully not too far) and arrived in the hall, or wherever, it is still to be hoped that the apparatus/tape recorder/equipment is in position, safe and works. The result of such imponderables is that a transition before a PE session is often unusually problematic and is likely to be characterized by a relatively weak level of rule-frame — unless a teacher takes specific steps to avoid this. Nor is putting things away, changing back into normal clothes and starting a new activity after a session likely to be much better.

A second set of factors which suggests why rule-frame is an inherent issue in Physical Education activities concerns the locations in which they take place. Open spaces seem to give children some sense of release and they often want to use the space to the full, in ways which they perceive to be exciting and worthwhile. A teacher may have different and more specific plans but the space and the provision of, say, apparatus or music may inspire some children to act in unanticipated ways. Often too the spaces in which physical activities must take place have more than one use and lessons must be organized among other equipment. Where school halls are concerned the common architectural decision to double them as corridors means that interruptions to PE lessons must often be anticipated. In addition many school halls have only limited noise dampening — a serious issue for those many teachers who feel that their competence is somehow in question if noise levels seem too high (Denscombe, 1980). This raises the issue of the public nature of many of the spaces in which physical activities take place. Whether lessons are conducted on a school field, playground or a school hall, teachers are likely to find themselves in more visible positions when taking Physical Education classes than they would be in their classrooms. Other teachers and children are likely to provide the main audiences, with parents no doubt taking an interest when they can. This both heightens the vulnerability of teachers and semi-disarms them — for some control techniques are only used in private.

A third issue concerning rule-frame involves the nature of PE activity itself. Almost by definition this involves a great deal of movement. This movement not only provides considerable scope for deviant or evasive activities but, once started, it has to be both lived with and then stopped. The latter may be no problem for those who have developed a clear switch-signal — 'aaand STOP' — but it remains crucial to the pattern of many movement and apparatus sessions in primary schools. These tend to follow a pattern of 'teacher presenting/giving instructions'→'child activity'→'teacher evaluation and restructuring'. At the crucial 'child activity' stage direct control is relatively slight. Control, in other words, must be pre-structured in many active Physical Education activities. This would be all very well if most teachers were full of confidence and knowledgeable about the teaching of PE. Given the nature of the constraints on the PE training of most primary teachers, this is rarely the case (see Howarth 1987). I would suggest that many lessons take place which rely on a routinized formula of groups rotating round 'big apparatus' or on broadcasts of movement activities in which the structuring is divorced from the immediate situation.

These points can be illustrated and a further set of factors introduced by considering an example of a movement lesson which took place at Hillside Junior.

The movement lesson was conducted by a stimulating and professionally aware female student teacher with twenty-eight 9-year-olds. She had planned the activities with care and had no serious discipline problems in her classroom. The lesson was intended to lead through warm-up activities into a group activity, related to the class topic on Greek myths, which simulated a voyage of Ulysses in a galley followed by feasting on arrival ashore. It took place after what some children described as 'a long and boring maths lesson' and was conducted in a central school hall to which six classrooms had direct access. Doors banged and people passed through almost continuously.

The children were lively from the start but a clear explanation of the initial activities was given and, despite a rising noise level, the warm-up exercises seemed to involve most of the children constructively — only one or two boys chose to investigate behind the piano and other obstacles on the perimeter of the space which had been cleared. The student called the activities to a halt and introduced the first part of the movement simulation. The voyage in the galley was to be enacted by the girls 'rowing' the galley in the centre of the room whilst the boys represented the wind swirling around them. A tambourine was to be used by the student to indicate the strength of the wind.

The 'wind' was calm as the girls, seated in line ahead, began to 'row'. As they picked up a rhythm the rowing became more dramatic and the sound of 'heaving' began to increase. Meanwhile the 'wind', in the shape of fifteen boys, had begun to get noisy and increasingly macho in its interpretation. The 'wind' begun 'crashing and zooming about' with an apparent unpredictability which began to disturb the student. Yet, despite the few boys who had again found their way behind the piano, there was a pattern in the wind's behaviour. It reflected that child art of distanced, subversive compliance in which a teacher's requirements are fulfilled but in a manner which plays to a quite different audience of peers. In this case it seemed as if the boys felt it necessary to outdo each other in registering their distance from the activity.

With a shout and a loud crash on the tambourine the student halted the action and gained the children's attention. 'OK, there's lots of movement but you've got to be quieter or we'll have to go back to the classroom.' The scene quietened and the student carefully began to restructure the activity. She reminded the children of the myth and clarified their dramatic roles. Then, to provide a good model of how 'wind' should present itself, she called upon Richard to demonstrate. Richard had been noticeable for his particularly agile and divergent movement which was a sensitive interpretation of the theme. He refused to move. 'Come on Richard, it was very good.' Richard, (who on other occasions played football for the city boys' team) shook his head. Continued encouragement was not enough and in the end the student changed her tactic and asked a group of boys, including Richard, to demonstrate. They did — boisterously — as if it was even more necessary to prove their lack of commitment to the activity.

After one brief further enactment the roles were reversed so that the boys were then required to 'row'. The girls now ran rapidly around the room, offering a progressively looser interpretation of their task. At the same time the oarsmen began to be overcome by the increasingly strenuous efforts and power which they invested in their rowing. Finally, amidst much grunting and banter someone 'caught a crab' and the order of the boat collapsed. The student felt that order in the lesson had been awash for a while and, drawing on her determination and reserves of authority, ordered the children to stop messing about, to be quiet and to return to the classroom.

In this example I would suggest that a normally competent teacher was caught out by some of the problems of teaching PE in schools. She would, in most circumstances, have been judged to have good relationships with her class and the working consensus and understandings about appropriate classroom behaviour were well established. Yet, despite her attempts to pre-structure the activity and to motivate the children with a topic-related theme, she encountered serious difficulties of control. It was certainly the case that the transition between sessions had been extended and was characterized by a weak level of rule-frame. From the confines of their classroom the children had moved into a large space where they were asked to attend to their teacher — despite the interruptions — and were required to enact the drama — despite the obstacles and scope for other activities which it made possible. In the end the student clearly felt that the activity could no longer continue because it was 'out of control' . In other words the activity made it possible for the children to do what they wanted to do — 'have a laugh', 'mess about', 'play around', and 'watch Miss as we do it'. It was no longer framed by the normal negotiated rules in which the teacher had had a major influence.

Yet this analysis, whilst necessary, is insufficient, for one of the most important factors involved in the case was gender. It was the boys' unwillingness to identify themselves with any activity which might be interpreted as undermining their masculinity which in a sense started the trouble. From there, self-consciousness took over and proved to be a more powerful force than teacher authority. Perhaps it was a strategic error to cast the girls and boys in different roles for an activity of this type, but, notwithstanding this probability, the potential of the children's gender awareness to provoke particular control problems in movement is highlighted. I would suggest that it is also a particular problem in other types of PE activity.

But consider another case from Hillside.

The bell went to signal that it was time for the third and fourth year juniors to get ready for games. A male student-teacher had responsibility for a class of 10-year-olds. There was a great deal of noise as the children started to change, the boys being particularly noticeable in their football strips. 'Less noise, or there'll be no games.' Games was a highlight of the week, particularly for the boys, and the children settled down. They prepared for the quarter-of-an-hour walk to the playing field. The file of children crossed the roads and eventually arrived at the field. As the children changed their shoes a small team cleared dog dirt from the pitches and marked goals and corners.

The girls went with a female teacher to play rounders. They played in a small corner of the field which was deemed 'not flat enough for football'. The boys had a choice of football or cricket. Of the majority, who opted for football, some were selected to play in full teams on the 'big pitch' by the male teacher who coached the school team. The remainder were to be supervised by the male student-teacher.

Two children, nominated as captains, chose their teams — the student insisting, as those available diminished in number, that 'no, nobody is rubbish'. And so to the game. This was played vigorously with much shouting, some skill and a great deal of commitment. The student refereed confidently as the game ebbed and flowed, judging 'offside', awarding free kicks and otherwise interpreting the rules. His authority was not questioned. A 'one all' scoreline heightened tension as the time ticked away. Members of each team urged each other on: 'Tank, pass!', 'Come on, get it, shoot!', 'Hard luck, Moony'. Then a boy fell, clutching his leg in pain. He looked hurt and the game stopped. 'Oh come on, John', said the student, 'Bobby Robson wouldn't do that. He'd play on. You've got to keep the game going.' John got up and hobbled until the end of the game. 'Two-one' — a 'great game' to the winners but a show of dissatisfaction elsewhere.

The potential for control problems in this session was considerable. The transition from the previous lesson was very inconvenient, the field had to be cleared and goals marked out, and large numbers of children had to be quickly involved in constructive physical activity. Perhaps it was for reasons like these that the teachers had developed routine procedures. However, these routines were not limited to getting across the roads, etc. Indeed, the most powerful organizational routine was that of structuring the session through competitive team sports. In the eyes of the deputy head of the school this was a response to the children's and parents' wishes: 'They are very competitive, ... they want to play a game and their parents are also very traditional like that.' But he also recognized that, 'anyway it's much easier just to let them get on with it'.

To some extent the football case stands as an example of how competitive team sport provides a ready-made control structure. The children pour their energy into the competition which the teacher is able to manage. By comparison the movement lesson clearly suffered from a lack of such an in-built rule-frame, for the framework within which collective dramatic expression should take place has far less social definition. In addition it is clear that, whilst the movement lesson expressly broke certain social expectations regarding gender, the football session both worked through and reinforced them. It was a macho event. First the girls were packed off, without choice, to the sidelines — albeit to play a competitive game of rounders. Then the male cultural obsession with winning football matches was indulged, with children like John being soon brought into line if they seemed to falter. Why did things work out like that?

Conclusion

I want to try to answer the question using the concept of 'hegemony' (Gramsci, 1978). The concept refers to the existence of a dominant set of ideas which supports a social and economic system and which permeates the thinking of the people living within it. Practices which support the interests of dominant interest groups are legitimized when they come to be regarded as 'natural', are implemented as 'common sense' and are thus internally regenerated. Such factors may relate, I would suggest, to competitive sport in schools for both boys and girls.

The first and most obvious point to make is that competition is regarded as being a necessity both for economic growth and for the smooth running of our capitalist system. Competition is regarded as 'natural', following Darwin, and as producing excellence. In addition, the post-war development of meritocratic ideas has provided a moral legitimation for success. Indeed, so strong have these ideas been that in the early 1980s the British Conservative Government could even contemplate the decline of whole industries, which had failed to compete, because of the 'strength' to which such 'rationalization' was expected to lead in the long term. In this context it is not surprising that the moral panic of 1986 should have been so powerful. The competitive sports lesson is thus legitimated as preparing children for the cut and thrust of their future lives and as a responsible national investment for future international survival. Yet upon whose vision of the future, whose assumptions, whose ideologies are these prescriptions based? It is hard to be specific, but the influential contributors to the moral panic seem to have been industrialists and representatives of traditional sports played at the international level — cricket, football and rugby. One might argue that they represent 'the establishment' but, although there seems to be some truth in such an argument, it would quickly have to be qualified to take account of the more popular groundswell. A more straightforward argument is that competition is primarily supported by men.

Perhaps then, whilst recognizing that some women are competitive, it is essentially a male vision that sees the necessity of competition. There seems to be a good deal of evidence at both macro- and micro-levels in support of this argument. Industry and international sport have been dominated by men for many years and, of course, men also form the bulk of the supporters of the major public sports. Perhaps being competitive and being strong are now so much a necessary part of the male self-image in our culture that they cannot be resisted. Certainly the gusto with which some boys engage in school sports where they can demonstrate these qualities is impressive, as, as we have also seen, is the extent to which they will go to evade acting in ways which they feel may compromise their incipient virility. Teachers have to control such forces when they set out to teach physical education and two old adages describe, in a nutshell, a set of very common strategies. First, 'if you can't beat them join them' — so we have evidence of many teachers unwittingly tuning their curricula to the interests of boys (Clarricoates, 1980), prioritizing interaction with them (Spender and Sarah, 1980) and engaging in the competitive activities which many boys particularly enjoy. The second adage is, 'divide and rule' — so competition, apart from being popular with some children, also makes it possible for a teacher to stand on the high ground as arbiter, judge and as the person 'in control'. Competition in school sport derives strength from its double articulation. It eases the difficulties faced by teachers and it is legitimated by a particularly powerful set of social expectations. Thus it seems like 'the way things ought to be'. Whether or not that is enough to justify it is another question.

Acknowledgments

I would like to thank the students, staff and pupils who worked in the schools studied for their help in preparing this paper. I am grateful too for the help and advice of John Evans, Sue Slocombe and Tony Clarke.

References

BECKER, H. (1963) *Outsiders: Studies in the Sociology of Deviance*, New York, Free Press.

CLARRICOATES, K. (1980) 'Dinosaurs in the classroom: A re-examination of some aspects of the "hidden curriculum" in primary schools', *Women's Studies International Quarterly* 1, 4, pp. 353–64.

COHEN, S. (1972) *Folk Devils and Moral Panics*, 1st ed., Oxford, Martin Robinson.

COHEN, S. (1980) 'Symbols of trouble: Introduction to the new edition', in *Folk Devils and Moral Panics*, 2nd ed., Oxford, Martin Robinson.

DENSCOMBE, M. (1980) '"Keeping 'em quiet": The significance of noise for the practical activity of teaching,' in WOODS, P. (Ed.), *Teacher Strategies*, London, Croom Helm, pp. 61–84.

DUNHAM, J. (1984) *Stress in Teaching*, London, Croom Helm.

GRAMSCI, A. (1978) *Selections from Political Writings*, London, Lawrence and Wishart.

HALL, S. *et al.* (1978) *Policing the Crisis: Mugging, the State and Law and Order*, London, Macmillan.

HEALTH EDUCATION COUNCIL (1986) *Physical Education Association Newsletter No. 3*, Health and Physical Education Project, London, Physical Education Association.

HOWARTH, K. (1987) 'Initial training in primary Physical Education', *British Journal of Physical Education*, 18, 4, pp. 152–3.

NIAS, J. (1984) 'The definition and maintenance of self in primary teaching', *British Journal of Sociology of Education*, 5, 3, pp. 267–280.

PHYSICAL EDUCATION ASSOCIATION (1984) *Physical Education within Primary Education*, A Report of the PEA Standing Study Group on Primary PE, London, Physical Education Association.

PHYSICAL EDUCATION ASSOCIATION (1986) 'Sports education in schools: A statement by the PEA's Executive Committee', *British Journal of Physical Education*, 17, November/December, p. 196.

POLLARD, A. (1982) 'A model of classroom coping strategies', *British Journal of Sociology of Education*, 3, 1, pp. 33–48.

POLLARD, A. (1985) *The Social World of the Primary School*, London, Holt, Rinehart and Winston.

SPACKMAN, L. (1983) *Teaching Games for Understanding*, Curriculum Development Centre, The College of St Paul and St Mary, Cheltenham.

SPACKMAN, L. (1984) *The Changing Focus of Physical Education*, Curriculum Development Centre, The College of St Paul and St Mary, Cheltenham.

SPARKES, A. (1986) 'The competitive mythology: A questioning of assumptions', *Health and Physical Education Project, Newsletter No. 3*.

SPENDER, D. and SARAH, E. (Eds) (1980) *Learning to Lose: Sexism and Education*, London, The Women's Press.

8
Changing the Face of Physical Education

John Evans and Gill Clarke

In recent years in Britain two innovations, Health Related Fitness (HRF) and Teaching Games for Understanding (TGFU), have caught the imagination of many within the PE profession. In this chapter we focus on one highly innovative coeducational comprehensive school which we call Forest Edge (see Clarke, 1987) in which the PE teachers were deeply committed to the development of both, largely in the belief that they have the potential to move the PE curriculum in the direction of a 'Physical Education for All'. We are especially interested in what we observed as a disjuncture between the ideas and intentions expressed by the teachers at Forest Edge outside classrooms and their actions inside them (Keddie, 1971). We claim that its origins lie outside the school context, where in recent years in Britain Institutes of Higher Education have become extremely important locations for the production of innovatory ideas on HRF and TGFU. In this direction they have been aided and backed by the Physical Education Association and its official publication, and widely disseminated within the PE profession. It is to be hoped that clarifying these connections will bring us closer to understanding the social and cultural production of Physical Education knowledge, the values and interests which underpin it, and the prescriptions which are made by what we describe below as its *official discourse* and in its silences. In the second part of the chapter we examine the perspectives and actions of teachers at Forest Edge and consider how the social production of PE knowledge inside classrooms may have been facilitated or constrained by this discourse.

In order to elucidate this argument, we first concentrate attention on HRF and TGFU innovations as they have been represented in what we may refer to as the new official discourse of PE teaching (Evans, 1987). By this we mean those images, ideas and prescriptions for action relating to the teaching of HRF and TGFU which are now to be found in the professional PE journals and other educational literature. This discourse contains and defines what, following Bernstein (1986b), we can call the 'official pedagogic practice', a set of ideas and rationales which not only define how the curriculum and teaching of PE ought to be, but also provide a philosophy of action, a way of thinking and talking about the place and purpose of the subject in the broader school curriculum. Practitioners in schools and PE departments such as the one at Forest Edge draw upon this discourse to construct both a rationale and a guide to their curriculum planning, *qua* subject content and pedagogy.

Initially our analysis calls upon the work of Lundgren (1977) and Bernstein (1971), from whom we take their concepts of 'frame' to interrogate the perspectives of individuals and examine and identify factors in the educational process which may either set limits to or facilitate their realization and development. They are also used to examine how decision-making and interpretive activity in different sites and at different levels of the educational process relate and connect. We have shown elsewhere (Evans, 1985, 1987; Clarke, 1987) how a useful amalgam of their frame-notions can serve as a conceptual tool to examine the processes of social and cultural production and to help us consider how PE is implicated in them. More specifically, we now draw heavily upon the recent work of Bernstein (1986a) in which he is critical of those in the sociology of education concerned with issues of social and cultural reproduction who, in his terms, have tended to treat pedagogic discourse (of and on schooling) as if it were 'no more than a relay for power relations external to itself: a relay whose form has no consequence for what is relayed' (p. 3, mimeo version). Following Durkheim, Bernstein reiterates concern for both the medium *and* the message, the importance of form *and* content. Interest in the latter, he argues (Bernstein, 1986b), has properly led sociologists of education to focus on the 'talk, the values, the codes of conduct' which underpin and constitute educational discourse and how these are 'biased in favour of a dominating group'. These values, codes, indeed

> privilege a dominating group, so such codes of communication are distorted in favour of one group, the dominant group. But there is another distortion at the same time; the culture, the practice and consciousness of the dominated group is distorted. It is recontextualised as having less value. Thus there is a double distortion. (p. 5)

However, Bernstein goes on to stress at an even more fundamental level, and in ways that have largely eluded recent analysts, that the work of social and cultural reproduction is achieved through the form as well as the content of what he calls the 'privileging text'. By this he means 'any text which confers class, gender, race privilege directly or indirectly. Text refers, amongst other things, to the dominating curriculum, dominating pedagogic practice and the rules whereby the material context is created' (p. 8). Following this line of analysis, we need to examine not only how children are differently positioned in *'relation to'* the privileging text by virtue of their cultural habitus but also the *'relations within'* the text, which at the micro-level of the school would refer to (again depending upon what we are here taking as its representation)

> the rules that place the text within the pedagogic discourses of the school within a course, within a curriculum, together with the organisational practice, that is, the rules regulating the relations between agents and contexts. At a relatively more macro level we would be referring to the rules regulating the construction of those discourses from which the initial 'privileging text' was derived, to the power positions within relevant pedagogic recontextualising fields and to the direct or indirect control by the State.
>
> Briefly, theories of cultural reproduction, resistance or transformation offer relatively strong analyses of 'relation to', that is, of the consequences of class, gender, race in the unequal and invidious positioning of pedagogic subjects with respect to the 'privileging text', but they are relatively weak on analyses of 'relations within'. (p. 11)

The analysis which follows draws attention mainly to the way in which pupils may be differently positioned in relation to the new privileging text of the official PE discourse and subsequently inside the PE classrooms at Forest Edge. It begins to identify the social rules and resources which are required of pupils to enter into and succeed at the learning process in new curricular practices within PE. We shall see that much work remains to be done on the nature of 'relations within' the discourse of PE.

The New Physical Education: Changing the Face

Over the past fifteen years the complex relationship between individual teachers, the organization and content of schooling and the role of the state in the educational process has been subject to redefinition and attempted radical alteration. We are at a point of potentially significant change in the level of autonomy granted to schools and the teachers within them. Since the late 1960s in Britain and indeed in the USA (see Apple, 1986) teachers have had to bear the brunt of powerful criticisms from all parts of the political spectrum, regularly disseminated by both the 'respectable' and other organs of the press and popular media. In the late 1960s the critique was voiced most loudly by the Black Paper writers, educationalists and politicians who succeeded in generating and establishing a view of teachers as responsible for declining educational standards and increasing ill-discipline. Blame was variously placed upon comprehensive schooling, the demise of a selective system, 'progressivism' and 'left-wing' teachers. The theme of 'school failure' was given further impetus and high public profile by Jim Callaghan (then Labour Prime Minister) in his speech at Ruskin College in 1976. That speech had two major separate but related strands of concern, *standards of behaviour* and the *supply of skilled manpower*, strands which have been developed and aired more noisily ever since in the conservative voices of the 'old humanists' and the industrial lobby (see Davies, 1986; Ball, 1988). Schools were, and continue to be, blamed for failing to equip pupils with the necessary skills and attitudes to cater for work. The bulk of this criticism has focused on the content of and access to the academic curriculum. In recent years, however, with innovation increasingly featuring in the PE curriculum, the issue of how the body is schooled has been brought firmly and squarely into the debate about educational practice and its relationship to post-school work *and* leisure (see Evans, 1987).

Innovations in the PE curriculum have been subjected to severe criticism by the popular press, the media, eminent sporting persons, the CCPR and political sources. This attack has centred largely upon what is presented as the lamentable demise or denudation of competition in the secondary school Physical Education curriculum. In the view of these critical commentators physical educationalists, like others in the educational world, are so caught up with fashionable egalitarian educational theories and practices that they are failing in their responsibility to the nation's economy (see Evans, 1987), its national identity and sporting prestige.

At the heart of these criticisms is the view that competition is being relegated, marginalized, or at worst dispensed with altogether in the PE curriculum. This view, whilst not empirically accurate, certainly has some claim to validity as far as it relates to the image of practice in the 'new privileging text of the official discourse'. While it would not be true to say that recent innovations (HRF, TGFU) ask the profession to dispense with competition altogether, they do, perhaps taking their lead from other and earlier libertarian philosophies in the USA and Britain, strongly challenge its nature, status and place in the PE curriculum. Within the 'official discourse' TGFU and HRF display a number of common features and prescriptive themes. Both start from a critique of conventional practice in PE, both challenge the content of the curriculum, especially its emphasis on competitive games, and its authoritarian pedagogical mode. Both claim to offer a curriculum which is not only more beneficial but also more accessible to the majority of pupils.

In the case of TGFU, for example, it is claimed (in contrast to traditional games) that success can be more easily achieved by the majority of pupils and that their aims are more relevant for children within today's society where it is desirable for all pupils to be offered equality in terms of experience. Here *equality* seems to imply the provision of a curriculum content and pedagogical mode which not only permits equality of *access* to each and every individual irrespective of their levels of physical ability or skill, but also some measure of equality of *outcome*. Everyone should experience some (but not necessarily the same) level of success, achievement, satisfaction, enjoyment along with an understanding of the principles which underpin different game forms.

The TGFU argument runs (Bonniface, 1987) that it is not possible in traditional games for *all* pupils to be offered equality of experience, because poor physical skill acts as a barrier to further learning. Thus the emphasis instead is placed upon the cognitive rather than the technical aspects of the game. While learning the full adult version of a game may present a long-term goal, in the eyes of those advocating an 'understanding' approach it is not the main purpose of games teaching in schools. Mini-games with adapted rules and equipment are more likely to provide all pupils with opportunities to make decisions concerning their play and the game itself whatever their physical ability. In this context all pupils will be given the opportunity to take responsibility for their learning and all/more pupils will be given the opportunity to experience the satisfaction of achievement and success. It is these experiences, achievement, satisfaction, enjoyment, which will form the motivational bases for a future of post-school involvement in physical recreation and sport.

The HRF literature also carries an image of educational practice in which organizational forms and curriculum content avoid the creation of losers and failures; but in this innovation the principle of equality of outcome is stressed even more strongly. The tone is against selection and the creation of ability hierarchies and for 'non-authoritarian', 'non-didactic' approaches to teaching. At the heart of this innovation too is a concern for the development of each and every individual's 'health career', their positive 'self-esteem' and 'decision-making skills'. Both the TGFU and the HRF initiatives in philosophy and content are radically *child-* rather than *subject*-centred. The focus is on 'individual needs rather than activities and on individual responses rather than marks of achievement' (Payne, 1985, p. 5). Together these initiatives have in recent years vied for a place not simply within, but as 'the privileging text', the dominating curriculum in the official discourse of PE. Both carry an image of practice in which relationships between teachers and pupils and between pupils and knowledge are significantly altered. Emphasis is upon a negotiated curriculum, on less didactic modes of teaching, upon pupils creating for themselves a curriculum (new game forms or personal HRF programmes) which is sensitive to individual interests, abilities and future life-styles. Theoretically at least these initiatives have the capacity radically to alter and challenge patterns of power and authority which have long featured in both the academic and physical curriculum of schooling.

The Limits of the Official Discourse: The Silences in the Privileging Text

While the new official discourse does seem to pose an important and powerful challenge to élitism in PE, we note with Joyce Sherlock (1987) and John Hargreaves (1986) that it does not totally reject competition. Challenged, played down, it is recommended as a separate activity for the gifted or alternatively as a purely extra-curricular activity. As Sherlock too points out, the values of competition are being questioned because it is this component of PE which is deemed 'to contribute towards turning children away from sport', not because physical educationalists are critical of competitive 'individualism' (p. 443). The new official discourse thus refocuses the emphasis in PE teaching, but it neither challenges nor reformulates in any fundamental way the categories and hierarchies of ability which have long prevailed in the PE curriculum.

In other respects too HRF and TGFU herald little that is new for the curriculum, especially for those involved in the teaching of girls' PE. The educational gymnastics, dance and movement education initiatives of the 1950s and 1960s were also explicitly child-centred in philosophy, curriculum content and pedagogical mode. They were, as John Hargreaves also points out, methods for developing in the individual child the 'qualities of flexibility and adaptability, the ability to explore and solve problems independently and to co-operate with others' (1986; p. 162), qualities which in Hargreaves' view were/are required for a competent occupational performance amongst the *new middle class*. Hargreaves's analysis, like that of Bernstein, asks us to examine how and in what way recent initiatives in PE, often lying alongside the old, are culturally encoded and to explore the conceptions of society and the person, of work, leisure and family life they embody. This is no mere abstract academic endeavour or interest. It is to consider such questions as, who is likely to succeed and fail in HRF and TGFU initiatives? What cultural (social class, gender or ethnic) capital or habitus is required of pupils to enter into the learning process and needed to provide a competent performance? Or, to use Bernstein's words, how are pupils differently positioned in relation to this 'new' 'privileging text'? The individual and social qualities described above — independence, flexibility, adaptability and cooperation — may not only be desired *outcomes* of the learning process, they may also be implicitly presupposed as requirements for *getting into* the curriculum in the first place. If Hargreaves' analysis is correct, HRF and TGFU initiatives may index a more widespread imposition of new middle-class values, through practices which indeed may be very satisfying and status-giving to teachers, but also highly removed from the experience and interests of a large number of pupils.

While we can see in this way that the new privileging text is culturally and socially impregnated, issues of class, gender, ethnicity and ability rarely enter explicitly into the 'official discourse' of recent HRF and TGFU initiatives. It is, to use Bernstein's words, as if both message and media were somehow 'bland, neutral as air'. We can see these silences are not unimportant to teachers who have to teach boys and girls together (sometimes for the first time), to deal with children differently predisposed to relate to the curriculum on offer. These silences seriously impair the ambitions of teachers who are trying to influence and change the attitudes and decisions of children towards teachers and each other, and to their school and post-school involvement in sport and leisure.

Facing the Change: The 'New' PE at Forest Edge

Forest Edge is a large (1350 on roll in 1986) coeducational comprehensive school on the outskirts of a city. It is a popular school with a largely middle-class intake of pupils. The PE department has five full-time members of staff, three male, two female, and one female part-time member. Curriculum change in the PE department at Forest Edge was initiated by the head of department, Mr Jones, soon after his arrival at the school in 1982. The origins of this change lay not untypically (cf. Sparkes, 1987) in a complex interplay of personal and professional motivations. In 1982 Mr Jones had attempted to effect change in the department by transposing to the Forest Edge boys' PE programme the kind of curriculum — with a strong emphasis on the teaching of traditional games, especially rugby — which had been very successful in his previous school. This initiative had faltered, badly. 'I tried to bring in the sort of scheme of work we'd been using at the previous school. It was successful there. Very quickly ... the boys didn't want to know ... the introduction was very gentle but ... they just didn't want to know ...' (Mr Jones). It was this failure, along with this teacher's desire to establish his own position and persona in the department by effecting curriculum change, which led him to begin, in his own words, 'to seriously question what we were doing.' It is at this point that we see in Mr Jones' actions that fusion of the highly localized and idiosyncratic interests and wider cultural and social conditions that Mills (1957) referred to as the conjunctive of biography and social movement. While the inspiration for change is the individual's own, both its logic and form are constituted elsewhere. In 1982 and 1983 debate on HRF and TGFU was increasingly taking place and space in the official PE discourse, a discourse which itself fitted well with a broader social and political ideology which was already redefining 'health' as an individual rather than a social concern and responsibility. Having attended a course on HRF run by the LEA, Mr Jones had returned to Forest Edge firmly committed to the view that the 'new' PE, in the form of HRF (and later TGFU) was ideally suited to the needs of the department. This was the first of a number of changes to be effected in the PE department, changes which were administered sensitively, cautiously and with the support and cooperation of all departmental members and the head of Forest Edge. The department subscribed to the professional journals so as to keep ahead with the new ideas, and other members of the department were encouraged to attend appropriate INSET courses. At the time of study (September 1986) both the head of PE and Mrs Smith, teacher in charge of girls' PE, were fully conversant with the rhetoric of the official discourse and were thoroughly committed to developing further and evaluating their curriculum innovations. The introduction of HRF and TGFU had led to major changes both in the content of the PE curriculum (detailed below) and in the way in which these teachers (and their colleagues) thought about their subject. The latter had undergone a substantial paradigm shift. Both teachers saw in these innovations a way of 'trying to break away from the élitism' of traditional team games; it was 'a deliberate attempt to try and get everybody to realize the benefits of PE and its health-related aspects ...', it was the means of valuing each child and providing an 'education for all'. The official discourse had been reconstituted in the thinking and the curriculum practice of both these teachers. Both were thoroughly committed to the principle of equal opportunities, *opening up access* to a physical education in which each and every child could experience success, satisfaction and enjoyment. It was hoped that these experiences would secure not only involvement in school PE, but also participation in post-school sport and leisure. The dominant motivation of these teachers, however, was unquestionably ameliorative and hedonistic rather than socially transformative. Theirs was a concern to alter the conditions of work for pupils, to change the form and content of PE toward goals of interest and enjoyment, the laying of the motivational bedrock upon which in later life each individual would build and develop their sport and leisure careers. Just as in the official discourse, theirs, initially, was not the business of directly confronting either extant, conventional categories of ability and conceptions of the body, or social class or gender inequalities or of challenging the social rules or roles governing social relationships inside or outside their classrooms.

Life in Classrooms

This 'neutrality' featured most obviously in the text of a booklet entitled *Fitness for Life*, which was distributed to every first year pupil during the first week at school. This booklet in effect constituted the HRF syllabus. Emblazoned on the opening page is the statement, 'Fitness is fun', and the text goes on:

> The Bad News. Keeping Fit Won't:-
> Make a small person tall!
> Make long noses shorter!
> Change the shape of your face!
> Change the shape of my bones!

and then

> The Good News. Keeping Fit Will Help To:-
> Make a fat person slim!
> Make a weak person stronger!
> Make me supple if I'm stiff!
> Make me look better and feel better!

Finally, it ends with the plea:

> Don't become a dull, pampered armchair athlete...
> get up ... get out ... get fit. ... Discover
> enjoyment, the excitement, the challenge ...
> USE IT OR LOSE IT

Now although this text is well intentioned, humorously presented and expertly designed (and may not be untypical of the style and content of presentation found in other HRF courses), clearly it is neither socially nor culturally neutral. Implicitly it carries a normative image of the healthy, acceptable individual. It is, to use Hargreaves' terms, an image *par excellence* of the 'active mesomorph' which in his view to all intents and purposes appeals to and is most easily accommodated within the thinking and outlook of individuals (pupils and parents) who occupy a middle-class world. While it is possible to take issue with the claim that it is only middle-class parents or children who aspire to this ideal body type, it is hard to deny that opportunities for people to achieve this ideal (to be healthy, active and happy) may be differently structured by the conditions of their class, colour or sex. The ideal body image and pupil performer typically present in the PE literature *is* happy, smiling and interested, neither fat nor thin. He or she is confidently self-assured and above all else always active. In Hargreaves' (1986) view it is an imagery which disguises profound social differences; we are not all of this type, neither do we all have the same opportunities or for that matter the desire to achieve it. As such it is an imagery that 'buttresses the impression of harmony and lack of social division' (p. 169). It also 'functions to devalue other body images in the culture, those of the ectomorph, the thin "skinny" body and the endomorph, the fat body type.' There is, in effect, a double distortion in this discourse. It not only represents or signifies one particular image of the body, it also devalues other 'bodies' which are 'recontextualised as having less value'. At Forest Edge children were thus differently positioned in relation to the text of the HRF booklet. Some pupils, those unable to approximate the physical ideal, would thus (prior to their active involvement in PE) already be placed in deficit. For such children PE would constitute a corrective exercise, a remediation process which would intentionally modify body, shape and mind.

For the first year pupils at Forest Edge Physical Education consisted of a diet of HRF, TGFU and educational gymnastics. Although we cannot here describe in any detail the content of these activities, or the forms of discourse and communication which featured within them (see Clarke, 1987), we shall try and identify some of the major and common social structural features of the HRF and educational gymnastics lessons of Mr Jones and Mrs Smith, and emphasize the social rules and roles which operated inside their classrooms. Educational gymnastic lessons typically involved the pupils working on movement sequences, alone or in pairs, either on apparatus or on floor mats. Typically, in the main phase of the lesson the teacher introduced a movement theme or concept, for example, 'travelling' and children were then encouraged to explore the different ways of doing this firstly in space defined by the mats on the floor and then (perhaps in subsequent lessons) on apparatus (see Clarke, 1987). As the lesson/s progressed new themes or concepts were introduced, 'levels', 'pacing', 'direction', etc. In these lessons the emphasis at least in theory was upon the children creating, exploring and discovering for themselves a range of movement possibilities and the limits of their own physical capacities. Within broad parameters set by the teacher (through the introduction of a theme or the provision of apparatus) pupils could control both the content and pacing of the lesson; in Bernstein's (1971) terms the lessons were 'weakly framed'. HRF lessons by contrast provided very little space for children to explore or control either the content or pacing of the lesson. They were in Bernstein's terms 'strongly framed'. These lessons took the form of a series of activities, e.g., short sprints, bench jumps, skipping, sit ups, etc., prearranged by the teacher, and around/through which the pupils progressed usually in pairs. Each individual spent perhaps a minute on an activity before receiving a minute's respite while her/his partner worked and before moving on to the next activity. These lessons were usually accompanied by background music, they were physically very demanding, but seemed to be enjoyed by the majority of children. In the closing minutes of the lesson pupils were called around the teacher for a short period of 'discussion'.

During the first weeks of term in HRF and educational gymnastics lessons both teachers spent much time socializing pupils into correct modes of behaviour. They were told, for example, where, when and how to sit: 'Right, let's have you sitting up. I know I say "sit down", but when I say "sit down" I also mean sit up' (Mrs Smith, Lesson 1), how and when to ask questions of the teacher and talk to each other: 'Can I remind you that when I do the Register I don't expect anybody to chatter' (Mrs Smith, Lesson 1), and 'Invasion, means games like hockey and rugby, netball, basketball and soccer, we shall be using [teacher stops as two boys are chatting] If you've got any comments to make would you like to make them to me at the end, alright' (Mrs Smith, Lesson 2). In these early encounters both teachers were also keen to stress that the activity of doing nothing was not permitted. Pupils were expected to be at all times 'busy, happy and good' (Placek, 1983). 'Don't just sit and watch, it's not a spectator sport, everybody should be involved and doing things that you know you are capable of' (Mr Jones, Lesson 1). Pupils also had to learn and be willing to adhere to technical rules relating to the performance of specific tasks. For example, Mrs Smith made it clear that she was 'a bit fussy in gymnastics and when I say a straight roll I mean legs straight, arms straight' (Lesson 1), and on another occasion stated: '... These things at the bottom of your legs they're called feet. A lot of them looked a bit like kippers, wet fish at the bottom of your legs 'cos they are all sort of floppy. What I'd like you to be doing with them is to be getting them nice and stretched' (Lesson 1). Despite the exploratory emphasis in educational gymnastics it was thus made clear that there is one correct aesthetic.

In all of the lessons observed it was the teachers' talk that pervaded the setting. It was they who controlled both the content and the pacing of the lesson:'Ah, right, sit down. Sit up, quickly. [Waits] Right, the whole point of me telling you what I expect you to do when you've got your mat is that we don't waste time. [Pauses] So far, I've seen a lot of people wasting time ...' (Mrs Smith, Lesson 2). But competence in the classroom involved far more than just knowing with whom, when and where one could talk. It also meant knowing how to answer the teacher's questions and having a willingness to participate in a system of turn-taking. The questions asked of pupils were, not untypically, closed, that is to say they involved little more than a pupil filling in the slots in the teacher's developing exposition, for example:

Teacher: What's the bone down the middle of your back called?
Girl: Spine.
Teacher: Yes, it's called the spine, do you know what it looks like? (Mrs Smith, Lesson 1)

Teacher: Right, can anybody tell me what's happening to your heart when you start to run for a long time or when you are doing any type of exercise, what's happening to your heart?
Simon: It speeds up.
Teacher: It speeds up. What actually happens then? (Mr Jones, HRF Lesson)

In the lessons observed it was the teacher who defined what was to be learned and how and when knowledge should be acquired. Even when questioning took a more open form, teacher knew the answer. In this example, taken from an educational gymnastics lesson, a pupil was required to give an opinion on a sequence of movement that they had just observed:

Teacher: Right, let's see Jenny's first of all. [Jenny shows her sequence to the class.] Very nice, give her a clap, well done, excellent. What was the most noticeable thing about Jenny's? Jack.

Jack: It flowed.

Teacher: Sorry, it flowed, it flowed nicely. Something else you noticed about it? Something that I'm always pestering you all about. Amy.

Amy: Tension.

Teacher: Tension, very neat and tidy. I don't think I saw her feet apart from that shape at all, lovely, well done.

The teacher steers the communication process so that eventually she receives the answer that she wants. She owns the conversation (Spier, 1966) and the children have restricted rights of access to it. The teacher decides who is to answer, how a reply should be given and what should be said.

We have not the space here to provide further detail on the teaching of HRF and educational gymnastics at Forest Edge (see Clarke, 1987) and we are conscious that the extracts provided hardly capture the quality of teaching displayed by Mr Smith and Mrs Jones, nor do they constitute ethnographic 'thick descriptions', which would reveal much more of the ambience, social dynamics and structure of the settings described. The data thus are limited and should be considered cautiously. We here present selected extracts only to help raise questions about what sort of change, if any, is occurring in the new initiatives of PE. On this sort of evidence the introduction of new content to the PE programme at Forest Edge had left unaltered the basic structure of centrally controlled interaction and centrally managed meanings which have long featured in PE and other curriculum areas. This form of discourse routinely demonstrates and reproduces the *teacher's* authority, knowledge and power. Teachers control the rights of the pupil and the limits within which pupil actions (replies and other behaviours) are to fall. Acting competently as a pupil in this setting requires not only a knowledge of the social rules and conventions governing didactic teaching (listening, turn-taking, etc.) but also a willingness to adhere to them. The teaching of HRF, TGFU and educational gymnastics at Forest Edge had not achieved any significant shift in the balance of power between teacher and taught in the classroom. For the pupils of Forest Edge life in PE classrooms meant learning a complex set of social rules and governing when, how and with whom they could talk, as well as technical rules governing how they should physically perform a task. These were teacher determined and non-negotiable. Pupils' control over their own learning was exercised within firm limits set and controlled by teachers.

Substantial curricular and organizational change had left largely unaltered relationships between teacher and taught and pupils and knowledge. They had also altered little in the relationships amongst pupils in the classrooms. Sex segregated traditional games gave away to a mixed-sex grouping for HRF, educational gymnastics and TGFU. To both teachers it no longer seemed necessary or efficient to separate boys and girls for games or HRF which after all no longer took on conventional 'gendered' forms. This organizational change was a concomitant of curriculum change, an initially unproblematic feature of the innovation. As the head of department later noted, the development of the curriculum content and the 'subsequent evaluation of the course programmes overshadowed the implications of mixed gender innovations.' There was little in the official discourse to suggest that this would or should be otherwise. As a result both teachers had few pedagogical resources to call upon to confront the issue of how boys and girls could be taught together.

Inside their classrooms we found boys and girls carefully managing the social spaces and boundaries between themselves. Gender ridden peer group practices, attitudes and friendships of the playground and wider social settings were re-enacted in the classroom. Girls and boys exhibited systematic reluctance to work together. Faced with this situation, Mr Jones intervened sensitively and carefully in their grouping choices. Children worked in mixed-sex pairs for at least part of the time and were then allowed to revert to single-sex pairs for the remainder. Unintentionally this may have had the effect of announcing rather than challenging the 'normality' of segregation. Mrs Smith felt that it was neither necessary nor particularly desirable that it should be otherwise. She was not altogether convinced that she should intervene in the relationships between boys and girls.

> If they wanted to work together they would do it. I know there is one group who frequently work together but it just seems as if you're putting extra work into it. Perhaps some of them, they may have worries about it already so why increase them and make them go with a boy or a girl if they really don't want to? You want to make the working conditions as easy as possible. ...

Although these comments express sensitive and rational appraisal of the worries and concerns of the children, they also affirm the mechanisms by which social and cultural divisions and hierarchies are emphasized and reproduced. At the heart of these teachers' practices (as in the official discourse) lay the desire, the intention, to improve the conditions of the school work place for every child, to make learning enjoyable and satisfying. They hoped to achieve greater equality of opportunity through ameliorative means, by steeping the individuals in powerful associations of physical activity and fun. In this way the person was to be both affectively and effectively imbued with the desire for more leisure. Within this ideological framework actively to create conditions of frustration or conflict, openly to generate tension and potential value disorder in order to confront the social/gendered roles of the classroom, would be to infract the deep consensual code (the 'privileging' rules) of the official discourse. As Mrs Smith's comments above suggest, it was not her or Mr Jones' intention to create problems of classroom order and control. Theirs was the ambition, as stated above, to keep pupils 'busy, happy and good'.

Despite the not insignificant and substantial paradigmatic changes in content and organization which had been effected by these teachers, there was very little pedagogical change of a kind which could challenge or change the authority relationships of the classroom or confront or alter the typical gendered attitudes and behaviours of children or indeed of the teachers. As Mrs Smith remarked, 'The boys can be a pain sometimes; it's a different way 'cos they are certainly always the first to answer questions, always the ones who will muck around with a football and not concentrate. Whereas the girls ... tend to sort of stand back a bit ...' and 'It's difficult because boys take your attention ... you start looking at them straight away ...' This teacher's endeavours to confront this 'domination' by bringing the girls more into the lesson had been resisted by the girls themselves. 'It's very difficult because sometimes you think the girls are very quiet and you'll try and bring them out but they don't want that, they'll try and stay in the background. ...' It was perhaps unsurprising to find that both teachers tended to identify more of the boys than girls as both more interested and more able performers in their classrooms. As Mrs Smith stated, 'When I think of 1A I think of three boys ...' and 'Yes ... very few girls stand out ... I think there's one that probably stands out (K), she lacks confidence and wants reassurance all the time. ...' Mr Jones commended the efforts of all his teaching group 1B but he also realistically noted that 'two or three [girls] need to be watched ... to be pushed. I think they've had a bad experience in their other schools and so now need to be pushed more. They can be silly, lazy... .' Most of the boys, it seems, could draw on a well established sporting capital to provide a socially competent performance. Many in Mr Jones' view had the motivational advantage of seeing PE as preparation for a sporting career. Few, if any, girls could or did think in this way.

Pupils who were unable or unwilling to call on the resources to display such social behaviours could be identified as deviant, or at the extreme socially or psychologically pathological:

there's one boy he's got a lot of problems he finds it very difficult to relate to other people and to work with them. I think he must have behavioural problems because it's all been documented about him. (He's a problem in other classes too.) He makes it very difficult.

Concluding Remarks

The new official discourse of PE and contingently the actions of teachers at Forest Edge school do contain radical elements. This discourse has constituted a sustained and well orchestrated attack on an élitism which has sometimes featured in the PE curriculum, on the high status and place given to the provision of a narrow image of traditional games and on the limits of didactic teaching. At Forest Edge the move away from a traditional games teaching programme towards TGFU, along with the time and emphasis given to HRF, had indeed marked a radical shift in the curriculum of the department and in the thinking of Mr Jones, Mrs Smith and their colleagues. Few schools in the area had taken such radical measures. These teachers saw in the new curricula the means of better realizing the potential of every child and of opening up opportunities for them within school and post-school involvement in physical activity and sport. We would stress too that as observers we, like Mr Jones and Mrs Smith, felt that the majority of children were thoroughly enjoying their lessons, that they were involved, challenged and happy. These outcomes of the new initiatives are neither unimportant nor insignificant; they constitute an important motivational resource which individuals may call on (perhaps in post-school life) to demand opportunities for and access to leisure. Our claim here is simply that the achievements in the new initiatives of PE are incomplete. They do little to challenge existing social or ability hierarchies or the social roles or rules which govern them. Changing the content of the PE curriculum has not brought with it changes in the deep structure of communication in classroom life, in the relationships between pupils and between teacher and taught, in the teacher's control over knowledge or in the way teachers think about ability and performance. The professional socialization and training of PE teachers has long centred upon didactic teaching and done little to make more complex how we think about ability and performance. John Hargreaves (1986) makes the point that the preferred recruit to the profession has long been a perceived physically adept performer and that notions of physical competence are strongly associated with a preference for the mesomorphic body type. He goes on to say that the image of the ideal body cuts across the movement education versus conventional PE divide in the profession. As we see at Forest Edge, the tension is equally evident in the new HRF and TGFU initiatives. Despite changes in appearance, the pedagogical process continues to produce and reproduce conventional body images and forms, albeit in different and perhaps more enjoyable ways.

Innovation at Forest Edge had certainly made teachers increasingly aware of the limits of their own professional training. It stood in the way of the achievement of a pedagogy which could emphasize student-centred learning, negotiated curricula and perhaps even challenge the asymmetry of the relationships between teacher and taught. Teachers are not helped in such quests by the new official discourse which hardly breaks free of existing conventions and the ideologies which sustain them. The official discourse celebrates individualism, personal power, control and responsibility but it remains largely silent on issues of class, race, gender and ability. These omissions can only serve to 'distort the text' and the practices to which it gives rise 'in favour of already dominant groups'. Thus the new official discourse of PE, just as the old, continues to function as 'a relay for power relations'. It does little to alter or challenge conventional hierarchies or patterns of power, authority and control.

But the innovations described above are incomplete and unfinished, and the teachers themselves had become increasingly aware of the limitations of their own practices, and especially of the difficulty of altering the means of communication in the classroom and challenging the attitudes and behaviours of children. It remains to be seen whether their initiatives can and do take on a more radical form. Our account also fails to convey either the high quality of the teaching that we routinely observed or the obvious enjoyment of the children. But these qualities are for us not directly at issue. The point we are making is that the initiatives described above are 'framed' or constrained within the parameters of convention set by the limits of the official discourse and a teacher's professional training. Consequently while HRF and TGFU innovations may successfully make more children more happy for more of the time inside PE classrooms, they may also do little to alter the way in which children think about each other, themselves, their bodies, their capacities to perform in sport and their suitability for involvement in physical activities as one form of leisure.

The existence of a form of educational practice in PE which is capable of providing 'an education for all' remains some distance away. Its arrival is likely to rest, amongst other things, upon a willingness to reconsider the social and cultural hierarchies which operate both inside schools and outside them and which define an individual's status, ability, performance, value and worth. The commitment to education either for health or leisure is unlikely to be realized unless within the classroom context teachers are resourced with a curriculum content, a form of pedagogy and evaluative criteria which together are able to help children better to understand and then challenge the expectations they hold about and for themselves and each other. Of course this quest to help children better understand each other and their lives (in and outside schools) is no simple task and cannot only be the preserve of the school or any single subject. The teachers in this study had worked and were working hard to bring both the personal and the social aspects of children's lives into their classrooms and to make contact with other like-minded teachers. Social class and gender issues had become their concerns. HRF and TGFU carry enormous potential and scope for pupils to generate data about themselves, others and their life-styles (through keeping diaries, fitness and activity profiles, etc.). This may be one way into a discussion of complex and sensitive issues about the social roles and rules which influence people's lives and of the limits which are set to leisure, work and health expectations and behaviours.

The new Physical Education may take space and time from what many politicians and parents recognize and consider as proper forms of Physical Education — competitive team games. As such it does seem to threaten that element of schooling which has long functioned to engender in individuals respect and commitment to one's betters, school and country. But on the evidence presented here critics of the new Physical Education need not have too much to fear from the kind of initiatives described above. They neither herald the end of competitive games nor a deterioration in standards or discipline, indeed they both foster and celebrate that very quality — individualism — which lies at the heart of conservative ideology and which many on the right expect schools and the individuals within them to cultivate and display.

Acknowledgment

Our thanks go to the teachers and pupils at Forest Edge for their cooperation and support. We are indebted to Pam Webster, Pam Ball and Ann Freeland for their patience, tolerance and expertise in preparing this paper. We are also grateful to Professor Brian Davies for his comments on an earlier draft.

References

APPLE, M. (1986) *Teachers and Texts*, London, Routledge and Kegan Paul.

BALL, S. (1988) 'Comprehensive schooling, effectiveness and control: An analysis of educational discourse', in SLEE, R. (Ed.), *Education, Disruptive Pupils and Effective Schooling*, London, Macmillan.

BALL, S. and GOODSON, I. (1985) 'Understanding teachers: Concepts and contents', in BALL, S.J. and GOODSON, I. (Eds), *Teachers' Lives and Careers*, Lewes, Falmer Press, pp. 1–27.

BERNSTEIN, B. (1971) 'On the classification and framing of educational knowledge', in YOUNG, M.F.D. (Ed.), *Knowledge and Control*, London, Collier Macmillan, pp. 47–90.

BERNSTEIN, B. (1986a) 'On pedagogic discourse', in RICHARDSON, J. (Ed.), *Handbook for Theory and Research in Sociology of Education*, Westport, Conn., Greenwood Press.

BERNSTEIN, B. (1986b) 'A sociology of pedagogic context', Unpublished mimeo, Institute of Education, University of London.

BONNIFACE, M. (1987) 'The changing Physical Education curriculum', Unpublished paper, Department of Physical Education, University of Southampton.

BUNKER, D. and THORPE, R. (1983) 'A model for the teaching of games in secondary schools', in *Games Teaching Revisited, Bulletin of Physical Education*, 19, 1, pp. 5–9.

CLARKE, G. (1987) 'Towards an Understanding of the Language of Teaching in Physical Education', MA (Ed) Dissertation, University of Southampton.

CLARKE, J. and WILLIS, P. (1984) 'Introduction', in BATES, I. *et al.* (Eds), *Schooling for the Dole?* London, Macmillan, pp. 1–17.

DAVIES, B. (1986) 'Halting progress: Some comments on recent British educational policy and practice', *Journal of Education Policy*, 4, 1, pp. 349–61.

EVANS, J. (1985) *Teaching in Transition: The Challenge of Mixed Ability Grouping.* Milton Keynes, Open University Press.

EVANS, J. (1987) 'Teaching for equality in Physical Education? The limits of the new PE', Paper presented to the Ethnography and Inequality Conference, St Hilda's College, Oxford, 1981.

EVANS, J. and DAVIES, B. (1987) 'Sociology, schooling and Physical Education', in EVANS, J. (Ed.), *Physical Education, Sport and Schooling*, Lewes, Falmer Press, pp. 1–11.

EVANS, M. (1985) 'An Action Approach to the Innovation of Mixed Physical Education in a Secondary School', Diploma Professional Studies dissertation, Kingston Polytechnic, London.

HARGREAVES, D. (1982) *The Challenge for the Comprehensive School*, London, Routledge and Kegan Paul.

HARGREAVES, J. (1986) *Sport, Power and Culture*, Cambridge, Polity Press.

KEDDIE, N. (1971) 'Classroom knowledge', in YOUNG, M.F.D. (Ed.), *Knowledge and Control*, London, Collier Macmillan, pp. 133–61.

LUNDGREN, U. (1977) *Model Analysis of Pedagogical Processes*, Stockholm, CWK Gleerup.

MILLS, C.W. (1957) *The Sociological Imagination*, New York, Oxford University Press.

PAYNE, S. (1985) 'Physical Education and health in the United Kingdom', *The British Journal of Physical Education*, 17, 1, pp. 4–9.

PLACEK, J.H. (1983) 'Conceptions of success in teaching: Busy, happy and good?', in TEMPLIN, T.H. and OLSON, J.K. (Eds), *Teaching in Physical Education*, Champaign, Illinois, Human Kinetics Publishers, pp. 46–57.

SHERLOCK, J. (1987) 'Issues of masculinity and femininity in British Physical Education', *Women's Studies International Forum*, 10, 4, pp. 43–45.

SPARKES, A. (1987) 'Strategic rhetoric: A constraint in changing the practice of teachers', *British Journal of Sociology of Education*, 8, 1, pp. 37–55.

SPIER, M. (1966) 'The child as conversationalist: Some culture contact features of conversation interaction between adults and children', in HAMMERSLEY, M. and WOODS, P. (Eds), *The Process of Schooling*, London, Routledge and Kegan Paul, pp. 98–104.

Today (1986) 'Barmy Britain', 11 July 1986, p. 1.

9
The Limits of Change in Physical Education: Ideologies, Teachers and the Experience of Physical Activity[1]

Lisa George and David Kirk

It is now widely accepted in the literature on change and innovation in education that the teacher plays a key role in determining the success or failure of a new initiative. Even within this view, though, the teacher's part in innovation often remains a fairly restricted one, centred on the efficient implementation of new content or methods within the classroom. In the face of this fairly 'technical' view of the teacher's function in the change process some writers have begun to argue that this role should be expanded because, they argue, the teacher is potentially an agent of social transformation through the educational process.

The developing body of literature that has grown up around this topic has been referred to as 'resistance theory' (Bullough and Gitlin, 1985). While we do not necessarily agree with this label's appropriateness, we consider that the work it refers to is extremely valuable. We take this to be built on a radical critique of schooling that has sought to highlight the part schools play in reproducing ideological configurations that serve to mask the interests of certain groups in society over others, reflected in particular along race, gender and class dimensions. Recent research in this field has been concerned to explore the role schools, and teachers within them, might play through their educative functions in undermining hegemonic definitions of power relations and prevailing orthodoxies in social practices (Bullough and Gitlin, 1985, 1986; Giroux, 1981).

We were interested in locating a study of Physical Education teachers within this developing field of research. This chapter is based on a study carried out in two Brisbane state high schools, Bankstown and Fielding, between September and December 1986.[2] One of the authors[3] conducted unstructured and semi-structured interviews with teachers in a range of subjects selected at random.[3] The particular focus for data collection was the Physical Education departments of both schools, and each member of the Physical Education staff was interviewed, some on a number of occasions. Special attention was paid to two first year teachers, one in each school, and they were interviewed and observed during in-school and out-of-school activities.

Our research was centred on the 'limits and possibilities' that exist for schools to promote emancipatory social change through education. The decision to focus on Physical Education as an appropriate arena in which to explore some of the issues raised by this research was influenced by several factors. As physical educators the first of these was our interest in and familiarity with Physical Education. The second related to Physical Education's unusual status as a curriculum topic which, until recently untrammeled by the pressures of the examination system, had a (relative) freedom to innovate unmatched by most other established subjects. The third reason related to physical educators' apparent lack of willingness to take advantage of this freedom from examination requirements, and their widely reported traditionalism and conservatism (Hargreaves, 1977). The juxtaposition of the second and third factors suggested to us an interesting site for investigation in relation to 'resistance theory', and in particular in relation to the amount of actual freedom or 'autonomy' teachers have available to them (Giroux, 1981).

The major message we want to communicate here is that in the schools we studied we saw little cause for optimism that Physical Education could be a site for the development of a 'critical pedagogy'; by 'critical pedagogy' we mean opening students' minds to domination, injustice and inequality (Kirk, 1988). This is because the conservative ideologies that saturate the ethos of Physical Education in schools and teachers' own experiences of physical activity are locked in a reproductive cycle that seems to have the power to cross generations of teachers. We want to illustrate this contention by outlining briefly some of the main in-subject ideologies that underwrote the teaching of Physical Education in our study schools, and then show how these interacted with PE teachers' experiences of physical activity to create aims and curricula for Physical Education that are uncritical and reproductive of the status quo.

Three Ideologies in Physical Education Teaching

We use the term 'ideology' here to refer to a set of beliefs and values that in some way distorts or masks reality (Apple, 1979). Beliefs and values serve an ideological function when they make less visible the extension and development of one group's interests to the disadvantage of other groups. Here we want to highlight three ideologies and illustrate how these work against radical teaching and learning in Physical Education, and at the same time mask particular sectional interests. These ideologies are *healthism, individualism* and *recreationalism*, and all three were embodied in the structure of the PE programmes in our study schools, in teachers' thinking and teaching, and in their experiences of physical activity.

Healthism we define as a belief in the attainment and maintenance of health as a self-evident good.[4] Typically the programmes in each school appeared to accept unquestioningly the 'obvious' link between organized physical activity and health. For example, the rationale on the front page of the work programme of the PE course at Fielding stated, 'Health and Physical Education promotes a healthy, active lifestyle by providing experiences which enable the student to choose behaviours which enhance healthy living and make informed, rational decisions as to involvement in physical activity.' This statement reveals that physical activity and health are believed to be unquestionably linked, and by virtue of this link the subject is seen to be rationally-based, wholesome and politically neutral. Moreover, the focus of the statement is the individual and his/her implied freedom to make informed choices about life-style.

These characteristics are significantly underpinned by an ideology of individualism. In the following list of aims for the Health and Physical Education (HPE) programme, which were very similar in both schools, there is a clear emphasis on the individualistic dimension of physical activity and health to the relative neglect of the wider societal factors that figure in the maintenance of health. These aims were:

> to develop an understanding of the structure and efficient physiological and mechanical functioning of the human body;
> to develop an understanding of roles and issues in leisure, recreation and sport in Australian society;
> to aid the selection of behaviours to enhance healthy living;
> to develop a personal concept of fitness;
> to develop individual potential through physical activity;
> to develop skills that facilitate participation in physical activities;
> to generate positive attitudes towards active participation in physical activities;
> to develop awareness of life-time physical activities;
> to encourage self-discipline and effective social interaction and behaviour.

We suggest that the interests these ideologies of healthism and individualism mask are those represented in advertising, particularly by the tobacco, alcohol and drug industries, by others involved in environmental pollution as by-products of industrial processes, food manufacturers and by the expanding health-care industry itself. Through this approach to Physical Education students are encouraged to view health as their own responsibility, and rarely as a matter dependent on wider social and mainly economically-based industrial processes. As Evans and Clarke (in this volume, Chapter 8) show, these ideologies are in the first place rooted in a 'middle-class view' of the ideal child who is an 'active mesomorph' and (borrowing Placek's phrase) is 'busy, happy, good'. Their point that 'opportunities for people to achieve this ideal (to be healthy, happy and active) may be differently structured by their class, colour or sex' remains a silent issue in the discourse produced by these ideologies.

The final aim on the list reminds us of Physical Education's historical association with medical care, social welfare and control; notions of 'encouraging self-discipline' and 'socially acceptable behaviour' suggest that some PE teachers in our study schools see as a priority the 'management' of individual students' lifestyles. 'Lifestyle management' has, indeed, become something of a battlecry for health-enthused physical educators, but rarely are the ideological dimensions of this notion acknowledged.

The third ideology, recreationalism, essentially plays down the educative functions of Physical Education and celebrates the hoary Cartesian myth of the mind's primacy over the body. This ideology strikes the deadliest blow to the idea of a critical pedagogy in Physical Education because it actively trivializes the educational experiences that can be gained through the physical. A 'wide range of activities' and 'freedom of choice' for students become the leading ideas in programme planning, and the notion that physical activity can be a medium for educational experience loses out to the idea that Physical Education is a hedonistic, playful break from the more rigorous demands of 'real subjects'. Recreationalism goes beyond the reasonable acknowledgment of the sensual pleasure to be derived from physical activity to celebrate 'enjoyment' as its *raison d'etre*.

After this brief outline of the three ideologies we now want to show how these were manifest in teachers' thinking, practice and personal experiences of physical activity.

Teachers' Experiences of Physical Activity

Healthism and individualism emerged strongly in our study in the structure of school PE programmes particularly, as we have already seen, in their aims. They also emerged significantly in the way teachers used physical activity in their own lives. For instance, Sam, one of the first year teachers in our study at Fielding, had maintained what might be described as a fairly intense involvement in physical activity. He had supported himself through his university course by playing professional rugby league, and he approached his recreational activities like surfing, golf and running with a similar degree of vigour. He was also a committed Christian and his religious beliefs, by his own admission, influenced his view of the purpose of physical activity as an exercise in catharsis, aimed at achieving spiritual fulfilment, personal harmony and inner balance. Being fit, healthy and encountering and overcoming personal physical challenges played a central role in Sam's life.

His approach to teaching Physical Education displayed a congruence with this perspective. While he considered games and sports to be useful media for developing positive social interaction, he bemoaned the lack of camping experiences available to students in his school. Camps, he considered, provide an opportunity for the concurrent development of the physical, social and spiritual. Similarly, in his volunteer work with a group of youths in a hostel for homeless men in Brisbane, Sam saw physical activity as a powerful 'cleansing' medium, a way of repairing the damage done by society, through the catharsis and sense of personal fulfilment vigorous physical activity could offer.

Of all the teachers in our study Sam probably connected most explicitly his personal experience of physical activity to his teaching. Interestingly, his intensity seemed to contribute to his popularity among the students as a 'good' teacher, and from our observations he had a strong impact on a number of pupils he had contact with. However, the messages the students received were, for us, far from radical. Rather, they represented a celebration of masculinity linked to spirituality and physicality, and displayed a level of personal conviction about physical activity, health and self-identity that admitted little questioning of these deeply felt beliefs.

While none of the other teachers in our study displayed the intensity of Sam's orientation to exercise, they nevertheless in a similar fashion reflected their personal involvement in physical activity through their teaching. For one teacher, a male head of department, teaching Physical Education and personal recreation were often for him the same thing.

> Yeh, I enjoy PE teaching ... you know, the kids are good and I think the courses we teach are good too. The activities we teach are the sort of recreational, whole-life sort of things and I enjoy taking them and participating with the kids. ... I like playing golf and badminton and squash and those types of things. (head of department, Bankstown)

Another of the first year teachers, Julie, strongly reflected this recreational orientation to her teaching, and also emphasized the social dimension of her personal involvement in physical activity. Indeed, Julie's life revolved around her social calendar. She was an extremely 'social person' and led what can only be described as a hectic life. In addition to her full-time teaching job she had a part-time job at a health and fitness centre where she conducted aerobic classes and supervised the gymnasium. On top of this she maintained a high level of social contact with many of the clients of the health and fitness centre. A large part of this involved participating in activities such as cycling, swimming and running. Recalling that Julie is a first-year teacher just out of college, the sheer physical effort to maintain these commitments was little short of awesome.

Julie's decision to become a PE teacher seems to have been influenced strongly by this view of physical activity as a medium for socializing and recreation. She said

> I guess typical of anyone who gets involved in PE you love sport to start with, so that this is the initial thing. You really enjoy sport ... and yeh, that was sort of basically it. The choices, I didn't know what else I wanted to do as much as this. I always enjoyed school, so it was easy to combine the two and not even think about it. (Julie, Bankstown teacher)

Recreational physical activity occupied a central place in Julie's life, and this personal involvement with physical activity formed the basis of her 'philosophy' of teaching. She claimed that her major contribution to the 'educational' (by which she meant 'academic') experience for her students was to help them pass examinations.[5] The curriculum activities she valued were those that offered themselves as life-time recreational pursuits.

> I think Bankstown is good ... I think it's got a good curriculum in that we do interesting things. Orienteering, lawn bowls, golf, I just think that is something different that the kids get the opportunity to do and they're life-style sports, they're not just normal school things that are just a passing phase. You know, golf is something that is played by all ages forever. (Julie, Bankstown teacher)

We would agree with Julie that Physical Education should make a significant contribution to students' recreative experiences. However, the ideology of recreationalism becomes problematic when it comes to represent an ultimate goal for teachers. The evidence suggests that this ideology was widespread among our study teachers, exemplified in this comment from Jenny, an experienced teacher at Bankstown.

> The biggest thing I would like to think I achieve would be that if I could at least encourage kids to continue with a sport or a fairly demanding recreational activity after they leave school, and to be aware of the need to do that. If they can leave school and be aware of the need for physical activity and good health then I think that would be my major achievement. (Jenny, Bankstown teacher)

We would argue that the healthism and recreationalism this statement reflects actively work against the use of Physical Education for educational ends. This is not to say that Jenny's aspirations have no value in themselves, but as they stand they trivialize Physical Education's potential to help students move towards the kind of understanding that seems to lie behind her comments. At the very least students are unlikely to be able to reflect on the need for regular exercise for good health by simply being fed a diet of recreational activities, never mind understand the limits of physical activity's impact on their health.

This is because recreationalism, healthism and individualism combine to depoliticize and trivialize the important understandings about physical activity, personal identity, well-being and society that an authentic Physical Education could promote; by 'authentic physical education' we mean the use of physical activity as a medium in, through and about which students are informed and their minds opened (see Kirk, 1988). The following comment from Elaine, another experienced teacher in our study, reveals in an explicit way the consequences of these ideologies for curriculum practice.

> I think as an educator my basic philosophy would be that the students enjoy themselves. I don't think that coming here and getting a High Achievement in English achieves very much. I don't think that education is governed enough towards life-skills. You know, I think there should be courses on running a home, budgets, especially for girls, how to balance your family life and have kids, the stresses that will be placed on you, things you can only learn through experience and that you can be divorced from. PE is fine because you're developing physical skills which kids will always use, running, jumping, they'll always use gymnastics, they'll use the different skills of body control. So I think PE is different from the other areas in that. (Elaine, Fielding teacher)

Here Elaine is arguing that there is a degree of relevance and meaningfulness in Physical Education that is lacking in other curriculum activities. Her response, though, can scarcely provide a means of moving towards the relevance she seems to want to achieve; by celebrating the physical and the concrete and omitting the cognitive and the abstract there seems to be a greater possibility of creating disjunctions in the student's experience of schooling than she claims already exist. This is not to say that all school subjects should be 'intellectual' pursuits, nor to claim that there should not be a balance between these and less abstract activities. We suggest, though, that notwithstanding the actual subject-matter, education is centrally concerned with enabling students to think intelligently about matters which are relevant and important to them and to the communities in which they live.

The HPE Syllabus in Queensland Schools

The structure of the HPE syllabus for use in Queensland high schools embodies these same contradictions that appear in our study teachers' own experiences of physical activity. The syllabus offers the possibility of creating local school programmes that can only with great difficulty allow teachers to surmount these problems.

In the first place the syllabus organizes the Physical Education curriculum into eight separate and distinct 'elements' (BSSS, 1986). By legislating that the elements must be applied in practice according to this structure, the syllabus effectively compartmentalizes knowledge. At any one time students can typically be experiencing concurrently units on sexually transmitted disease, biomechanical principles of movement, soccer and abseiling. Not only are these activities taught as discrete, self-contained units in ways that discourage teachers and students from cross-referencing, but this way of organizing the curriculum forces the separation of 'theoretical' from 'practical' activities as well. Information in biomechanics that may be of relevance to participating in abseiling and soccer can thus find no official medium for expression. Because of the linear conception of 'theory to practice' this arrangement implies, health education topics are left in the even less enviable position of being seen to be entirely theoretical and so as having no practical application at all.

The crux of our criticism is that the structure of the syllabus itself discourages teachers from using physical activity as a means and a medium for authentically educative experiences. Instead, it reproduces and legitimates age-old prejudices both inside and outside the subject for and against the potential of Physical Education to open students' minds, inform them and help them better to understand themselves and the world around them.

Conclusion

On the basis of this study we have little cause for optimism that a critical pedagogy can be practised through current Physical Education programmes in Queensland high schools. While we are aware that the specifics and details of educational practice differ from place to place, we suggest that there are at least four issues arising out of our data that have a bearing on schools other than those in our study.

First, it appears that there is an anti-intellectualism among the Physical Education profession, reflected, for instance, in their programme goals, choice of subject matter and separation of theoretical and practical activities, that actively prevents the critique of prevailing orthodoxies. There is also a celebration of physicality that seems to accept the separation of mind and body.

Moreover, the Queensland experience of examinations has failed to challenge this emphasis, and has instead reinforced it by tacking on to the curriculum a spurious academicism. Rather than challenging orthodoxies, Physical Education through this orientation simply helps to reproduce and legitimate them.

Secondly, the ideology of recreationalism seems to be firmly rooted in many teachers' own experiences of physical activity and this has led to a trivialization of the educational potential of Physical Education. Teachers have been correct to mistrust the thin attempts to make Physical Education look 'academic' for examination purposes by the adoption of watered-down tertiary courses in Exercise Science. Their reaction to this trend has been to emphasize the hedonistic dimensions of participation in physical activity. However, mere enjoyment and a frivolous sense of play do scant justice to the authentically educational experiences we believe Physical Education can promote.

Third, there is in all of this a rather passive acceptance by teachers of 'health' and 'recreation' as necessary goods. There is, to the best of our knowledge, little questioning of the more deep-seated reasons why we have a greater amount of leisure time that needs to be filled. Nor is there examination of the wider social practices that create ill-health, particularly the 'modern diseases' of cancer, coronary heart disease and stress.

Finally, there seems to be a widespread and unquestioning acceptance that there is always a strong and positive link between physical activity and health, and that both are our individual responsibilities to maintain. If we are overweight, drink excessively or catch AIDS, physical educators would tell us that we only have ourselves to blame. We have simply mismanaged our life-styles and need to refrain from eating cream cakes or promiscuous sex. In this study we rarely witnessed teachers questioning phenomena such as advertising, social conditioning or ideology itself as significant contributors to ill-health. Physical educators have, in a sense, transferred the élitist values of the traditional curriculum based on competitive sport to a new competitive individualism that pits itself against illness and socially undesirable behaviour rather than against players in a game.

We are conscious of the pessimism of our conclusions, and do not wish to convey the impression that we see no hope for Physical Education as a medium for educational experiences. But, before this can be realized in curriculum practice, we need to acknowledge the extent of the problem facing anyone who wishes to promote social transformation through education. Evans and Clarke (in this volume, Chapter 8) argue that changes in content by themselves do little to alter the structural power that acts through institutionalized practices in schools. The evidence presented here lends support to this claim, and by focusing on how ideologies work through people's own lived experiences, shows that bringing about genuine change in and through education will involve changing teachers as well as the curriculum.

Many teachers come to Physical Education teaching *because* they have had particular experiences of physical activity that are often, in themselves, reproductive of existing orthodoxies. Not only this, but these teachers *believe in* the values they hold and so not surprisingly pass them on to their students through their teaching. Any attempt to incorporate teachers into the effort to use education as a socially transformative device must recognize that many teachers are, in the first place, the most likely front-line defenders of orthodoxies. Or, at the very least, they represent a sizeable group who may see themselves as having much to lose and precious little to gain personally by beginning to question the status quo.

Continuing research in the area of 'resistance theory' has much to offer physical educators, because it highlights the possibility that teachers can take an active part in steering their own professional practice, and in providing their students with authentically educative experiences. On the basis of this study we are convinced that this possibility will only become reality when teachers begin to think of themselves not as mere transmitters of information but as transformers and creators of new knowledge. But for this to happen we need to learn much more about how life in schools and classrooms is shaped and structured by wider social forces, and how teachers can use this knowledge in their own personal and professional growth.

Notes

1 A version of this paper was presented at the British Educational Research Association Annual Conference, Manchester, September 1987.

2 The names of the schools and the teachers cited in the text have been changed. We wish to thank all of the teachers and students who participated in the study, and the Queensland Department of Education for permission to enter the schools.

3 The paper draws on data collected by Lisa George as part of her honours thesis in the Department of Human Movement Studies, University of Queensland. See L.F. George (1986) 'Investigating the Limits and Possibilities of Teacher Resistance in Physical Education', Unpublished Honours Thesis, University of Queensland.

4 We wish to thank Derek Colquhoun at Sunderland Polytechnic (formerly University of Queensland) for drawing our attention to this notion.

5 Health and Physical Education became an examinable junior and senior subject in Queensland high schools in 1976 (see BSSS, 1986). The senior award can be counted towards the tertiary entrance score.

References

APPLE, M. (1979) *Ideology and Curriculum*, London, Routledge and Kegan Paul.

BOARD of SECONDARY SCHOOL STUDIES (1986) *Junior and Senior Syllabuses for Health and Physical Education*, Brisbane, Queensland Government Printer.

BULLOUGH, R.V. and GITLIN, A.D. (1985) 'Ideology, teacher role and resistance', *Education and Society*, 3, 1, pp. 65–73.

BULLOUGH, R.V. and GITLIN, A.D. (1986) 'Limits of teacher autonomy: Decision-making, ideology and reproduction of teacher role', *New Education*, 8, 1, pp. 25–34.

EVANS, J. and CLARKE, G. (this volume) 'Changing the face of Physical Education', Chapter 8.

GIROUX, H.A. (1981) *Ideology, Culture and the Process of Schooling*, Lewes, Falmer Press.

HARGREAVES, J. (1977) 'Sport and Physical Education: Autonomy or domination', *Bulletin of Physical Education*, 13, pp. 19–25.

KIRK, D. (1988) *Physical Education and Curriculum Study: A Critical Introduction*, London, Croom Helm.

10
The Micropolitics of Innovation in the Physical Education Curriculum

Andrew C. Sparkes

Most teachers will readily admit in private that they are surrounded in school by forms of 'wheeling and dealing' through which different people attempt to advance specific interests. Indeed, Burns (1961) maintains that most modern organizations actively stimulate various kinds of politicking because they have built into their design certain systems of simultaneous competition and collaboration, which means that people may collaborate in pursuit of a common task, yet are often pitted against one another in direct competition for limited resources, status and career opportunities. In such situations Burke (1969) believes that 'conspiracy is as natural as breathing' (p. 166), whilst Gronn (1986) claims that in schools today it is conflict rather than consensus which is the norm. Others adopting a pluralistic-conflict stance (see Ball, 1981, 1985, 1987; Bell, 1986; Evans *et al.*, 1987; Kirk, 1987; Riseborough, 1981; Sparkes, 1986, 1987a, 1987b) have suggested that if we are to understand the limits and possibilities of educational change, then schools and departments should be regarded as 'arenas of struggle', contexts in which power is unevenly distributed amongst members and in which there are likely to be ideological differences and conflicts of interests. These conflicts provide the basis for the rich dynamic of school life in which the diverse interests of teachers can just as easily collide as they can coincide.

Figure 1 indicates the relationship and tensions that can often exist for teachers between 'doing' the job (task), their long- and short-term career aspirations, and their personal values and life circumstances in operation beyond the school gates (extra-mural interests). These three domains of interest can interact (the shaded areas) but may also remain separate, and it is the attempts by each teacher to maintain a balance of interests (as perceived by the individual) in a changing environment that create the tensions within, and between, the perspectives of teachers which lie at the heart of political activity.

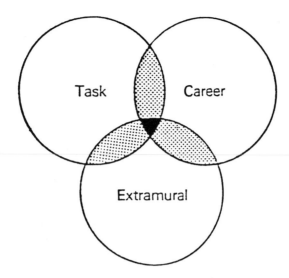

Figure 1. Organizational Interests: Task, Career and Extra-mural

Source: Morgan, 1986, p. 149.

That the area of complete convergence of interests is often minimal (the darkest area) is but one reason why organizational (or task) rationality is the exception rather than the rule for teachers, as these interest domains are contested in schools both *between* and *within* subject subcultures. Studies of innovation are particularly useful in highlighting these tensions and conflicts. As Ball (1987) points out:

> Innovations are rarely neutral. They tend to advance or enhance the position of certain groups and disadvantage or damage the position of others. ... It is not surprising that innovation processes in schools frequently take the form of political conflict between advocacy and opposition groups. (p. 32)

During periods of stress within an institution the deep-rooted and often implicit 'subterranean issues' that Lacey (1977) talks of are raised forcefully to the surface as teachers strive to protect their interests. This reveals the darker side of organizational life involving the world of micropolitics which Hoyle (1982) conceptualizes as embracing those 'strategies by which individuals and groups in organizational contexts seek to use their resources of power and influences to further their interests' (p. 88). In these terms innovation may be seen as an *interactive political process*.

This chapter focuses directly upon the micropolitical strategies that teachers develop to cope with the tensions they experience when they attempt to balance task, career and extra-mural interests in order to gain some measure of control over what happens to them in their world of work. It suggests that in the creative production of solutions to their daily recurring problems in school, teachers not only create but legitimate a theory-practice divide that allows 'traditional' teaching roles to remain intact despite attempts to change them, so that the type of education offered to children itself remains unchanged. This dislocation between theory and practice means that whilst changes may occur in the organization and content of the curriculum (subject paradigm), there need be no corresponding change in the individual's teaching method or mode of transmitting knowledge (subject pedagogy) to children in the classroom (see Ball and Lacey, 1980). Thus, 'innovation without change' often takes place (Evans, 1985), whereby the deep-rooted assumptions embedded in the perspectives of teachers remain unchallenged and taken-for-granted as they continue to engage in classroom practices which serve socially and culturally to reproduce the inequalities within society in terms of gender, race, ability and class (Apple, 1979; Carrington and Leaman, 1986; Giroux, 1983; Hendry, 1981; Kirk *et al.*, 1986; Scraton, 1986, 1987).

The data presented are drawn from a three-year (1983–1986) case study of teacher initiated innovation within a PE department of seven specialists at a large English urban coeducational comprehensive school which will be called Branstown. Here, a newly appointed head of department, called Alex, attempted to introduce structural changes in the PE curriculum which involved the abolition of streaming by ability in games lessons in favour of mixed-ability groupings. In addition, he attempted to reorientate the educational philosophies of those in his department towards his own. The confusions, anxieties and conflicts caused by these proposals for change were witnessed by me during the fieldwork phase of the research which began in September 1983. During this academic year I adopted the role of 'researcher-participant' (see Gans, 1982) within the department and used 'reflexive' interviews (Hammersley and Atkinson, 1983) to focus upon the early adoption phase of the innovative process when Alex began to conceive of changing the curriculum and started to introduce his ideas to the department. From September 1984 to September 1986, interviews only were used to enhance my interpretation of the adoption phase and to examine the consequences of the innovations for the teachers involved, once they had been implemented in September 1984. Importantly, the categorization of 'change as micropolitical' emerged during the course of the study as a 'grounded' concept (Glaser and Strauss, 1967; Glaser, 1978) within the frame of reference of both the teachers involved and myself as each attempted to understand an innovative process which could only be sensibly interpreted in terms of the micropolitics of the department and school.

Competing Perspectives: The Context for Conflict

According to Becker *et al.* (1961) perspectives are:

> A co-ordinated set of ideas and actions a person uses in dealing with some problematic situation, to refer to a person's ordinary way of thinking and feeling about and acting in such a situation. These thoughts and actions flow reasonably, from the actor's point of view, from the ideas contained within the perspective. (p. 34)

Prior to the arrival of Alex as the new head of department in 1983, all the members of the department held to varying degrees the equivalent of what Ball (1981) has termed an 'academic' perspective, which when transferred into the context of PE takes the form of a 'sporting' perspective. This is subject-centred, concerned with the development of physical skills and maintaining 'standards' within a meritocratic system where the focus of attention is on the élite performer and more able pupils in order to produce successful school teams. The most visible expression of this perspective in action was the organization of the 'games' lessons in PE, where both boys and girls were 'streamed' and the Physical Education specialists took the most able in the 'top-group' which contained the potential school team players. The boys' curriculum in particular was heavily 'skewed' (Glew, 1983) towards the major team games at the expense of individual activities in the quest for inter-school sporting success. The female members of the department provided more individual activities for the girls' curriculum, such as dance, but they still organized their games lessons in the same way as the men and used the 'élitist' top-group system. As a young female member of the department comments:

> I have a top-group in hockey for first years. That's quite nice because it gives you a chance to work with your team players. ... Also you can move a bit faster, where the bottom groups are still dribbling or hitting, with the top-group you are working out a system of taking corners, something very complicated. ... If it went over to mixed ability it would slow the progress that you made. (interview transcript)

If perspectives are taken to be dimensional rather than dichotomous two-member typologies (Hammersley, 1977), then at the opposite end of the dimension was the 'idealist' perspective held by Alex on his arrival at Branstown School. This is child-centred, egalitarian and concerned with personal and social development via individual self-paced activities, such as, educational gymnastics and swimming. It is essentially anti-élitist and anti-traditional, and whilst the idealist perspective is not uncommon amongst teachers in general it was the first time at Branstown School that a physical educator had held such views.

At the extremes of the dimension the two perspectives in operation within the department were subcultural worlds apart, neither accepting nor understanding the view of the other. From within each perspective the physical educators made sense of, and negotiated, their world of work as they engaged with the curriculum at a 'deep personal level' (Woods, 1984), and it was only after a period of 'orientation' (Sparkes, 1986) during his first term at the school in the summer of 1983, when Alex was involved in coming to terms with the organization of his new school and attempting to develop friendly working relationships with those in his department, that he realized the prevailing curriculum was capable of negating his own expression of self. Commenting upon his early involvement with the extant curriculum, he notes:

> I had that terrible experience of that Autumn term, and I really did start to struggle there. I just couldn't accept that form of system — I was definitely under increased pressure — how can I put it? Internally I was under pressure. It was totally against my philosophy, I couldn't cope with it — I felt I couldn't live with myself because it was so bad, it was so élitist. Honestly, I would come back in after a games lesson and some of the teaching made me despair. I felt like crying sometimes. I would come home and I'd be angry and I was desperate — 'What can I do?', 'Where can I go?', 'Do I change everything — or what?'. (interview transcript)

As with Nias' (1984) junior school teachers, the problem for Alex was that of creating a work setting that would be congruent with, and allow for, his own sense of 'substantive-self' (see Ball, 1979) to be expressed. There were additional pressures upon him since he believed that he had been appointed specifically to promote his idealist perspective within the department, and that this had implications for his own career aspirations. He notes:

> I think that the Headmaster thought the department was a mess, and a bit too traditional and not moving in the direction he wanted. There was a mess, and no real direction in the curriculum, it was a bit behind, and really needed updating and bringing into line with school policy — and obviously I was under pressure to do that. ... I was appointed for my philosophies and beliefs, and I like to think that they fit in with the comprehensive ideal. If I didn't end up with the majority of my ideals and philosophies within the department, then I wouldn't have done my job, and been seen to be doing my job properly. (interview transcript)

As a consequence of these pressures Alex began, during the early part of the autumn term 1983, to consider making changes in the curriculum which involved the abolition of the streamed top-group system in games in order to make all lessons mixed-ability for both boys and girls. This structural change in the curriculum would allow Alex his self-expression but it also constituted a threat to the self-expression of those holding the sporting perspective who themselves engaged with the curriculum at a deep personal level. They believed that streaming by ability in games lessons was essential for producing school teams and catering for the able children which they saw as a central element of the PE teacher's role. As one such teacher comments:

> I do think that school teams are important, and this new fangled thing that's coming around where school teams ought to be dropped and we concentrate on everyone. I don't really think that is a good idea at all. ... I think that if you dilute it too much, and if you keep the good ones together with the less able ones and you do a course that is for everybody, without concentrating on the élite at some stage. I think that's doing a disservice to the good kids. (interview transcript)

In contrast, Alex wanted to reduce the emphasis on the major team games and inter-school sport in order to offer a broader curriculum to cater for *all* the pupils. He notes: 'There has been a strong emphasis on games within the school, and it's going to take time to get away from that, and get other people away from the idea that we simply produce good teams and PE is just about games' (interview transcript).

Thus, the opposing perspectives within the department contained 'competing systems of interpretation' (Silverman, 1970) over what should be included in the PE curriculum, and how it should be taught. These differences of interpretation were a source of anxiety, confusion and conflict throughout the study as the teachers involved struggled to come to terms with the implications of change. However, there was one concern that *all* the department shared which formed a point of unity and this related to subject status.

The Superordinate Goal of Status Enhancement

If the teaching profession in general is prone to 'status panic' (Mills, 1951) then physical educators may be under a phobic stress, and Hoyle (1986) claims they are 'particularly given to pondering status issues' (p. 43). He suggests that whilst there is little comparative data available, one suspects that PE is universally lower rather than higher in the pecking order of school subjects, despite its 'periodic elevation' (Woods, 1983) in terms of presenting a public image of the school.

In the PE department at Branstown School status was a burning issue and all the members of the department felt that theirs was a position of 'marginality' (Hendry, 1975). In 1983 all those in the department, including Alex, claimed their subject had low status in the school with regard to prestige, wealth and authority (see Biddle and Thomas, 1966; Biddle, 1979). In terms of prestige they felt they were viewed by the rest of the staff, including the headmaster, as anti-academic (see Cannon, 1964; Scotland, 1964) and suffered from what Glew (1984) describes as an 'image problem'. They felt that their subject was classified as non-serious, only being useful for the cathartic discharge of pupils' energies in order to make them more docile in academic lessons.

In terms of wealth the low scaling of the department was taken as an indicator of their low status in the school. Most heads of department in the school were on a scale 4.[1] Alex was a scale 3 along with the heads of art and music which were also classified by the physical educators as marginal subjects. Of the rest of the department only Monica as head of girls was on a scale 2, the rest of the department were scale 1s. Concerning this low scaling of her department, Rachel, a probationary teacher, commented:

> I think that the PE department hasn't got enough scale points in it. I think that Alex should be on a 4, whereas he's on a 3. So I think that shows that they [the senior management] don't care very much. If they did they would pump more points into the department. (interview transcript)

The final criterion of 'authority' also reinforced their perceptions of marginality, as they believed that the school senior management had consciously excluded them from positions of power in the school where they would have the opportunity to exert an influence over other subject areas. In combination, these status concerns were crystallized during 1983–1984 when the headmaster initiated a major curriculum review in the school which entailed every subject justifying its place in the curriculum. The physical educators saw the review as a prelude to rationalization in the school in which some departments would 'survive' and some would 'go to the wall'. Commenting upon the importance of PE justifying its place in the curriculum as part of this review, Alex notes, 'It could make or break this department in terms of its position within the school over the next ten years', whilst Monica, the head of girls, claimed, 'The cake is only so big, and every department is trying to grab as much as it can. If we don't justify our subject we could just end up with the crumbs.' In such a climate the school curriculum was viewed by those in the department as an 'overstaffed environment' (Barker, 1960) in which there is intense competition between different subject areas for limited time and resources.

Gaining access to time and resources depends upon the relative power and negotiating skills of staff (Pollard, 1982); the higher the status of the subject the better the prospect for the teachers involved with regard to staffing ratios, higher salaries, more graded posts and better career prospects (see Goodson, 1981, 1984). Therefore, the struggle for status is intimately linked to the career prospects of each subject teacher and subject community. In this struggle at Branstown School the physical educators were well aware that status meant strength, and strength meant bargaining power for the finite resources available in the school. Thus, in order to advance their interests in the career domain they had to enhance the status of their subject in the eyes of other staff, which involved changing their 'image'. Commenting upon the 'battle' to change the perceptions of other staff, Monica, head of girls, notes:

> If we don't think it's possible, we might as well give up, and I just think that we will end up getting drowned when they come to sort the system out — certainly in this school, into a faculty based system. I think we will find ourselves right at the bottom of the heap. (interview transcript)

However, whilst all the department recognized the need to raise their subject status within the school, just *how* this was to be achieved was contested. Those holding the sporting perspective felt that the production of successful school teams was the most appropriate mechanism for aligning their 'organizational' categories with those 'institutional' categories of the school's significant publics', such as the headmaster and senior teachers (see Meyer and Rowan, 1978; Meyer, 1980; Reid, 1984). As one male member of the department comments:

> When I started teaching I fell on my feet in-so-much as the first team I took won every game of the season. ... For people to look and say, 'Oh, the 1st and 2nd years are doing well — who's taking them?' I mean it could have been bloody King Kong, it wouldn't have made a difference, they would still have won. But as a new teacher that gave me a lift, because people would say, 'It's really going well, keep it up, well done!' That surely has got to be a smaller version of the PE department. If you can produce successful school sides and get a good reputation, then people will look to the school sides and say, 'Well done, congratulations'. (interview transcript)

In contrast, from within the idealist perspective Alex believed that the status of PE could only be raised by arguing for its importance in 'educational' terms. This involved an 'aims-objectives' alignment, whereby the aims and objectives of the PE department were presented to the senior management as congruent with those of the school in general. Commenting on the headmaster, Alex notes:

He's a chap that thinks. He goes right back to basics and says, 'What is your subject doing for the child?' He wants to know just that. He really doesn't want to know what the 1st XV or 1st XI are doing. He wants to know what you are doing and how it affects that child ... obviously I have taken every opportunity to speak to him on the importance of my subject. ... I don't think that we are doing enough in pushing the importance of our subject to other members of staff in the school, and senior management. I haven't just got to convince him, I've got to convince all the other senior members of the hierarchy within the school as well as the Heads of Department. I have to convince them of the importance of my subject before I can go back to him and say in black and white — 'I want more scales for my department.' (interview transcript)

Therefore, whilst the rest of his department felt that the headmaster was impressed by, and desired, school sporting success, Alex believed he did not value these achievements very highly. Indeed, Alex considered that a continued emphasis upon the production of school teams would undermine the quest for subject status. Consequently, during 1983–1984 he dominated the weekly departmental meetings and utilized them as a platform to articulate his idealist perspective to the department and impress upon them the need to argue for subject status in educational terms. It was in these same terms that he forcefully argued the case for innovation. His proposals, however, met with strong resistance from those in the department holding the extremes of the sporting perspective and mild resistance from those holding its weaker version.

The strategy used by Alex to secure the cooperation of his department involved the use of a stylized language form, which borrowed concepts from educational theory to substantiate and to legitimate his proposals for innovation and undermine the claims of the sporting perspective. Significantly, this language form was gradually adopted by the members of the department, even though several strongly disagreed with its content, since it allowed each of them to maintain the delicate balance between their task and career interests. In effect they began to learn from Alex a 'language of change' which provided a means of enhancing personal and subject status, whilst at the same time safeguarding teacher autonomy and allowing their classroom practices to remain unchanged.

Killing Two Birds with One Stone: The Emergence of a Pragmatic Coping Strategy

There were pressures acting upon the seven physical educators from several directions: from their head of department to accept and implement his curriculum innovations, from the need to justify themselves as part of the curriculum review, from their desire to raise subject status, their career aspirations, and their desire to maintain the preferred practices of the classroom which allowed for their expression of self. In order to 'juggle' (Pollard, 1982) their self-interests in relation to these pressures, together they developed a pragmatic coping strategy. As Monica notes:

> We decided as a department, it was Alex who got us thinking about it, but we decided that we ought to improve the status of the department in the eyes of the whole school. ... So we had to become well versed in the changes that were taking place, in case people asked us about it in meetings. (interview transcript)

This coping strategy involved a form of talk or language that I have referred to elsewhere as a 'strategic rhetoric' (Sparkes, 1987b), which was directed specifically at the school senior management team in order to 'justify' the subject and raise its status. It hid from public view the conflicts within the department and cloaked the realities of the classroom where pedagogy changed very little for the three teachers holding the weak sporting perspective, and not at all for the three who held the extremes of this position. This is to say that during the study those holding the weak sporting perspective occasionally 'experimented' in a few of their lessons on a 'one-off basis' to 'try out' some of Alex's ideas, and these teachers gradually became more sympathetic to the idealist perspective towards the end of the study. However, during the adoption phase of the innovation in 1983–1984, despite these occasional 'experimental' lessons, their routine daily practices in the classroom remained unchanged as did the practices of those holding the extremes of the sporting perspective. In this period a strategic rhetoric was used by these teachers to defend themselves against the pressures of and for change in order to reduce their feelings of marginality and to enhance the status of the subject.

This 'rhetorical justification' involved the use in everyday discourse of concepts borrowed from educational theory and introduced to them by Alex, such as 'core experiences', 'developing the whole child', 'negotiated curriculum', 'individual learning styles' and 'relevant life skills'. It was then claimed that the existing curriculum and the proposed changes by Alex were ideally suited as a medium for the realization of such experiences. Significantly, this form of rhetoric was used *only* in the educational context of the school, that is, in the staffroom, at staff meetings, in job interviews and in conversations with the school senior management team (see, Keddie, 1971).

The concepts and language form provided by Alex allowed the department to act in the educational context as a 'performance team' (Goffman, 1959), creating the 'front' of a unified group with a coherent and homogeneous philosophy. Creating the impression of a unified department was seen as essential by Alex in relation to his negotiations with the school management team, of which he was a member by virtue of his position as head of department. Reflecting on the role of the rhetorical justification in this impression management, he notes:

> It was very important, otherwise I would have been arguing the case in one way in the staffroom or whatever, and they would have undermined it by not arguing it in the same way — that would have put me in a weak position. It would have seemed that the department was not behind me. ... We had to present a unified front to make an impact upon the rest of the staff. What went on out on the games field is another matter as I'm sure you know. (interview transcript)

Here Alex makes it clear that he was aware that the classroom practices of those in his department did not match the content of the rhetoric they used in the staffroom. In this sense rhetorical justification played an essential part in a 'curriculum negotiation' (Macdonald and Walker, 1976) where fundamental value conflicts were subsumed beneath a common rhetoric to which all apparently subscribed. The day-to-day realities of departmental life at Branstown School were rarely congruent with the content of this rhetoric which promoted a 'public image' to others that centred upon intentions not actualities. This included such statements as, 'We are trying to teach cooperation in team games', 'By children supporting each other in gymnastics we hope they gain a sense of responsibility'; 'The curriculum changes will allow us to meet the needs of the less able.' The unchanged practices of the classroom and the intra-departmental conflicts were not recognized or alluded to in the rhetoric; they remained hidden from view in the educational context of the school.

The Separate World of the Classroom

Phenomenologically distinct from the educational context is the 'classroom context' which Keddie (1971) claims involves the world of *is* rather than *ought*, a pragmatic world focused upon deeds not words, practice not theory. In this context Cole (1985) suggests that the 'practical' mode of consciousness is dominant in which teachers draw up their tacit commonsense knowledge to survive in the classroom. Here the physical educators were concerned to express themselves in terms of control, achievement, competence, enjoyment and autonomy, and if rhetorical justification was used at all it was framed in humorous terms. As an example, prior to a rugby lesson Simon jokingly said to Peter, 'I suppose you're going to do a bit of the old games-for-understanding today then.' To which Peter laughingly replied, 'You must be bloody joking. You had this lot last year didn't you? They can just about understand how to get their boots on.' Concerning this private classroom arena of practice, Ball (1987) notes:

> The simple arguments of the debate are invariably overwhelmed by the complexities and messy realities of classroom life. The language employed here is the everyday discourse of pragmatism. The high-flown rhetoric must be adapted to the immediate physical and material constraints of survival at the chalk face. (p. 39)

In addition, due to his respect for teacher autonomy, Alex made no attempt to intervene directly in lessons in order to impose changes in pedagogy, and claims 'I can try and get them to change their ideas about PE and hopefully that will lead to them changing their teaching, but I can't force anyone to change how they teach.' In 1986 Alex was aware that those holding the strong sporting perspective in his department had not changed their classroom practice at all, but he was pleased that at least they were representing the department more positively in the educational context of the school. He notes:

> That's how it's got to be if you want to gain recognition for your subject. That's one of the main arenas of, if you like, being on show. It's where you impress colleagues that you understand educational matters and just don't play sport all day. They are much better now at that, that's very pleasing to me, it strengthens my case, I'm backed up. ... It's a skill [rhetorical justification] they've learnt. ... (interview transcript)

As such, the use of rhetorical justification in relation to the proposals for innovation became legitimized as an effective means to enhance individual subject status only in the educational context of the school. Thus it reinforced a theory–practice gap which deflected the physical educators from considering the implications of the content of the rhetoric for their own practice. The use of rhetoric was situationally specific, it served different 'interests-at-hand' (Schutz, 1962). As an example, Simon, who held a very strong sporting perspective, openly disagreed with the views contained within the idealist perspective and admitted that regardless of any changes in subject pedagogy that Alex instigated, his own classroom practice would remain unchanged. However, the same teacher clearly saw the advantages of using rhetorical justification to create the 'illusion' of being an 'idealist' in the interview situation if it was to his advantage, as the following interview extract indicates:

Simon: It sounds really waffly, 'games-for-understanding' to me, but I mean people are impressed, yes, if you can talk the language, you know the jargon. People 'understand' by

	that, that you are well read and well versed, and they like some proof of the fact that you are changing. ... But at the end of the day there is a lot that you can say in interview that you can get away with, that you didn't have to do after if you get the job.
Researcher:	How do you mean?
Simon:	Well, 'Would you be willing to take on a health-related-fitness course?' 'Oh yes please, I'd *love* to do that!' [laughs]. You would say that even if you didn't have a bloody clue — you would still say it, and say that you could do it. ... PE is full of theory now, as long as you can spout the theory you can get on. The fact that you may be a bloody good teacher means bugger all — or it seems that way to me. You spout it all out if you want to get on.
Researcher:	Even if you don't agree?
Simon:	Of course. Whether you agree or not has nothing to do with it — it's giving out all the right bullshit to the right people at the right time, which is so ridiculous when you think of it.

Like teachers elsewhere (cf. Hilsum and Start, 1974) the physical educators at Branstown School believed that success as a classroom teacher was not influential in gaining promotion — although they felt it should be. Hence, the use of rhetorical justification was seen as a legitimate strategy under the prevailing conditions in the school to enhance status and promotion prospects, even though the content of the rhetoric often had little in common with the privately held beliefs and intentions of the individual.

Rhetoric, Self-Presentation and Exerting Control in the Work Place

Rhetorical justification may be interpreted as a pragmatic strategy developed by the physical educators at Branstown School to cope with the tensions of balancing individual and group interests in the task and career domains (see Figure 1). This coping strategy was both adaptive and *creative* (see Hargreaves, 1978) in that it allowed them skilfully to manipulate their self-presentations within the different contexts that the school provided, such as the staffroom, classrooms and departmental meetings.

Importantly, as Goffman (1968) points out with regard to such impression management, individuals not only have the right to control the type of information about themselves that is made available, but also the right of choice as to the audience who will receive this information. As indicated, the physical educators directed rhetorical justification at 'target' members of the school's significant public, such as the headmaster, and this rhetoric contained only selected information. As such it was an *intentional* goal-directed behaviour and functioned to control the level of trust and intimacy in the relationship, influence the amount that 'others' learnt about the teacher, and affected the relative *power* of the relationship. Thus the control of self-relevant information had implications for how the teacher *should* behave, and how they *are* and *should* be defined, regarded and treated by others in the school.

This controlling of self-relevant information made skilful use of teacher autonomy within the prevailing structure of the school which reinforced the separation of the educational and classroom contexts. Both Bidwell (1965) and Lortie (1975) have indicated that the immediate work situation in schools serves continually to redefine the conception of teacher autonomy, with the former noting the temporal and functional differentiation which characterizes the job. In the five-period day at Branstown School the teachers were split into separate teaching areas and segregated during lesson times, whilst work was organized into concurrent lessons where each teacher was responsible for separate portions of subject-matter based on a loosely defined syllabus. All this built a sense of autonomy into their everyday practices. They were rarely in a position to observe, supervise or control the activities of colleagues in their own department, and similarly other teachers rarely saw the physical educators in action. Such structural looseness coupled with the privacy of the 'closed classroom' (see Denscombe, 1985) meant that the significant publics, such as, the headmaster and senior teachers, who were the targets for rhetorical justification, were rarely in a position to assess the congruence (or lack of it) between the content of this rhetoric and the realities of the classroom. As one member of the department explained:

> I mean the Headmaster has *never* come into one of my gymnastics lessons — he'd have to walk too bloody far [laughs]. He might see me teaching rugby from far off for a while, but I shouldn't think that he stands there analyzing if I'm doing games-for-understanding or whatever. (interview transcript)

At Branstown School the physical educators felt anxious and threatened, and in such a situation they acted accordingly to gain some control of the situation. They were clearly aware of the 'pragmatic efficacy' of rhetorical justification and they had *chosen* to project different self-images to different people, in different contexts, by manipulating the realities of the educational process (cf. Reid, 1984; Williams, 1985) in order to control the impressions that others formed of them.

All relationships which people have to one another are based on their knowing something about the other, therefore, by controlling the information available the individual gains greater control over the interactive process. Dawe (1973) claims that the basic principles of impression management are based on concealment, calculation and gamesmanship. If this is so, then the use of rhetorical justification can be classified as a 'strong' form of political behaviour that has machiavellian overtones, involving a *conscious deception* in the hope of maximizing gains in both long- and short-term interests. Christie and Geis (1970) suggest that machiavellians are adept at resisting the influence of others, at least when it is to their advantage, and are skilled at finding ways to circumvent complying with another's requests and persuasions. They tend to excel in face-to-face situations where they are permitted some latitude in the type of behaviours they use. The development and use of this skill by the physical educators should not be viewed in a pejorative fashion, since in the circumstances that prevailed in their school it may have been one of the few legitimate tactics available for protecting their interests in a social system characterized by increased competition for time and resources. Indeed, as Smith (1983) found elsewhere, in a contracting educational system many teachers may be forced by their situation into adopting machiavellian tactics to secure ends either for themselves or for their departments.

For the physical educators at Branstown School, learning the skilled use of rhetoric to control self-representations was essential, not only for subject survival and career development but also for the survival of self as expressed through the curriculum. This ability came to be defined as a central criterion of 'competent membership' (see Denscombe, 1980) for this particular depart-ment. A central aspect of this competence involved the ability to switch from operating in the discursive mode of consciousness in the educational context of the school, to operating in the practical mode of consciousness when in the classroom context. In learning and demonstrating this ability, the physical educators utilized the prevailing structure of the school to legitimate a theory-practice gap which they skilfully manipulated to protect their task interests by resisting the pressures from Alex to change their classroom practice, whilst simultaneously promoting their career interests in the educa-tional context by using a strategic rhetoric.

Thus, Alex's calls for innovation were deflected by his department into the educational context where they adopted his rationale for change in order to present an image to others of 'informed and innovative educator', yet the progressive ideals contained within this rhetoric were not translated into their daily routine classroom practices.

In effect, Alex had been able to introduce mixed-ability *grouping* but not mixed-ability *teaching*, and in this sense there was innovation without change. In these situations Evans (1985) claims: 'Stratification, social division, inequality of educational opportunity stand largely unscathed, despite the hustle and bustle of curricular activity which on the surface suggests that substantial educational innovation is afoot' (p. 147). The strategic rhetoric developed by the physical educators to cope with the material and structural constraints in operation at Branstown School, allowed them to gain a measure of control over their working conditions without challenging the taken-for-granted role of the teacher, or changing the type of education offered to children in their lessons. Their manner of coping indicates that teachers are not passive, unreflective 'over-socialized' dupes but active participants in the construction and maintenance of those structures which act upon them (see Giddens, 1976). The structure of the school does have a profound influence upon teacher behaviour, but it does not fully determine it as teachers always retain some degree of autonomy enabling them to resist structural constraints and act in unpredictable ways (see Bullough and Gitlin, 1986). The events at Branstown School bear testimony to the power of teacher autonomy and the ways in which teachers can utilize it to resist change and maintain the delicate balance between their interests in the task and career domains.

Concluding Remarks

Creating change in schools is an extremely long and complicated process involving conflict and resistance as teachers utilize the limited resources available to them to protect their self-interests. In this process it is essential to recognize the micropolitical matrix of the institution as a powerful mediator when teachers attempt to innovate in their own schools. At Branstown School the lack of significant change at the classroom level was fundamentally related to the micropolitics of the institution which created both the limits and possibilities for educational change. Importantly, the rhetoric made available by Alex assisted some of his department in resisting his calls for change, but it also helped others to become aware of alternative ideas and practices allowing them to widen their definition of what was considered appropriate practice. The occasional 'experimental' lessons of those holding the weak sporting perspective may be the early part of an evolutionary process in which new ideas are translated into daily routine practices, but whether these practices are maintained and developed remains to be seen.

The events at Branstown School highlight the need for teachers to communicate and critically examine their own practices and those of colleagues holding different perspectives. Creating the conditions in which teachers feel secure enough to engage in open and frank dialogue would be a necessary step in reducing teacher isolation and closing the theory-practice gap which frustrates so many attempts to promote change. Reducing teacher isolation is a difficult task and involves providing teachers with time to come together and reflect deeply about their actions and situations as a prelude to modifying both. This requires a great deal more than a 'cosy chat' since the dialogue needs to illuminate the underlying assumptions contained in the perspectives of those involved in order to promote new ways of thinking about teaching. Efforts need to be made to encourage teachers to discuss individual concerns, share problems and examine how their own aims, values and belief systems can play a vital role in influencing their pedagogical decisions and actions which may simply serve to reproduce social inequalities. Should the teachers themselves decide that change is desirable they can then creatively utilize their autonomy to challenge the prevailing structures in the school and experiment with alternative forms of pedagogy, as the traditional teaching role is slowly modified and transformed. In this change process, the meaning and perspectives of teachers in the complex milieu of the school and classroom have to be placed centre-stage in order that they can be critically examined by the *teachers themselves*, since only by engaging teachers in the transformation of their own practice can teacher isolation and the theory-practice gap be reduced, allowing for the possibility of innovation *with* change to occur in our schools.

Note

1   On each scale teachers progress one increment each year. Once at the top of the scale no further increase in salary occurs until promotion is gained to a higher scale; movement up the scales is not automatic.

References

APPLE, M. (1979) *Ideology and Curriculum*, London, Routledge and Kegan Paul.

BALL, D.W. (1979) 'Self and identity in the context of deviance: The case of criminal abortion', in WILSON, M. (Ed.), *Social and Educational Research in Action*, Milton Keynes, Open University Press, pp. 189–217.

BALL, S.J. (1981) *Beachside Comprehensive*, Cambridge, Cambridge University Press.

BALL, S.J. (1985) 'School politics, teachers' careers and educational change: A case study of becoming a comprehensive school', in BARTON, L. and WALKER, S. (Eds), *Education and Social Change*, London, Croom Helm, pp. 29–61.

BALL, S.J. (1987) *The Micro-Politics of the School: Towards a Theory of School Organisation*, London, Methuen.

BALL, S.J. and LACEY, C. (1980) 'Subject disciplines and the opportunity for group action: A measured critique of subject subcultures', in WOODS, P.E. (Ed.), *Teacher Strategies*, London, Croom Helm, pp. 157–77.

BARKER, R.G. (1960) 'Ecology and motivation', in JONES, M.R. (Ed.), *Nebraska Symposium on Motivation*, Lincoln, Nebr., University of Nebraska Press, pp. 127–43.

BECKER, H., GEER, B., HUGHES, E. and STRAUSS, A. (1961) *Boys in White*, Chicago, Ill., University of Chicago Press.

BELL, L. (1986) 'Managing to survive in secondary school Physical Education', in EVANS, J. (Ed.), *Physical Education, Sport and Schooling: Studies in the Sociology of Physical Education*, Lewes, Falmer Press, pp. 95–115.

BIDDLE, B.J. (1979) *Role Theory: Expectations, Identities and Behaviours,* London, Academic Press.

BIDDLE, B.J and THOMAS, E.J. (1966) *Role Theory: Concepts and Research*, New York, Wiley.

BIDWELL, G.E. (1965) 'The school as a formal organization', in MARCH, J. (Ed.), *Handbook of Organization*, Chicago, Ill., Rand McNally, pp. 201–19.

BREAKWELL, G.M. (1985) 'Society, culture and change', Open University Course D307, *Social Psychology: Development, Experience and Behaviour in the Social World*, Milton Keynes, Open University Press.

BULLOUGH, V.R. and GITLIN, A.D. (1986) 'Limits of teacher autonomy: Decision-making, ideology and reproduction of role', *New Education*, 8, pp. 25–34.

BURKE, K. (1969) *A Rhetoric of Motives*, Los Angeles, Calif., University of California Press.

BURNS, T. (1961) 'Micropolitics: Mechanisms of organizational change', *Administrative Science Quarterly*, 6, pp. 257–81.

CANNON, C. (1964) 'Some variations in the teacher's role', *Education for Teaching*, 64, pp. 29–36.

CARRINGTON, B. and LEAMAN, O. (1986) 'Equal Opportunities and Physical Education', in EVANS, J. (Ed.), *Physical Education, Sport and Schooling: Studies in the Sociology of Physical Education*, Lewes, Falmer Press, pp. 215–26.

CHRISTIE, R. and GEIS, F. (1970) *Studies in Machiavellianism*, London, Academic Press.

COLE, M. (1985) '"The teacher trap?" Commitment and consciousness in entrants to teaching', in BALL, S.J. and GOODSON, I.F. (Eds), *Teachers' Lives and Careers*, Lewes, Falmer Press, pp. 89–104.

DAWE, A. (1973) 'The underworld view of Erving Goffman', *British Journal of Sociology*, 24, pp. 246–53.

DENSCOMBE, M. (1980) 'The work context of teaching: An analytic framework for the study of teachers in classrooms', *British Journal of Sociology of Education*, 1, pp. 279–92.

DENSCOMBE, M. (1985) *Classroom Control: A Sociological Perspective*, London, George Allen and Unwin.

EVANS, J. (1985) *Teaching in Transition: The Challenge of Mixed Ability Grouping*, Milton Keynes, Open University Press.

EVANS, J., LOPEZ, S., DUNCAN, M. and EVANS, M. (1987) 'Some thoughts on the political and pedagogical implications of mixed sex grouping in the Physical Education curriculum', *British Educational Research Journal*, 13, pp. 59–71.

GANS, H.J. (1982) 'The participant observer as a human being: Observations on the personal aspects of fieldwork', in BURGESS, R. G.. (Ed.), *Field Research: A Sourcebook and Field Manual*, London, Allen and Unwin, pp. 53–61.

GIDDENS, A. (1976) *New Rules of Sociological Method*, London, Hutchinson.

GIROUX, H. (1983) *Theory and Resistance in Education: A Pedagogy for the Opposition*, London, Heineman.

GLASER, B.G. (1978) *Theoretical Sensitivity: Advances in the Methodology of Grounded Theory*, Mill Valley, Calif., Sociology Press.

GLASER, B.G. and STRAUSS, A.L. (1967) *The Discovery of Grounded Theory: Strategies for Qualitative Research*, New York, Aldine Publishing Company.

GLEW, P. (1983) 'Are your fixtures really necessary?', *British Journal of Physical Education*, 14, pp. 126–8.

GLEW, P. (1984) 'The image', *British Journal of Physical Education*, 15, pp. 183–4.

GOFFMAN, E. (1959) *The Presentation of Self in Everyday Life*, New York, Anchor Books.

GOFFMAN, E. (1968) *Asylums*, New York, Anchor Books.

GOODSON, I. (1981) 'Becoming an academic subject: Patterns of explanation and evolution', *British Journal of Sociology of Education*, 2, pp. 163–80.

GOODSON, I. (1984) 'Beyond the subject monolith: Subject traditions and sub-cultures', in HARLING, P. (Ed.), *New Directions in Educational Leadership*, Lewes, Falmer Press, pp. 325–41.

GRONN, P. (1986) 'Politics, power and the management of schools', in HOYLE, E. and McMAHON, A. (Eds), *World Yearbook of Education: The Management of Schools*, London, Kogan Page, pp. 45–54.

HAMMERSLEY, M. (1977) 'Teacher perspectives', Open University Course E202, *School and Society*, Milton Keynes, Open University Press.

HAMMERSLEY, M. and ATKINSON, P. (1983) *Ethnography: Principles in Practice*, London, Tavistock Publications.

HARGREAVES, A. (1978) 'The significance of classroom coping strategies', in BARTON, L. and MEIGHAN, R. (Eds), *Sociological Interpretations of Schooling and Classrooms: A Reappraisal*, Driffield, Nafferton Books, pp. 73–101.

HENDRY, L.B. (1975) 'Survival in a marginal role: The professional identity of the Physical Education teacher', *British Journal of Sociology*, 26, pp. 465–76.

HENDRY, L. (1981) 'The family, society and leisure: The hidden curriculum', *Proceedings of an International Seminar on Leisure and Family*. Brugge, Belgium.

HILSUM, S. and START, K.B. (1974) *Promotion and Careers in Teaching*, Slough, National Foundation for Educational Research.

HOYLE, E. (1982) 'Micropolitics and educational organizations', *Educational Management and Administration*, 10, pp. 87–98.

HOYLE, E. (1986) 'Curriculum development in Physical Education 1966–1985', in *Trends and Developments in Physical Education: The Proceedings of the VIII Commonwealth and International Conference on Sport, Physical Education, Dance, Recreation and Health*, London, E. and F.N. Spon, pp. 35–48.

KEDDIE, N. (1971) 'Classroom knowledge', in YOUNG, M.F.D. (Ed.), *Knowledge and Control*, London, Collier-Macmillan, pp. 133–60.

KIRK, D. (1987) 'Researching the Teacher's World: A Case Study of Teacher-Initiated Innovation', Unpublished PhD Thesis, Loughborough University of Technology.

KIRK, D., MCKAY, J. and GEORGE, L.F. (1986) 'All work and no play? Hegemony in the PE curriculum', in *Proceedings of the VIII Commonwealth and International Conference on Sport, Physical Education, Dance, Recreation and Health*, London, E. and F.N. Spon, pp. 170–7.

LACEY, C. (1977) *The Socialization of Teachers*, London, Methuen.

LORTIE, D. (1975) *School Teacher: A Sociological Study*, Chicago, Ill., University of Chicago Press.

MACDONALD, B. and WALKER, R. (1976) *Changing the Curriculum*, London, Open Books.

MEYER, J.W. (1980) 'Levels of the educational system and schooling effects', in BIDWELL, C.W. and WINDHAM, D.M. (Eds), *The Analysis of Educational Productivity, Vol. 2*, Cambridge, Mass., Ballinger, pp. 15–63.

MEYER, J.W. and ROWAN, B. (1978) 'The structure of educational organizations', in MEYER, J.W. and MARSHAL, W. (Eds), *Environments and Organizations*, San Francisco, Calif., Jossey Bass, pp. 78–109.

MILLS, C.W. (1951) *White Collar: The American Middle Class*, New York, Oxford University Press.

MORGAN, G. (1986) *Images of Organization*, London, Sage.

NIAS, J. (1984) 'Definition and maintenance of self in primary teaching', *British Journal of Sociology of Education*, 5, pp. 267–80.

POLLARD, A. (1982) 'A model of classroom coping strategies', *British Journal of Sociology of Education*, 3, pp. 19–37.

REID, W. A. (1984) 'Curriculum topics as institutional categories: Implications for theory and research in the history and sociology of school subjects', in GOODSON, I.F. and BALL, S.J. (Eds), *Defining the Curriculum: Histories and Ethnographies*, Lewes, Falmer Press, pp. 67–75.

RISEBOROUGH, G. (1981) 'Teachers' careers and comprehensive schooling: An empirical study', *Sociology*, 15, pp. 352–81.

SCHUTZ, A. (1962) *The Problem of Social Reality: Collected Papers I*, The Hague, Martinus Nijhoff.

SCOTLAND, J. (1964) 'The Physical Education teacher', *Scottish Bulletin of Physical Education*, 1, pp. 4–7.

SCRATON, S. (1986) 'Images of femininity and the teaching of girls' Physical Education', in EVANS, J. (Ed.), *Physical Education, Sport and Schooling: Studies in the Sociology of Physical Education*, Lewes, Falmer Press, pp. 71–94.

SCRATON, S. (1987) '"Boys muscle in where angels fear to tread": Girls' sub-cultures and physical activities', in HORNE, J., JARY, D. and TOMLINSON, A. (Eds), *Sport, Leisure and Social Relations*, London, Routledge and Kegan Paul, pp. 160–86.

SILVERMAN, D. (1970) *The Theory of Organizations*, London, Heinemann.

SMITH, J.T. (1983) 'On being political', *Educational Management and Administration*, 11, pp. 205–8.

SMITH, L.M. and KEITH, P.M. (1971) *Anatomy of Educational Innovation: An Organizational Analysis of an elementary school*, New York, Wiley.

SPARKES, A.C. (1986) 'Strangers and structures in the process of innovation', in EVANS, J. (Ed.), *Physical Education, Sport and Schooling: Studies in the Sociology of Physical Education*, Lewes, Falmer Press, pp. 183–91.

SPARKES, A.C. (1987a) 'The Genesis of an Innovation: A Case Study of Emergent Concerns and Micropolitical Solutions', Unpublished PhD Thesis, Loughborough University of Technology.

SPARKES, A.C. (1987b) 'Strategic rhetoric: A constraint in changing the practice of teachers', *British Journal of Sociology of Education*, 8, pp. 37–54.

WILLIAMS, E.A. (1985) 'Understanding constraints on innovation in Physical Education', *Journal of Curriculum Studies*, 17, pp. 407–13.

WOODS, P. (1983) *Sociology and the School: An Interactionist Viewpoint*, Lewes, Falmer Press.

WOODS, P. (1984) 'Teacher, self and curriculum', in GOODSON, I. and BALL, S. (Eds), *Defining the Curriculum: Histories and Ethnographies*, Lewes, Falmer Press, pp. 239–61.

11
Control and Responsibility in Outdoor Education: Residential Experience and YTS Students

Anthony Rosie

This chapter takes a story, the experiences of two groups of unemployed young people who underwent rather different forms of residential courses while on a particular type of vocational scheme, and it examines some of the social dynamics of those particular situations. Residential experience is taken here to refer to an organized curriculum activity with pupils/students being taken to a centre for a period of time, typically a week in length, where they live and engage in organized (usually outdoor) activities that characteristically differ from their regular school/college curriculum experience.[1] The story-telling motif is a deliberate one in that the account given here arose from a two-year ethnographic project I conducted between 1984 and 1986 into the lives of 16-year-old school leavers who joined a vocational scheme for young people who in the view of Careers Officers were unlikely to enter employment easily.[2]

The Youth Training Scheme (YTS) was introduced in Britain in 1983 as a one-year scheme and since 1986 has been extended to two years of training as part of a national training policy for unemployed school leavers. The research upon which this chapter is based was carried out before the extension of YTS to two years of training. The Manpower Services Commission (MSC) has been the body responsible for developing and overseeing the project although there is considerable variation between different schemes.[3] Thus on the one-year scheme as set out in policy documents (see MSC, 1982), each student receives fifty weeks' training accompanied by a weekly trainee allowance in lieu of social security payments and the training involves both work experience and general and vocational education. Courses for students who Careers Officers felt were unlikely easily to enter work could reduce the work experience element and increase the general education and vocational training components.[4] A number of official documents describing the creation of YTS refer to the desirability of residential experience as part of a YTS course (see MSC, 1984; FEU, 1984). Although a residential course was not required to offer Outdoor Activities as part of its programme in many cases scheme organizers approached residential experience with Outdoor Activities high on their agenda.

The YTS course reported on here was required to recruit primarily from a pool of young school leavers with learning and behavioural problems. Most of the annual intake of twenty-five students had previously attended special schools but two or three students each year came from units for adolescents who had been expelled from school. The majority of students each year had originally attended special schools because they could not cope with the work in mainstream schools, but in addition a number had been sent to special schools because of their violent behaviour. A few students suffered from physical disabilities and this is taken up in the ensuing account since it was clearly relevant to student participation in Outdoor Activities. Of the fourteen young women and eleven young men joining the course in 1984/85 twelve came from special schools but in 1985/86 seventeen of the intake came from the special school sector. The 1985/86 intake consisted of nine women and fifteen males.

Special education and pupils with special needs have received increased attention from sociologists in recent years,[5] including accounts of such young people on vocational courses (Atkinson *et al.*, 1981), and a feature of this work has been its concern with how the actions and thinking of these young people are structured and controlled. The account here, in line with much of this recent literature, will suggest that the term 'special needs' can function as a label implying criticism of those students not seen as amenable to forms of social control. Student behaviours are not being regarded as the product of psychological qualities inherent in the individual. Rather they are considered as 'practices' (see Willis, 1983) that involve an interplay between individuals' personal biographies and their membership of social classes. In this case social class membership includes experiencing positions of dominance or of being dominated and is based on arguments developed in Willis (1981, 1983). The young people I studied came from working-class homes and cultures, but I am not suggesting that their cultural experience was necessarily uniform; indeed there were important differences between students including, amongst other features, the effects of gender, position and status within the student's family. Some of these points are taken up in Rosie (1988). It will be seen below that residential course staff perceived some students critically and considered them to present problems of control. This perception was often supported by a staff belief in the presence of a cultural lack or deficiency in these students' lives.

However, the term 'control problem' does not refer solely to aspects of behaviour management but also includes the level and type of supervision required in order to maintain student safety on a residential week.

During the two years of the investigation I was in overall charge of 'college course' as it became known. This was a fifty-week YTS course for young people with special needs where the students could choose two of the following four option courses and study them for part of the year: catering, computing, office and typing skills, woodwork. In addition students had to take courses in social and life skills while in college. This college-based course of general and vocational education was interspersed with blocks of work experience with each student having a different work placement. Each of the four option classes was run by a specialist tutor and the work experience elements were organized by two tutors (Mrs Lane and Mrs Thompson) who also contributed to social and life skills work. The residential week took place when the students were in college and their normal timetable was suspended for the duration of the week. Mrs Lane as course tutor was responsible for much of the day-to-day running of the course and she and I worked closely on all aspects of course organization.

I was involved in teaching the group for social and life skills and between 1984 and 1986 I collected data for a research study into the students' lives. During the early fieldwork I conducted interviews with students and teachers on a number of different YTS projects in the county to provide a series of comparisons. My analysis of the text contained in MSC publications and of the practices I saw within particular work places revealed a series of goals for youth training programmes in this particular county. These goals included helping students to develop personal initiative, group cooperation, self-presentation, which were all behaviours that had to be both recorded and assessed (MSC, 1984). One particular industrial company in the area was keen to send YTS students on a residential week and sought a residential course providing an opportunity to develop these skills through both Outdoor Activities and an organized project based on business and marketing concepts. As a result the county Association of Boys' Clubs, which was a part of the county's youth service provision, organized residential weeks at a coastal centre not just for the company that had requested the provision but for all the local YTS courses wishing to participate. During 1984/85 the college course accepted this provision and so part of the research reported on below was conducted at this centre. In 1985/86 Mrs Lane, Mrs Thompson and I as the tutors most involved with the residential work decided to organize a residential week independently of the official provision and we took the students in this particular year to a different centre. We felt the residential centre we had used in 1984/85 and which the Association of Boys' Clubs hoped we would use again in 1985/86 tended to see women students as less able to cope with both Outdoor Activities and project work than their male counterparts, and we felt that an association with the term 'Boys' Clubs' in its title was symptomatic of this. As a result the account given below draws upon my observations of two different residential centres.

Interpreting Residential Experience

Gidden's discussion of Weber's methodological essays makes clear that there are no obvious relationships between motives and conduct (1971, p. 149). Thus an observer cannot straightforwardly infer the reasons or motivations for actions from the behaviours he/she observes. Interpretations of residential tutor activity can consider how far such tutor knowledge of students draws upon a prior categorization of young people in terms of expectations of differential performance from students with different educational backgrounds. Such knowledge frequently remains implicit although it may well inform taken-for-granted routine activities. The ethnographic research described below explored some aspects of these implicit understandings by concentrating on a small series of incidents where the routine and expected order of the residential course were upset. Such incidents when examined allow us to unravel some of the understandings that informed these residential tutors' perceptions of students and contributed to their strategies for organizing student groups.

I was a 'stranger' (Schutz, 1964) in the two centres I chose to study and within them I sought to be accepted by the established adults present, namely, tutors with a specialist involvement in outdoor pursuits. The students visiting the centres were also 'strangers' and it was their acceptance or rejection by the adults present that contributed to the ways in which the courses were organized. Residential tutors could draw upon their 'sedimented knowledge' (Berger and Luckmann, 1966) to effect routines which they followed from one course to the next. These routines were taken-for-granted; they were unproblematic and unquestioned. As such they constituted organized strategies which remained implicit but guided the often decisive actions that residential tutors took. The questions I asked and the discussions I held both as a participant and as an observer were largely directed towards making explicit those strategies that tutors took for granted. This revealed strategies that indicated not only the tutors' personal perspectives upon Outdoor Activities but also their expectations of those using the centres as part of their YTS programmes (industrial trainees and students from colleges). The following account starts from the 'rational' construction of the purposes of a residential week for young people as expressed by both YTS trainers and specialist residential course staff before exploring processes of modification that occurred during the particular weeks observed.

Residential weeks by their very nature tend to be highly intensive for all involved in them and it is possible for goal-setting, organizational adjustments and personal change to take place very quickly in such a context. This pattern was observed here and one can depict two 'official' forms of curricular intention embodied in organizational practices that guided the initial reception of students. It is not being suggested that there is a finite number of perspectives structuring residential experience but rather that there is a complex interplay between overt demands on centres by those paying to send students and the often implicit beliefs and personal philosophies of specialist tutors that guide their organizational practices. These organizational practices include both a curriculum philosophy and a pedagogy designed to realize curricular goals. The interplay of these demands, beliefs and curricular practices becomes most susceptible to observational study when a crisis occurs that threatens to reveal a contrast between what tutors claim to be the purposes of residential experience and how they actually respond to particular students who threaten the smooth running of the course.

An Industry-Based Approach to Residential Experience

In the case of the company mentioned above which sought a residential course for its YTS trainees, and thereby created a pattern for all other YTS training programmes in the particular county, there was an insistence upon trainees carrying out a separate project as part of the course. This project involved trainees in setting up a company, devising a product and marketing it. The students had to work in groups, brainstorm ideas, produce written reports and appropriate mathematical representations of their data. In keeping with MSC (1984) there was an assumption that successful performance in Outdoor Activities, which the company also valued, would transfer to the business programme because confidence would be built up and students would be more prepared to tackle unfamiliar tasks. The particular centre chosen by the Association of Boys' Clubs, and called Lakeside here, was valued highly by the local MSC Area Assessors for its work and was used by the college course in 1984/85.[6] YTS personnel were not involved in the residential programme on this course other than being invited to a presentation session at the end of the week when they could judge the achievements of their students in presenting their business projects. As a result YTS trainers made no direct contribution to the Outdoor Activities programme.

An Education-Based Approach to Residential Experience

By contrast the college course placed less emphasis upon the business element because tutors felt that such activities were beyond the capabilities of the majority of the students with learning difficulties which the course received. Thus in 1985/86 the college course students attended a residential week based at a centre called 'Knollton' where the college course tutors were involved in designing the programme. The YTS tutors still desired an emphasis upon Outdoor Activities and relinquished to the specialist programme organizers full responsibility for this aspect of the course though they themselves organized an evening programme for the college YTS group. The emphasis in this model was upon personal accomplishment and self-confidence rather than the completion of a predetermined set of goals.

Residential Experience and the College Course: An Overview

In February 1985 twenty-three students from the 1984/85 college intake attended the coastal residential centre, Lakeside, together with seventeen students from the industrial company mentioned above. The centre warden, Steven Kemp, had a background in PE teaching and hired qualified staff on a contract basis. From small beginnings in the early 1970s the centre had developed and now found itself a popular venue for groups from far afield including secondary schools, YTS organizations, industrial training schemes and adults on management training courses. The centre itself offered a range of activities including climbing, canoeing, orienteering, all taught in mixed-sex groups. Achieving a full complement of pupils/students was important and it was quite common to find a number of different YTS courses in residence at one time for a 'YTS week'. This meant that while the YTS courses present may well have differed substantially among themselves the students followed a common programme and were assigned to groups in such a way that each specialist tutor had a group containing students from all the YTS courses in residence at that particular time.

At the same time the warden and his staff had their own ideas of what constituted a successful course and therefore there was an attempt not so much to impose alternative goals on top of the industrial training requirements but to mesh their own approach to outdoor pursuits and residential organization with the industrial rationale. The composition of the college YTS group had been discussed with Steven earlier in the year and it was clear that the centre was not used to taking a 'special needs' intake on a 'YTS week' so an alternative evening project had been discussed. However, the centre staff clearly felt that all YTS students were similar and should follow a common programme no matter which scheme they came from. Since YTS tutors were only permitted to join the course on the last day there was little opportunity for renegotiating the curriculum directly. Lakeside, in common with many centres, required a list of any student medical conditions likely to affect performance in Outdoor Activities to be made available before the course began but as far as physical disability was concerned they felt no student should be debarred for coordination difficulties. The issue here is the way in which organizational strategies adopted by Steven and his tutors at the centre changed in response to college YTS student characteristics including performance in outdoor pursuits.

Although I was not expected to play a part during the week, after three days the centre telephoned and asked me to collect a student, Michelle, who they felt could not cope with the course. I went down and spent a day at the centre before returning with Michelle and during the day was able to carry out observations and ask questions. The centre saw Michelle as unable to participate fully because she was reticent in speaking to people she did not know and also because she found some physical activities particularly difficult. Centre staff were adamant that it was unfair on all other students and indeed Michelle herself if she remained; Michelle indicated that she wanted to come home because she was unhappy.

The difficulties which centre tutors had with students such as Michelle, together with our feeling at the college that the course was not responding to our particular special needs student intake, meant that we sought a different residential course the following year. On this occasion only eighteen students attended and the group contained seven female students and eleven males. Knollton was a rural centre in a mountainous area which had opened in 1983 and was staffed by two tutors, Jem Smith and Dave Preece, with a background in youth work rather than in teaching. As with Lakeside, the centre catered for a varied clientele but would only take one group at a time no matter what size that group was. The week's programme was worked out in consultation with the YTS course organizers who were expected to participate in all activities which included climbing, potholing, canoeing, orienteering, pony trekking and walking as the main Outdoor Activities. These were supervised by one of the two team leaders at the centre although they drew on outside help for climbing and potholing. On this occasion Sue Thompson, a tutor, and I took the group for the week.

The students were divided into two smaller groups and Sue and I led one group each with specialist help from Jem while Dave for this week organized the catering arrangements. Knollton, therefore, follows the educational model described above in that Sue and I devised the evening programme in cooperation with Jem and Dave. For this we concentrated upon a diary of key events to be presented as a series of news bulletins. However, as with Lakeside, the specialist staff had particular goals which they wanted to foster and also an attitude to student control which again drew upon their perceptions of performance in outdoor pursuits although it was only a series of unexpected events that revealed this.

Residential Staff Perspectives: The Initial Stage

Residential staff tutors specializing in outdoor pursuits inevitably evaluate and assess student performance from the time that they first meet a new student group, and as Jem indicated there is a necessary concern over the safety demands that individuals are likely to make. The perspectives of staff at the two centres can be illustrated by their depiction of the purposes of the week.

For Steven Kemp at Lakeside it was clear what a residential week ought to be able to offer all students:

> We stress that what's important is having a go. Nobody gets laughed at ... we see to that and it's important. One lad can be laughing at someone one minute and then find himself having problems the next so it's important that they learn not to laugh at each other. Competition is important, you can't get away from it but what's important here is that no-one competes against anyone else. It doesn't matter how long it takes one of them to climb a wall or handle a capsize ... we're very patient ... what matters is that they push themselves. They're competing against themselves but they are all part of a group. They surprise themselves by what they can do. It takes time for some of them, but then you find the quiet one who surprised himself on the climbing wall and he comes alight, he comes out of his shell and you'll see that spread to his project and to all the other things they do.

This suggests that a corporate entity is built up and there is an emphasis upon personal achievement. In fact as Steven indicated everyone was required to participate and specialist tutors would insist that all students attempted the various tasks on offer. Michelle had been seen in negative terms partly because she had failed to meet these demands although this was compounded by her difficulties in communicating with people she did not know well. However, residential tutors working with groups containing college students who found tasks such as rock climbing and canoeing difficult inevitably compared them with individuals or groups who completed such activities more readily.

Dave and Jem at Knollton took a rather different view and explained their approach as follows:

> It's about confidence and personal success. We try not to put pressure on especially when it's too much. We never force anyone to do any of

the activities although we encourage them to have a go. For some climbing or potholing just isn't on and that's OK. But we're careful not to draw attention to anyone who doesn't do it. I don't know if you've done any climbing ... well you'll know you can be shaking like a leaf ... we want them to push themselves but no-one must be hurt in this. As I said it's about confidence.

When asked specifically about the problems two college course students with restricted limb movement might face and whether they should join the course, Jem and Dave were quite clear on the desirability of these students attending. Both emphasized the importance of personal accomplishment and saw themselves as entering into a relationship with the group on an individual basis. It was stressed that success in terms of good physical performance was not important since what mattered was personal achievement no matter how slow and laborious this might be. The course at Knollton differed from Lakeside in that while Jem and Dave and their wives were happy to form an audience for a presentation of the students' evening work on the last day, they took no part in either organizing this or helping students; this was an area for the college tutors to supervise. Jem and Dave tended to view the evening activity as a means of keeping a group together and did not see it as related specifically to the outdoor pursuits programme.

In the course of the research I was interested in how or whether the designation 'YTS student' carried any implication for how residential course tutors viewed performance in outdoor pursuits at the outset of a course. At Lakeside, Mary, Steven's wife, who ran most of the catering arrangements but was not involved in the Outdoor Activities, was clear that there was a difference between YTS students and other groups. In her view YTS students tended to be noisier, more cocksure, possibly more rude and certainly less able than school pupil groups. She commented on how the specialist staff found it more demanding to encourage a YTS group to complete outdoor activities than other groups. Steven also felt that a substantial number of YTS students found outdoor pursuits difficult and were less inclined to have a go than other groups and he spoke strongly of the need for YTS training as a form of motivation. We can, therefore, suggest that outdoor pursuits may be seen by residential staff not only as a motivating force in order to accomplish the personal goals referred to above by Steven but also the industrial goals which YTS can be said to promote.

At Knollton YTS groups were not perceived at the outset as being any different from school-based parties. In fact Dave and Jem took considerable note of how visiting tutors with a group organized their students, built up relationships with individuals and how they established patterns of control. Their assessment of a group could be seen to include both tutors and students.

Residential Staff Perceptions of the YTS Group: Crisis and Strategy Change

Any group on a residential week is compared favourably or unfavourably with other similar groups by specialist tutors who build on past experience and their sedimented knowledge. By the time I was asked to collect Michelle from Lakeside, Steven and his staff had established a clear view of the student group. With my visit a change of organizational direction was discussed more fully in the light of the college course students' performance. In brief, the students were seen not as 'difficult' but as 'limited' and 'less able to benefit from the experience than others'. By this Steven meant that the college students compared less favourably with the YTS students from industry. Many college students found the learning tasks particularly difficult and in turn centre staff found them reluctant to join in with the other YTS students. Since YTS students in general were perceived less favourably than school parties anyway, we reach a point where the college students are being positioned in strongly negative terms.

> Now they're limited ... we don't mind that ... we do weeks for the handicapped as I've explained to you and some of these fit in there. Some of them have poor coordination and apart from Mandy and Liz none of them can plan anything easily. Of course they're frightened and sometimes I do bark but they know it's not meant as a threat. We should have known they were like this. You see they can't keep up with the others [YTS students from industries] and they hold them back. They don't join in the same way because they can't. Now some are coming on but Chris had to spend all day with some of them in the water getting them confident when he could have done more with some of the others. (Steven)

Clearly a differentiation between YTS students has taken place which arises from two sources: performance at outdoor pursuits and response to the group project task. There may have been an initial expectation that all YTS students would be unmotivated but after only a few days those students from industrial training are being seen as potentially good students while the college students are seen as less adequate.

Time was an important feature of the week since each specialist tutor had a set of objectives to cover with their groups. The college course students were seen as hindering this process partly because they lacked both confidence in their ability and also certain highly valued planning and organizational skills relevant to both physical pursuits and the group project. Steven thus voiced a general centre concern, stating that the YTS groups from industry were doing all the work and were receiving little backup from the college-based students.

The criteria for differentiation included the amount of help students needed and the time they took to complete a task whether it was in Outdoor Activities or in the project. The college students found the written reports and the production of graphs very difficult in this particular setting although back at college most of them had completed similar tasks. Thus there was an assumption that it was the college students' deficiencies that stopped them completing tasks. It was never suggested or considered that both the Outdoor Activities and the projects were being structured in ways that impaired their development and sharpened the differences between them and the other YTS students.

The distinction between the college students at Lakeside and the other industrially sponsored YTS students led to a change in teaching organization. The college students were now largely separated for both the daytime activities and the project. As a result they were given easier routes on the climbing wall and only a selected few were allowed to attempt abseiling. Most of them were given a shorter and easier route for a midnight trek. Steven explained that his priority was both to extend those YTS students sponsored by industry and above all to ensure that the college students were operating within their limits and did not find themselves too discouraged or downhearted. In the evenings the groups were reconstituted and two college YTS groups were created for those who Steven and his staff felt were most at sea with the report-writing tasks and these students were given extra help. They were allowed to present a project based on the approach we at the college preferred, i.e., a diary of the main events of the week. The move to accept the YTS tutor view of a project involved a realization on the part of centre staff that other goals could feature in the course; but as we shall see this accommodation did not lead to an acceptance of such goals. As a result of these changes most of the students felt there was less pressure on them later in the week. They felt that they were being given more time and were no longer being compared to the other YTS students. However, two college students regretted quite strongly that they had not been able to join the abseiling group and one student commented on the tutors not letting her do as much as she wanted.

The position at Knollton was different in that since the project was under YTS tutor control and the crucial judges of the success or otherwise of the week's programme were the very tutors who had come to participate, the specialist residential staff did not need to work to a tight time schedule. Thus their perception of student performance in outdoor pursuits was guided solely by the task at hand. However, Jem identified a group of male students consisting principally of Terry and Billy whom he regarded as very trouble-some. Terry was extremely good at rock climbing and revelled in his superiority but was likely to belittle other students, whereas his friend Billy had no desire to climb and unfortunately sat and passed comments on other students' efforts. Responding to this situation became (quite reasonably) an issue for the YTS tutors. Later Jem began to discuss Billy in strongly critical terms and linked Billy's admittedly insensitive attitude to other students both to the way he tried to avoid participating in other activities and to his friendship with Terry. A colleague, Sue Thompson, and I discussed our understanding of the students with Jem and it became clear that by this point his attitude to more problematic students was based on a perception of how much constant tutor supervision they required and also how far such students were likely to impede the progress of others.

There was no shift in organizational strategy in respect of their behaviours as such until a dramatic event occurred which impinged on all activities. In brief, Billy and Terry broke a window one night, climbed over a roof and then went down to a hotel before moving to a field where they made a considerable nuisance of themselves. A midnight telephone call from an irate farmer led to the swift return of the students but a physical confrontation between Jem and Terry led the latter to pull out a knife and threaten violence. This incident, coming as it did after a series of problems presented by Billy and Terry, was the last straw for Jem who now would not countenance Terry and Billy staying at the centre any longer. As a result I took them home as their presence clearly meant that further conflict was likely.

The issue here, however, is not whether this action was the appropriate one in the circumstances but rather that of the manner in which the problem of control was resolved. Jem's rationalization for this decision to remove Billy and Terry revolved around the following considerations: the risk to safety posed by a student seizing a knife, the clear desire of the two students to disrupt the week as evidenced by their comments on other students, the fact that other students did not receive as much tutor attention as they deserved because so much tutor time was taken up by Billy and Terry. Again the question of tutor time emerged to reveal that there are implicit assumptions about the amount of tutor support students should receive. The resolution to the problem of negative student behaviour also involved a shift in the pattern of authority and control. Dave and Jem owned the house which provided the centre and so were establishing legitimate proprietor rights in their decision to exclude two students. However, this decision was reinforced in Jem's case by what he saw as a breakdown in control; that is to say, in his view the two YTS tutors were not succeeding in establishing a necessary pattern of effective control because they were not resourced to do so: 'This lot are like an IT group[7] but there you have one member of staff to two students. You can't do it with just two of you. Most of them are nice kids but you can't spend enough time with them' (Jem).

At Knollton the residential course staff saw the visiting tutors as largely responsible for all aspects of supervision apart from situations arising in

Outdoor Activities. This can be contrasted with the programme at Lakeside where specialist tutors took over all aspects of control. Thus at Lakeside specialist staff were expected to succeed in completing a prearranged programme with a group, and problems that arose could be interpreted by the staff in terms of the deficiencies and needs of the students. On the other hand, at Knollton visiting YTS tutors were seen as responsible for the deficiencies in their students, and therefore the level of control maintained by YTS tutors could influence the outcome of the Outdoor Activities programme. As stated earlier there is no obvious link between means and ends and, while the particular incident with Billy and Terry reflected a dramatic issue, other forms of problematic student behaviour had occurred during the week which did not involve these students and which did not bring about organizational change. The contrasting feature was that incidents which did not threaten the operation of the daily programme and which by their very nature were dealt with by YTS tutors without drawing public attention to them did not threaten the stability of the centre's curriculum philosophy and pedagogy.

We have seen how at Lakeside students were differentiated on the basis of how they coped with both Outdoor Activities and project work and criticisms of students were made largely against individuals. At Knollton there was less concern with individual performance since there was no pre-set standard prescribed by industrial sponsors but instead there was a concern with ways in which individual students supported or hindered each other. A group of students who were prepared to try their best at any physical activity but who ran the risk of being exposed to ridicule needed to be protected from the often cruel taunts of others. Thus both residential centres differentiated students in ways that suggested student deficiencies associated with special needs caused problems of control for specialist tutors.

The End of the Week

Sue Thompson, Sandra Lane (college course tutors) and I visited Lakeside for the final day, as did the YTS industrial sponsors, to see the students present their projects. These presentations were conducted very formally with each group having up to fifteen minutes and then being subjected to questions. The industrial students responded to this challenge with gusto (they had already been prepared for it as part of their training course) while the college students looked on glumly. The audience made appropriate allowances for the different styles of presentation and in fact the college students surpassed themselves. Steven Kemp's closing speech reiterated the values of the course as set out originally, with the assumed transfer of learning between outdoor pursuits and work-based activities. Thus the shift to accommodate the YTS college perspective was not officially recognized at the close and instead the original ideals of the residential week were restated in ways which not only supported the industrial model referred to above but served to mark the distance between students with special needs from the college course and industrial trainees. However, as the students departed Steven and his staff said farewell to the college students on an individual basis and stressed how well they had done and how 'they had not disgraced themselves'. Again this emphasized that the industry-based YTS students provided the norm by which the college students were evaluated and found wanting. In particular this was manifested by different levels of accomplishment at outdoor pursuits.

At Knollton the aftermath of the departure of Billy and Terry had to be responded to. The adjustments that Dave and Jem made saw them becoming fully involved in the last two days with all aspects of the work including the preparation of the lighthearted sketch based on incidents during the week. Dave and Jem moved more closely to the total supervisory role they had hitherto avoided despite the rhetoric of their initial approach having stressed that they would adopt this approach.

Thus at the end of the week at Knollton organizational adjustment occurred with a coming together of specialist tutor and YTS tutor perspectives but this sharing of responsibility was not a feature of the week at Lakeside.

Conclusion

The organizational goals of the two courses have certain common dimensions. Both ascribed a great deal of importance to the business of spending time with individual students but the differences between the centre approaches embody their different philosophies. On the surface it would appear that at Lakeside outdoor pursuits have an intrinsic value linked towards goals of self-improvement and motivation within a group context, and this philosophy supports the explicit goals of youth training as traditionally prescribed by both industry and the MSC. At Knollton outdoor pursuits are related more closely to individual needs and personal development. However, when a notion of crisis occurred at Knollton there was a brief but clear change in organizational strategy while at Lakeside a series of adjustments allowed the dominant organizational form to continue. These adjustments at Lakeside involved a differentiation between the college YTS students and the YTS students sponsored by industry, with the college students eventually being given an alternative programme, but this did not alter significantly the pedagogic strategies and curricular philosophy of the specialist residential tutors. At Knollton the crisis led the two specialist residential tutors to change their own practices so that they accorded with the curricular philosophy and pedagogy they had espoused at the outset.

At Lakeside the thinking and actions of some tutors that linked the values of performing outdoor pursuits with the goals of youth training enabled residential staff to label the college students as 'limited' and thereby position them as deficient. There was little scope for the students to occupy a more favourable position because they were seen as a largely homogeneous group. On the other hand, at Knollton students were more likely to be perceived by specialist tutors in individual rather than group terms. Thus once Billy and Terry had been excluded from the course the stress on individual and personal accomplishment and cooperative endeavour meant that the remaining students were able to achieve success as a group.

The organization of residential experience can be considered as a process of student management in that the goals of the centres became more difficult to achieve when tutors were faced by a student group that could be readily defined as deficient in ways which affected the actual management of the course. At both the centres forms of social control were related to the perceived problems the students posed for staff. The organizational strategy at Lakeside embodied implicit assumptions whereby specialist tutors linked achievement in Outdoor Activities with the goals of youth training and in this case the college students were positioned in negative terms. Here the perceptions and values of the college tutors were subordinated to these goals and so became marginalized. However, this emphasizes the power relations in play in that the needs of industrial trainees being sponsored by a large company take precedence over a group of students with substantially different needs. At Knollton the emphasis upon personal effort and individual accomplishment for its own sake was only realized as a pedagogic strategy when the authority and control of centre staff were threatened. Although the overt curriculum philosophy was closer to the college perception the pedagogic practices did not at first support this and it was only through the pedagogic adjustments following the incident described above that pedagogy and curriculum philosophy came closer together.

Notes

1 Outdoor Activities are commonly included on residential courses although they do not always form a central part of the curriculum. Both centres described here treated such activities as essential to their courses, and Outdoor Activities is taken as an inclusive term for at least the following curricular possibilities: outdoor pursuits, outdoor education, outward bound courses, see Humberstone (1986). I have followed Humberstone in referring to outdoor pursuits and related outdoor

activities as those physical activities involving potential danger and so requiring a high concern for student safety.

2   The research has been carried out for a thesis in progress and all names have been changed.

3   The history of the MSC is a complex one. See CCCS (1981) for an account of the development of the organization up to 1980. Aspects of the history of youth training include Gleeson (1983), Fiddy (1983), Raffe (1983), Finn (1986, 1987). These accounts contain a substantial critique of both the form of vocational training offered through YTS and the role of the state.

4   When YTS was introduced in 1983 there were two types of course. Mode A schemes were organized by employers and tended to maximize the work experience component, while Mode B schemes were largely provided by colleges and voluntary organizations and were in effect subcontracted by the MSC. Within the Mode B category there were finer distinctions and a number of alternative courses. Since 1986 and the advent of the two-year YTS the distinction between the two modes has been removed although provision for young people with special needs still remains.

5   See Barton and Tomlinson (1984), Oliver (1985), Bines (1986), Quicke (1986).

6   In 1985/86 I was asked by an MSC Assessor why I was no longer using the same residential centre as in 1984/85 since it provided a course which insisted upon this business programme. While I would not discount the value of such a programme in specific circumstances, I would not accept it uncritically.

7   Intermediate Treatment as a programme for 'young people at risk' followed the implementation of the Children and Young Persons' Act 1969 as a court sanction which was 'intermediate' between home-based supervision and custody. Young people receiving this provision are often referred for treatment by schools and probation officers as well as by the courts. In the main Intermediate Treatment Centres are run by Social Services Departments, and the presence of residential weeks as part of their programme is well established.

References

ATKINSON, P., SHONE, D. and REES, T. (1981) 'Labouring to learn? Industrial training for slow learners', in BARTON, L. and TOMLINSON, S. (Eds), *Special Education: Policy, Practices and Social Issues*, London, Harper and Row, pp. 235–57.

BARTON, L. and TOMLINSON, S. (Eds) (1984) *Special Education: Policy, Practices and Social Issues*, London, Harper and Row.

BERGER, P. and LUCKMANN, T. (1966) *The Social Construction of Reality*, Harmondsworth, Penguin Books.

BINES, H. (1986) *Redefining Remedial Education*, London, Croom Helm.

CENTRE for CONTEMPORARY CULTURAL STUDIES (CCCS) (1981) *Unpopular Education*, London, Hutchinson.

FEU (1984) *Supporting YTS*, London, Further Education Unit Publications, DES.

FIDDY, R. (1983) 'The emergence of the Youth Training Scheme', in FIDDY, R. (Ed.), *Youth Unemployment and Training*, Lewes, Falmer Press, pp. 27–39.

FINN, D. (1986) 'YTS: The jewel in the MSC's crown?' in BENN, C. and FAIRLEY, J. (Eds), *Challenging the MSC*, London, Pluto Press, pp. 52–76.

FINN, D. (1987) *Training without Jobs*, London, Macmillan.

GIDDENS, A. (1971) *Capitalism and Modern Social Theory*, Cambridge, Cambridge University Press.

GLEESON, D. (Ed.) (1983) *Youth Training and the Search for Work*, London, Routledge and Kegan Paul.

HUMBERSTONE, B. (1986) '"Learning for a change": A study of gender and schooling in Outdoor Education', in EVANS, J. (Ed.), *Physical Education, Sport and Schooling: Studies in the Sociology of Physical Education*, Lewes, Falmer Press, pp. 195–215.

MSC (1976) *Instructional Guide to Social and Life Skills*, Sheffield, Manpower Services Commission.

MSC (1982) *Youth Task Group Report*, Sheffield, Manpower Services Commission.

MSC (1984) *Guide to the Revised Scheme Design and Content*, Sheffield, Manpower Services Commission.

OLIVER, M. (1985) 'The integration-segregation debate: Some sociological considerations', *British Journal of Sociology of Education*, 6, 1, pp. 75–93.

QUICKE, J. (1986) 'A case of paradigmatic mentality? A reply to Mike Oliver', *British Journal of Sociology of Education*, 7, 1, pp. 81–7.

RAFFE, D. (1983) 'Can there be an effective youth employment policy?', in FIDDY, R. (Ed.), *In Place of Work*, Lewes, Falmer Press, pp. 11–26.

ROSIE, A. (1988) 'An ethnographic study of a YTS course', in POLLARD, A., PURVES, J. and WALFORD, G. (Eds), *Education, Training and the New Vocationalism: Experience and Policy*, Milton Keynes, Open University Press.

SCHUTZ, A. (1964) *Collected Papers, Vol 2*, The Hague, Martinus Nijhoff.

TOMLINSON, S. (1982) *A Sociology of Special Education*, Henley, Routledge and Kegan Paul.

WILLIS, P. (1981) 'Cultural production is different from cultural reproduction is different from social reproduction is different from reproduction', *Interchange*, 12, 2/3, pp. 48–67.

WILLIS, P. (1983) 'Cultural production and theories of reproduction', in BARTON, L. and WALKER, S. (Eds), *Race, Class and Education*, London, Croom Helm, pp. 107–38.

Notes on Contributors

Kevin Bruce is a recent MS graduate in Physical Education from Purdue University and teaches in Dearborn, Michigan.

Robert Burgess is Director of CEDAR(Centre for Educational Development, Appraisal and Research) and Senior Lecturer in Sociology at the University of Warwick. His main teaching and research interests are in social research methodology, especially qualitative methods and the sociology of education, in particular the study of schools, classrooms and curricula. He is currently writing an ethnographic re-study of a comprehensive school. His main publications include *Experiencing Comprehensive Education* (1983), *In the Field: An Introduction to Field Research* (1984), *Education, Schools and Schooling* (1985) and *Sociology, Education and Schools* (1986) together with nine edited volumes on qualitative methods and education.

Bruce Carrington has been a Lecturer in Education at the University of Newcastle upon Tyne since 1979. Before taking up this post he was a Lecturer in Sociology at St Mary's College, Twickenham and a primary school teacher in North London. He has a long-standing research interest in 'race' and ethnicity and has published extensively in the area. His book with Geoffrey Short, *Race and the Primary School: Theory and Practice* (NFER-Nelson), is due to appear in 1988. He is also co-editing *Children and Controversial Issues: Strategies for the Early and Middle Years of Schooling* (Falmer Press) with Barry Troyna.

Gill Clarke taught Physical Education in comprehensive schools before becoming a Senior Lecturer in Human Movement Studies at the West Sussex Institute of Higher Education. In her spare time she is an international hockey umpire. Her research interests centre on the study of communication and discourse within Physical Education classrooms.

Brian Davies is Professor of Education at University College, Cardiff. He was formerly Senior Lecturer in Sociology at the University of London Institute of Education and lectured at Goldsmith's College London after a period as a school teacher. He has written widely on the sociology of education and is author of *Education and Social Control* (1986) and the editor of an issue of *Educational Analysis* which dealt with the *State of Schooling.*

John Evans teaches the sociology of Physical Education and the sociology of education in the Faculty of Educational Studies, University of Southampton. He is author of *Teaching in Transition, The Challenge of Mixed Ability Grouping* (1985) and edited *Physical Education, Sport and Schooling* (1986) (Falmer Press). He has published widely in the sociology of education.

Lisa George graduated with first-class honours in Human Movement Studies from the University of Queensland. Her main research interests are in the sociology of Physical Education and youth culture. She is currently teaching Health and Physical Education in a Brisbane secondary school.

Linda Hart is a Physical Education teacher at Lafayette Jefferson High School, Lafayette, Indiana.

David Kirk is a Lecturer at the University of Queensland. His current research interests are in the processes of curriculum and social change. He has published papers on a range of curriculum issues in Physical Education, and is author of *Physical Education and Curriculum Study: A Critical Introduction* (1988).

Oliver Leaman is a Lecturer in Philosophy at the Department of Education, Liverpool Polytechnic. He is author of *Sit on the Sidelines and Watch the Boys Play: Sex Differentiation in Physical Education* (1984) and 'Physical Education, dance and outdoor pursuits', in Craft, A. and Bardell, G. (Eds), *Curriculum Opportunities in a Multicultural Society*, (1984). His research interest is in Physical Education and equal opportunities.

Andrew Pollard is Reader in Primary Education at Bristol Polytechnic. He has taught across the primary age range and is author of *The Social World of the Primary School* and *Reflective Teaching in the Primary School* (with Sarah Tann).

Anthony Rosie taught English in London comprehensive schools for twelve years. He now lectures in Education at the College of St Paul and St Mary, Cheltenham.

Patricia Sikes at the time of writing this paper had two part-time jobs as a Research Fellow at the Open University working on TVEI evaluation and as Director of Evaluation at the Counselling and Career Development Unit at the University of Leeds. She is now a Lecturer in Education at Warwick University. She is co-author, with Linda Measor and Peter Woods, of *Teacher Careers: Crises and Continuities* (1985) and her PhD study investigated the ways in which secondary school teachers perceived and experienced teaching as a career at a time of contraction.

Andrew C. Sparkes is a Lecturer in the School of Education, Exeter University. He has taught Physical Education and Biology in comprehensive, public and special schools. His particular research interests are in the sociology of innovation and the development of naturalistic-interpretive methodologies on which he has published a number of papers.

Thomas Templin is an Associate Professor of Physical Education and Education at Purdue University in West Lafayette, Indiana. He has published widely in the area of professional socialization in Physical Education and is co-editor of *Teaching Physical Education* (1983) and *Socialisation into Physical Education: Learning to Teach* (fall 1988 publication).

Trevor Williams is the Director of the Sport Research Unit and a Senior Lecturer in the Department of Physical Education and Creative Studies at Sunderland Polytechnic. Over the past seventeen years he has taught Physical Education in England and Canada and currently teaches research methods and the sociology of sport and leisure. His research interests include sport subcultures and ethnicity, and he is the research co-ordinator for a Sports Council National Demonstration Project on the integration of sensorially and physically disabled young people in school Physical Education and community sport.

Index